Business M600 /

TABLE OF CONTENTS & ACKNOWLEDGEMENTS

HARVARD | BUSINESS | SCHOOL

9-502-006
REV: AUGUST 9, 2005

JOHN T. GOURVILLE

The Medicines Company

"When people first hear our business concept, they think we're crazy," stated Clive Meanwell, the founder, president, and CEO of the Medicines Company. Formed in 1996, the Medicines Company "acquired, developed, and commercialized pharmaceutical products in late stages of development," meaning that it purchased the rights to drugs that other companies had abandoned. As Meanwell explained it:

> We founded our company on the premise that sometimes there is still value in drugs that fail to meet a developer's initial expectations. Companies develop drugs with particular applications, users, price points, and market sizes in mind. When clinical testing calls these expectations into question, companies often halt development. But drugs that seem unprofitable for one application or user group might prove quite profitable for others. Our job is to find such drugs, acquire them at reasonable prices, complete their development, and bring them to market.

By early 2001, this strategy seemed to be working. Four years earlier, the company had acquired the rights to Angiomax, a blood-thinning drug, or "anticoagulant," that Biogen had abandoned after $150 million and seven years of development. On December 17, 2000, after completing the required clinical trials, the Medicines Company received U.S. Food and Drug Administration (FDA) approval to sell the drug for use in conjunction with an artery-clearing procedure known as an angioplasty. (**Exhibit 1** provides a newspaper account of this drug approval.)

In spite of this good news, several issues remained for Meanwell and his management team. The first issue involved pricing. Angiomax was positioned as an alternative to "heparin," the most widely used anticoagulant in emergency coronary heart care. The problem was that heparin cost about $2 per dose. While it was clear that the Medicines Company would price Angiomax above heparin, the question was "how much above?"

The second issue involved the need to develop a product portfolio. Meanwell had long argued that the company's success depended on the development of a drug pipeline. However, the company had run into problems with its second acquisition—a migraine headache drug—and had halted its development. This setback and Angiomax's recent FDA approval had Meanwell wondering whether there truly was the need for a drug pipeline.

Finally, as a public company, the Medicines Company faced the realities of the stock market. In fact, many investors had expected a sharp stock price increase with the approval of Angiomax. Instead, the company's stock (Nasdaq: MDCO) fell over 25% in the month following FDA approval (see **Exhibit 2**). This caused some people to question the company's core business strategy.

Professor John T. Gourville prepared this case. HBS cases are developed solely as the basis for class discussion. Cases are not intended to serve as endorsements, sources of primary data, or illustrations of effective or ineffective management. Some nonpublic company data have been disguised and some business details have been simplified to aid in classroom discussion.

The Drug Development Industry [1]

By any measure, prescription drugs were big business. At the manufacturer level, prescription sales in 2000 approached $220 billion worldwide, with growth projected at 10% per year through 2010. The largest market for these drugs was the United States, accounting for 50% of all sales.

The United States was also home to most of the world's major drug companies (see **Exhibit 3**). The largest of them was Pfizer/Warner-Lambert, with annual drug revenues in excess of $25 billion worldwide and $14 billion domestically. As for profitability, the U.S. drug industry ranked first among all major industries, with net incomes at almost 20% of revenues in 1999.[2]

In 2000, several trends were impacting the U.S. drug market. They included:

- An aging population. In 1999, people aged 65 or over accounted for 15% of the population but 33% of prescription drug sales in the United States. Between 2000 and 2020, this population was expected to grow from 35 million to 55 million.
- Increased price pressure. Prescription drugs accounted for 9% of medical expenses in 2000 and were growing at a 20% annual rate. As a result, managed care organizations (which paid for 70% of all prescription drugs) and the government (which paid for 10%) were pressuring drug companies to contain or lower drug prices.
- The growth in generics. As a rule, a generic drug came to market soon after the patent on a branded drug expired, typically at a price 25% to 75% below the price of the branded drug. Between 2000 and 2010, generic sales were expected to grow from $10 billion to $60 billion as several blockbuster drugs came off patent.

Drug Development

Historically, new drugs were the lifeblood of the pharmaceutical industry, drugs under development at any point in time representing the potential blockbuster drugs that would drive the industry 5 to 10 years later. The successful development of a new drug was far from easy, however. Beginning in 1938, the FDA required drug developers to follow a complex process designed to prove the safety and effectiveness of any proposed new drug. Accordingly, pharmaceutical firms followed a sequential drug development process:

- In *preclinical/animal trials*, a candidate drug was identified, studied for its chemical properties, and tested on animals to assess safety and effectiveness. Most drugs were eliminated at this stage due to unacceptable side effects or failure to work as expected.
- In *Phase I clinical trials*, the drug was given to a small number of healthy people in order to test safety. Initially, small doses were administered, with dosage increased over time to assess safety at higher levels.
- In *Phase II clinical trials*, the drug was given to people suffering from the condition that the drug was intended to treat. This stage usually included a larger number of people and a longer period of time than in Phase I.

1 Much of these data were drawn from S&P's industry survey, "Healthcare: Pharmaceuticals," December 21, 2000.

2 "Health's Price Tag," *The Boston Globe*, March 28, 2001, p. D4.

- *Phase III clinical trials* were the most critical of the four stages.[3] They were the largest, most complex, and most rigorous of the human trials, designed to test fully the safety, effectiveness, and dosing levels of the drug on actual patients.
- An *FDA submission* typically followed a successful Phase III trial. It came in the form of a new drug application (NDA) seeking FDA approval for the commercial release of the drug. Each year, the FDA approved about half of all the NDAs it received.

This drug development process was remarkable in several respects. First, as outlined in **Figure A**, for every drug that received FDA approval, approximately 4,000 candidate drugs began the process. Second, the process took an average of 10 years to complete successfully. Third, the process was capital intensive, with U.S. drug companies spending $26 billion on drug development in 2000 (**Exhibit 4** provides a breakdown of how this money was spent). Finally, a company generally applied for (and received) a 20-year patent for a drug it had under development. After completing development, however, only about 10 to 15 years of patent protection remained (for instance, in the United States, the Angiomax patent was due to expire in 2010).

Figure A Stages of Drug Development (average years in each stage in parentheses)

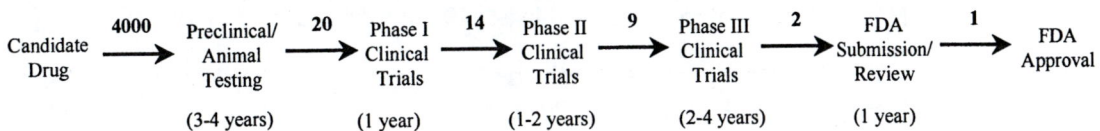

Candidate Drug —**4000**→ Preclinical/ Animal Testing (3-4 years) —**20**→ Phase I Clinical Trials (1 year) —**14**→ Phase II Clinical Trials (1-2 years) —**9**→ Phase III Clinical Trials (2-4 years) —**2**→ FDA Submission/ Review (1 year) —**1**→ FDA Approval

These factors combined to create an industry that relied heavily on "blockbuster drugs"—premium-priced breakthrough drugs that generated in excess of $1 billion in sales per year. In 1999, 19 drugs met this threshold in the United States (see **Exhibit 5** for the 10 top-selling domestic prescription drugs). Meanwell described this focus on blockbuster drugs in the following fashion:

> In any given year, only about 90 drugs receive FDA approval. Across 40 drug companies, this means that the average drug firm is turning out only one or two new drugs a year—maybe three in a good year. If you are Merck, with over $10 billion in sales and your investors expect 10% growth per year, these one or two drugs have to generate a lot of revenue. A drug that brings in $200 million just won't do it for you.

The Medicines Company History

The Medicines Company was founded in July 1996 by Meanwell and a small group of investors on the premise that there was opportunity where other companies saw failure. Their corporate strategy was to acquire drugs that were in the late stages of product development but were undervalued by their developing companies. Once such drugs were acquired, the Medicines Company planned to complete product development, navigate the regulatory process, and commercialize the drugs in the United States and abroad.

[3] Typically, Phase II and Phase III clinical trials were done across several hospitals, with doctors administering the candidate drug to a random sample of patients seeking treatment for the target disease. Quite often, the process was "double-blind," with neither the doctor nor the patient knowing what drug was administered.

While some questioned the logic of this business model, 15 years of experience in international drug development had convinced Meanwell that such a strategy made sense. As director of product development for Hoffman-LaRoche, one of Europe's largest drug developers, Meanwell had come to believe that drug firms often overreacted to clinical results, sometimes abandoning drugs that still had value. *The Boston Globe* described Meanwell and his company's business strategy as follows:

> You might say Dr. Clive Meanwell is a bit of a scavenger. ... After all, he founded a company four years ago based on the idea that there was money to be made off drugs other companies cast aside. His Cambridge start-up ... picks through and rescues products languishing because of lackluster results, shifting corporate priorities, or development problems.[4]

Of course, the first task for Meanwell and his colleagues was deciding what drugs to "rescue." To guide them in their acquisitions, Meanwell and his colleagues looked for drugs that met the following criteria:

- Required less than four years to get to market
- Required less than $60 million to get to market
- Had at least a 65% chance of getting to market
- Had the potential to generate at least $100 million per year in sales

Beginning in late 1996, the team spent six months reviewing potential acquisitions—starting with 3,000 candidates, quickly weeding those down to 20, and then seriously considering 3 or 4. By early 1997, they had settled on Angiomax, an anti-blood-clotting drug that Biogen had been developing as a more effective alternative to heparin, the anti-clotting drug most widely used in the acute treatment of coronary heart disease. In 1994, Biogen had halted development of Angiomax after clinical tests suggested that it was no more effective than heparin. Upon reviewing Biogen's clinical test results, however, Meanwell became convinced that a market still existed for the drug. Thus, in March 1997, the Medicines Company acquired all rights to Angiomax and set out to complete the clinical trials that Biogen had started. Finally, in December 2000, the Medicines Company received FDA approval for the use of Angiomax in the prevention of blood clots during a coronary procedure known as an angioplasty.

Following a similar screening process, in 1998 the Medicines Company acquired the rights to IS-159, a drug designed to treat acute migraine headaches. And in 1999 it acquired the rights to CTV-05, a drug designed to treat gynecological infections in women of childbearing age.

During its four-year effort, the Medicines Company relied upon two sources of funds. From its inception through mid-2000, the company received approximately $100 million in several rounds of funding from several private equity firms. Then, in August 2000, the company raised $101.4 million (after fees) from an initial public offering of 6,900,000 shares at $16 per share.

Through early 2001, these funds were used almost exclusively to acquire and develop the company's three drugs. In fact, through December 2000, the company had yet to report revenues of any kind (see **Exhibit 6**). At the same time, the company had close to $100 million in cash and short-term assets to finance the commercial launch of Angiomax and the continued development of its other products (see **Exhibit 7**).

---

[4] "The Rescuers," *The Boston Globe*, September 13, 2000.

Angiomax

Without question, Angiomax was The Medicines Company's lead product, representing the company's first attempt at rescuing a seemingly failed drug. The specific application for which Angiomax received FDA approval was for the treatment of "high-risk" patients undergoing a balloon angioplasty. A balloon angioplasty was a procedure developed in the 1970s to restore normal blood flow to arteries in the heart clogged by a fatty buildup called plaque. In an angioplasty, a small incision was made in a blood vessel in the groin and a long flexible tube with a deflated balloon was threaded through an artery until it reached the clogged artery in the heart. The balloon was then inflated, compacting the plaque against the artery wall and opening the artery to increased blood flow.[5]

Sometimes, this procedure would lead to the formation of an unwanted blood clot in the area of the angioplasty. This blood clot had the potential to reclog the artery, leading to chest pains and a possible heart attack. Angiomax was designed to reduce the likelihood that such a clot would form.

Coronary Heart Disease

Through the late 20th century, coronary heart disease was the leading cause of death in the United States, accounting for 1 in every 5 deaths. It involved the narrowing of the arteries of the heart due to the gradual buildup of plaque on the inside of the artery walls. Over time, this buildup would narrow the artery and reduce the flow of blood and oxygen to the heart muscle, often resulting in chest pains following physical exertion. This type of pain was called stable angina.

Sometimes, a portion of the built-up plaque would tear or break off, triggering the rapid formation of a blood clot at the site of the tear. This blood clot would further reduce the flow of blood to the heart, causing steadier and more intense chest pains called unstable angina. In extreme cases, the blood clot would completely cut off the blood supply to the heart and cause a heart attack. If the blood supply were cut off for a long enough period, the cells of the heart would die, leading to permanent disability or death.

By the late 1990s, an estimated 14 million Americans had some form of coronary heart disease, 7 million of whom suffered from stable angina. Of these, about 1.5 million experienced unstable angina each year, another 1.1 million suffered a full-blown heart attack, and close to 500,000 died.

While patients suffering from stable angina were treated with a regimen of diet, exercise, and a variety of slow-acting drugs, patients with unstable angina or full-blown heart attacks required emergency care. Typically, such patients immediately received a combination of several fast-acting drugs, including TPA, which was meant to break apart the clot that had formed, and an anticoagulant, which was meant to prevent a new clot from forming.

Shortly after this initial treatment, most emergency care patients underwent either a balloon angioplasty or coronary artery bypass surgery (CABG), which involved surgically replacing the clogged coronary arteries with healthy blood vessels taken from the patient's leg. In 1999, roughly 700,000 angioplasties and 400,000 CABGs were performed in the United States. Both types of operations had the potential to further disrupt arterial plaque, leading to the formation of a new

---

5 In about 65% of cases, in addition to the angioplasty, a small metal mesh tube called a stent was threaded through the artery and placed at the site of the blockage. This tube was meant to permanently prop open the artery to restore blood flow.

blood clot. Therefore, anticoagulants also were widely administered to prevent blood clots from forming before, during, and after these procedures.

Heparin

By far, the most widely prescribed anticoagulant in acute coronary heart treatment was heparin. Discovered in 1916, heparin was initially used to prevent the coagulation of blood samples drawn from patients. By the 1990s, however, it was the primary drug used to prevent unwanted blood clots from forming as the result of unstable angina, heart attacks, and coronary surgery. Having never been subject to patent protection, heparin was viewed as a commodity drug and sold by many different manufacturers at about $2 per vial. As reflected in **Table A,** Meanwell estimated that about 3.5 million coronary care patients received heparin each year to prevent unwanted blood clots.

Table A Heparin Use Across Treatments

Treatment	# of Patients Per Year Receiving Drug
Unstable Angina (i.e., elevated chest pains)	1,300,000
Heart Attack	1,000,000
Balloon Angioplasty	700,000
Coronary Artery Bypass Surgery	400,000
Other	100,000

Source: Medicines Company estimates.

Despite its almost universal use, heparin was not without it shortcomings, however, as Meanwell was quick to point out. These included:

- Unpredictability. Both within and across patients, the anticlotting effect of heparin was unpredictable. Its use required very close monitoring.
- High risk of bleeding. Some patients who received heparin had a high incidence of uncontrolled bleeding.
- Adverse reaction. In 2% to 3% of patients, heparin caused a sometimes fatal immune reaction called heparin-induced thrombocytopenia or HIT.

These shortcomings led some medical experts to question the ongoing use of heparin. As one cardiologist pointed out:

> Heparin is easy to use, but difficult to use properly. Its effectiveness depends on achieving a certain degree of anticoagulation in the blood. Too much anticoagulation and the patient can suffer from uncontrolled bleeding. Too little anticoagulation and you might not prevent a blood clot. But that window of proper dosing differs across patients and across time. As a result, you need to monitor the patient very closely. Making the problem more complex, it takes several hours for the effects of heparin to kick in and wear off. This means that you might have to wait three or four hours to see if a given dose of heparin has the desired effect.[6]

[6] Reflects comments obtained from a cardiologist in interviews conducted by the Medicines Company.

To assess the prevalence of this viewpoint, the Medicines Company conducted a random survey of 90 leading interventional cardiologists (the doctors who perform angioplasties) that asked them to rate their satisfaction with heparin. (Results of this survey are shown in **Figure B**.)

Figure B Overall Satisfaction with Heparin among Interventional Cardiologists

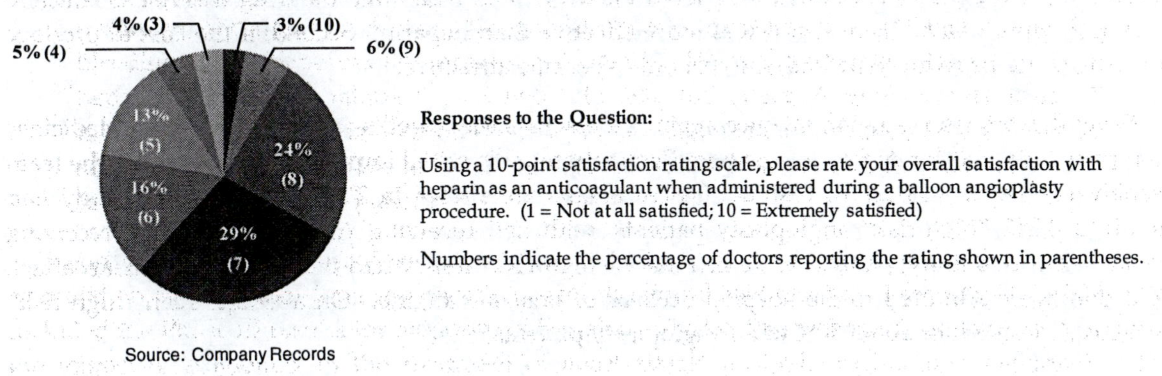
4% (3)
3% (10)
5% (4)
6% (9)
13% (5)
24% (8)
16% (6)
29% (7)
Responses to the Question:
Using a 10-point satisfaction rating scale, please rate your overall satisfaction with heparin as an anticoagulant when administered during a balloon angioplasty procedure. (1 = Not at all satisfied; 10 = Extremely satisfied)
Numbers indicate the percentage of doctors reporting the rating shown in parentheses.

Source: Company Records

Biogen's Angiomax: A Replacement for Heparin

Angiomax began its life in the mid-1980s in the laboratories of Biogen. Biogen's insight into Angiomax began with the observation that certain animals, such as leeches, drew blood from their victims without triggering the victim's blood-clotting process. Armed with this insight, Biogen isolated the chemicals in leech saliva that caused this anticlotting response. Once isolated, Biogen was able to reproduce it using recombinant technologies.

As initially conceived, Angiomax was to replace heparin for use during angioplasties. According to Meanwell, Biogen expected the typical angioplasty patient to require about four doses of the drug. Longer term, Biogen hoped Angiomax would replace heparin in almost all applications.

Over the next 7 years, Biogen spent $150 million bringing Angiomax through to Phase III trials. In 1994, however, Biogen came to two unsettling conclusions. First, its Phase III clinical trial involving "high-risk" angioplasty patients suggested that Angiomax was only slightly better than heparin at preventing blood clots. Second, given the complexity of the drug, Biogen expected that it would cost $100 per dose to produce Angiomax. In an industry where the typical "price" to "cost of goods sold" ratio was 10 to 1, this implied a selling price of $1,000 per dose. Reluctantly, Biogen halted development of Angiomax, concluding that its benefits did not justify such a price. Meanwell described Biogen's decision as follows:

> In 1994, Biogen was at a bit of a crossroads. To that point, they had licensed products to other drug companies. But, in the summer of '94, they had two drugs in Phase III trials—their first attempts to bring a product to market. One was Angiomax. The other was Avonex, a drug to treat multiple sclerosis. In July, the Phase III Avonex study showed very promising results. Then, in September, the Phase III Angiomax study showed mixed results. As a result, Biogen decided to pour its resources into Avonex and to shelve Angiomax. In the end, this may have been the right decision. Biogen received FDA approval for Avonex in 1996 and quickly turned it into the world's best-selling multiple sclerosis drug. In 2000, they sold over $750 million worth of Avonex.

The Decision to Acquire Angiomax

Following its decision to shelve Angiomax, Biogen actively shopped the drug to other biotech and pharmaceutical firms in the hopes that one would acquire or license the drug. One such firm was Hoffman-LaRoche, where Meanwell was head of drug development. While he decided not to pursue Angiomax, two things struck Meanwell about the drug. First, although the drug was not as effective as Biogen would have liked, it still was more effective than heparin. Second, if the cost to produce the drug could be reduced by half, the economics became attractive.

Several years later, Angiomax once again came across Meanwell's radar screen as the Medicines Company searched for its first acquisition. Remembering his initial impressions of the drug, the team reanalyzed Biogen's Phase III results. (These results are shown in **Table B.**) Biogen's study had involved 4,312 "high-risk" angioplasty patients, with half receiving Angiomax and half receiving heparin. For this study, patients were defined as "high-risk" if they had previously had a heart attack or if they were admitted to the hospital because of unstable angina. On average, such "high-risk" patients accounted for about 50% of all angioplasty patients.[7]

Table B Phase III Results for "High-Risk" Patients Undergoing an Angioplasty

Outcome within 7 days of treatment (number of patients in condition)	Heparin (2,151)	Angiomax (2,161)
Death	0.2%	0.2%
Heart Attack	4.2%	3.3%
Need for a Repeat Angioplasty	2.8%	2.5%
Experienced Major Bleeding	9.3%	3.5%

Source: The Medicines Company.

In addition, the Medicines Company found that for a particular subgroup of "high-risk" patients—those who had experienced a heart attack in the two weeks immediately preceding the angioplasty—the benefits of Angiomax were more pronounced. (**Table C** provides a comparison of heparin and Angiomax for these "very high-risk" patients.) On average, these patients represented 20% of the "high-risk" patients (or 10% of all angioplasty patients).

Table C Phase III Results for "Very High-Risk" Patients

Outcome within 7 days of treatment (number of patients in condition)	Heparin (372)	Angiomax (369)
Death	0.5%	0.0%
Heart Attack	5.6%	3.0%
Need for a Repeat Angioplasty	3.5%	2.4%
Experienced Major Bleeding	11.8%	2.4%

Source: The Medicines Company.

7 For the remaining 50% of angioplasty patients—that is, "low-risk" patients—Meanwell estimated that the relative benefits of Angiomax over Heparin were about half as great as those shown in **Table B.**

When asked to account for these results, Meanwell noted that Angiomax did not have many of the drawbacks that heparin had. Specifically, he noted:

> Unlike those of heparin, the effects of a dose of Angiomax are very exacting and very crisp. Physicians who use Angiomax have been pleasantly surprised by how predictable their results are, which is important in an acute-care setting where you are trying to minimize uncertainty. Second, the product works better among patients at risk for bleeding, where heparin often proves problematic. Third, the product works faster than heparin. Instead of taking 2 to 3 hours to take full effect, Angiomax only takes 30 minutes. Finally, there is no immune reaction to Angiomax, so you don't have to worry about unexpected reactions to the drug. These benefits seem to have the greatest impact for the "very high-risk" patients.

Based on their reanalyses, Meanwell and his colleagues agreed to acquire all rights to the drug's formulation, its manufacturing specifications, and its clinical trial results. These clinical trial results included the Phase III results for angioplasty but also included Phase II results for studies looking at the impact of Angiomax in the treatment of heart attack, unstable angina, and heparin-induced thrombocytopenia (HIT) .

The cost of this acquisition was an up-front fee of $2 million, a commitment to invest another $28 million in the continued development of the product, and a future royalty that started at 6% of sales and rose to 20% of sales as sales volumes increased.

Bringing Angiomax to Market

Upon acquiring Angiomax in 1997, the Medicines Company set out to address several issues. First, the company conducted a confirmatory clinical study using "high-risk" angioplasty patients, obtaining results similar to those shown in **Table B**. On the combined strength of Biogen's initial studies and this confirmatory study, the Medicines Company submitted a new drug application (NDA) in early 2000 and on December 17, 2000, obtained FDA approval to market Angiomax for use in "high-risk patients undergoing a balloon angioplasty." Meanwell estimated that the Medicines Company spent a total of $12 million in finishing these clinical trials and gaining FDA approval.

The second thing that the company did was to focus on bringing down the cost of using Angiomax. This was accomplished in two ways. First, rather than four doses of Angiomax, further clinical testing revealed that about 70% of angioplasty patients would require a single dose, with the other 30% requiring two or three doses. Second, in 1999 the Medicines Company contracted out production of Angiomax to UCB Bioproducts, with the understanding that UCB would attempt to develop a second-generation manufacturing process to bring down the cost of production. The Medicines Company contributed almost $10 million to this development effort. The result was a new production process that reduced the cost of goods sold from $100 per dose to about $40 per dose.

The third thing the company did was to push forward on the other Angiomax clinical trials. In particular, it undertook additional studies to confirm the benefits of Angiomax (1) for patients experiencing heart attacks and unstable angina, (2) for patients at risk for HIT, and (3) for patients undergoing coronary artery bypass surgery. By early 2001, the company had five sets of clinical trials either completed or under way, as reflected in **Exhibit 8**.

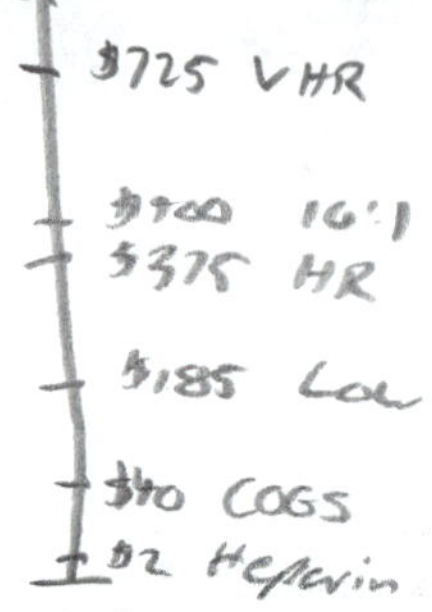

The Marketing of Angiomax

Making the case for Angiomax As it became apparent that Angiomax would gain FDA approval, the company's next big task was to establish a "going to market" strategy for the drug. As part of this strategy, the company hired Dr. Stephanie Plent as senior director of medical policy. Part of Plent's job was to communicate the benefits of Angiomax to cardiologists and hospital administrators. She explained these benefits in the following fashion:

> When a hospital performs an angioplasty on a patient covered by insurance, it is reimbursed at a predetermined rate. Currently, that rate is $11,500. In most cases, this more than covers the cost of the procedure—an angioplasty with no complications costs a hospital about $9,500 to perform.
>
> In a small percentage of cases, however, complications do arise. But insurance companies do not reimburse the cost of these complications. Instead, hospitals are forced to absorb these added expenses. On average, a hospital incurs an additional $8,000 to treat a person who has a heart attack, requires a repeat angioplasty, or experiences major bleeding. These added costs are largely due to the fact that the patient's hospital stay is extended by four or five days. Even a death costs the hospital an additional $8,000. Angiomax helps avoid some of these costs.

At the same time, Plent noted that this message had a different impact on the various members of the hospital staff. She pointed out that there were three major groups that influenced the purchase and use of any new drug: (1) the doctor who would use the drug, (2) the hospital pharmacist who would carry the drug, and (3) the hospital administrator who would approve the drug for ongoing use within the hospital. Each of these groups had a different set of incentives, as Plent pointed out:

> Selling a premium-priced new drug into a hospital is a tricky process. First, there are the doctors. You have to convince them that the drug works. They are not concerned with price so much as they are with results. Next, there are the hospital pharmacists. They have an annual budget for all the drugs they dispense and are rewarded for meeting or beating that budget. Replacing a widely used $10 drug with a $100 drug really kills that budget. Unless they can justify the cost of the new drug to the hospital administrators and get the added expense incorporated into their budgets, it is unlikely they will carry it. Finally, there are the hospital administrators. They take the big picture into account—does this drug make economic sense. Unfortunately, drug companies rarely have direct access to these administrators. Rather, we have to work through the doctors and the pharmacists and get them to push for the drug.

Assembling a sales force The task of selling Angiomax into this complex network of hospital personnel fell to Tom Quinn, vice president of sales and marketing. It was Quinn's job to assemble a sales force, promote the use of Angiomax, and ramp up sales over time.

According to Quinn's analysis, 1,300 medical centers around the country performed angioplasties, with the typical center staffed by 5 to 20 interventional cardiologists. Across these 1,300 centers, Quinn decided to focus on those 700 centers responsible for 92% of all angioplasty procedures. These 700 angioplasty centers were divided into five sales regions.

10

To service each of these five regions, Quinn hired a regional manager and outsourced to a marketing services firm for 10 to 15 account reps. Quinn explained his thinking behind this approach:

> When we looked at what we needed to do, we realized we needed people with existing relationships within the acute coronary care community. Also, we wanted to ramp up rapidly. The answer was Innovex, a marketing services firm. They provided us with fully dedicated salespeople with an average of 5 years of sales experience and with existing relationships with the doctors and pharmacists we wanted to reach. As for our regional managers, we hired them as Medicines Company employees to retain control and to create stability over time.

Quinn was also responsible for educating the marketplace. This included publication of academic journal articles, presentations at trade shows, and the advertising of Angiomax in medical journals. Beginning in the fall of 2000, for instance, Quinn's marketing department started drawing attention to the shortcomings of heparin. Such an approach was made necessary by FDA regulations that forbade the marketing of a drug not yet approved for use. Therefore, at medical trade shows and in medical journals in October, November, and December, the company presented material designed to get doctors to question the safety of heparin. One such bit of material was an academic article on the deficiencies of heparin that appeared in the *Journal of Invasive Cardiology*. Once Angiomax was approved, the company followed with trade show presentations, journal articles, and advertisements in medical journals identifying Angiomax as the preferred alternative to heparin. (**Exhibit 9** provides an example of one such ad.)

Finally, Quinn sought to create advocates within the medical community. Through early 2001, the company sponsored four weekend getaways for thought leaders (and their families) in the cardiology community. These invitees were handpicked by the sales force and included 400 cardiologists, 75 nurses, and 30 pharmacists. Over the course of two days, they would participate in about eight hours of presentations designed to educate them on the company and the product. Quinn estimated that the Medicines Company spent about $3 million on these efforts.

Other Drugs Under Development by the Medicines Company

In addition to Angiomax, the Medicines Company had acquired two other "abandoned" drugs. In July 1998, the company acquired the rights to IS-159, a nasal spray designed to treat acute migraine headaches. And in August 1999, it acquired the rights to CTV-05, a drug designed to treat gynecological infections in women of childbearing age.

IS-159

Acquired from Immunotech S.A. of France, IS-159 was an acute migraine drug in Phase II trials that promised rapid absorption into the bloodstream. Under the acquisition agreement, the company paid an up-front fee of $1 million, was obligated to pay an additional $4.5 million upon reaching certain development milestones, and would pay a 5% royalty on sales upon commercialization of the product. At the time of the acquisition, Meanwell noted that the drug had shown promise in its Phase II trials, offering "an impressively rapid onset of action and a convenient form of administration." At that time, Meanwell estimated the migraine drug market to be about $2 billion.

By mid-1999, however, development of IS-159 had been halted by the Medicines Company. After spending an additional $6 million in clinical trials, the company had run into problems with the drug's formulation. Specifically, for the nasal spray to be absorbed into the bloodstream, an additive was needed. The additive being used was modified coconut oil. However, while modified coconut oil had gained FDA approval as an additive in oral medications, it had not yet gained FDA approval as an additive in nasal medications. As a result, the company faced the daunting task of either finding a new additive or conducting clinical trials to show the safety and effectiveness of coconut oil as a nasal additive. Meanwell estimated that either course of action would cost as much as $30 million and take five years.

CTV-05

With Angiomax looking like it would gain FDA approval, the failure of IS-159 in mid-1999 presented a problem. With plans to go public in the near future, all parties felt that it was critical to have a second drug under development to avoid the appearance that the company was a one-drug enterprise. IS-159 was supposed to have been that other drug. With its failure, the company was forced to rescue some other drug that was underappreciated.

That drug turned out to be CTV-05, a drug designed to treat bacterial vaginosis (BV), an infection common in women of childbearing age. By one estimate, 10% to 15% of college-age women suffered from BV, which often resulted in premature termination of pregnancies and in low-birth-weight babies. Under the terms of the acquisition, the Medicines Company obtained worldwide rights to the drug for an up-front fee of $1 million and future royalties of about 5%.

Upon reflection, Meanwell noted that the company's acquisition of CTV-05 was quite different from the company's earlier acquisitions. As he pointed out:

> With Angiomax, we knew the drug worked. Even with IS-159, we knew the drug worked—we just hadn't anticipated problems with its formulation. With CTV-05, we were taking a bit of a flier. We needed another drug under development, but there were no obvious alternatives. We didn't know if CTV-05 worked—it was only in Phase I trials—but we knew we could get it at low cost. So far, we have been happy with the results. We have invested about $4 million and we are currently completing Phase II trials. What started out as a high-risk investment is showing a lot of promise.

Looking Ahead

Moving forward, Meanwell knew that he and his colleagues had several decisions to make. First, they had to decide on the pricing of Angiomax. On the one hand, he felt that the product warranted a vast premium over heparin. On the other hand, he knew that replacing a widely accepted $2 drug with *any* drug costing many times more would raise a few eyebrows. Second, he had to decide whether the business strategy that brought the company to this point still made sense moving into the future. In particular, while a productive drug pipeline would be a nice thing to have, was it essential? Finally, Meanwell wondered how success with Angiomax would change the company and its underlying business model.

For the moment, however, Meanwell and his colleagues enjoyed the feeling of having rescued a drug with the potential to make a difference in people's lives.

Exhibit 1 Excerpt from *The Boston Globe,* December 19, 2000

Medicines Co. Receives FDA Approval for Blood Thinner

Drug up against cheaper heparin

by Naomi Aoki
Globe Staff

Medicines Co. yesterday said it won regulatory approval to market its first product, a blood thinner designed as an alternative to the 85-year-old standard treatment, heparin.

The drug, called Angiomax, was approved by the US Food and Drug Administration for use in an artery-clearing procedure known as angioplasty. The drug was developed to prevent blood clots that can lead to heart attacks.

... Angiomax [is expected to be] significantly more expensive than heparin, which sells at about $10 a vial. But the Cambridge company said data from more than 4,300 patients [showed the drug to be a superior alternative to heparin].

"Obviously, this is a very major milestone for Medicines Co.," said Dr. Clive Meanwell, the company's president and chief executive. "We think it is also a major milestone for the field of interventional cardiology. But most of all, we think it should be a significant milestone for patients."

Meanwell also hailed the approval as a confirmation of the young company's business model, based on the idea that there is money to be made off drugs that other companies cast aside.

Since other companies bring the products through the early stages of development, Medicines Co. bears less risk. Still, there is no guarantee that the products—sometimes shelved because of lackluster test results or unresolved developmental problems—will get to market.

In fact, at one time, the deck seemed stacked against Angiomax. The drug was discovered by Biogen Inc., among the nation's oldest and biggest biotechnology companies, but was abandoned after disappointing results from broad-based clinical trials.

Biogen's disappointment became Medicines Co.'s first project. The company licensed the drug from Biogen in 1997. ...

Jay B. Silverman, a senior biotech analyst with Robertson Stephens Inc. in New York, said he expects Angiomax to perform well against heparin. ... The challenge will be to persuade doctors and hospitals to change from heparin to Angiomax, he said, efforts that are already underway.

"That is always the challenge with these hospital products," Meanwell said. "Doctors are appropriately demanding of the data. They want to know how this drug will impact practices and costs."

The company has plans to conduct clinical trials at hundreds of hospitals nationwide to allow doctors to gain hands-on experience with the drug, Meanwell said. It anticipates a series of articles to be published in upcoming issues of independent, peer-reviewed scientific journals.

Meanwell said the company has gathered a team of experienced sales and marketing executives to head the 52-person sales force. And the product will be launched officially next month, after a weeklong educational meeting for the sales staff. ...

"This approval is about the best Christmas present I could get," Meanwell said. "We're very excited, very relieved, and very grateful."

Source: *The Boston Globe,* December 19, 2000, p. C3.

Exhibit 2 The Medicines Company Stock Performance—August 8, 2000 to January 31, 2001

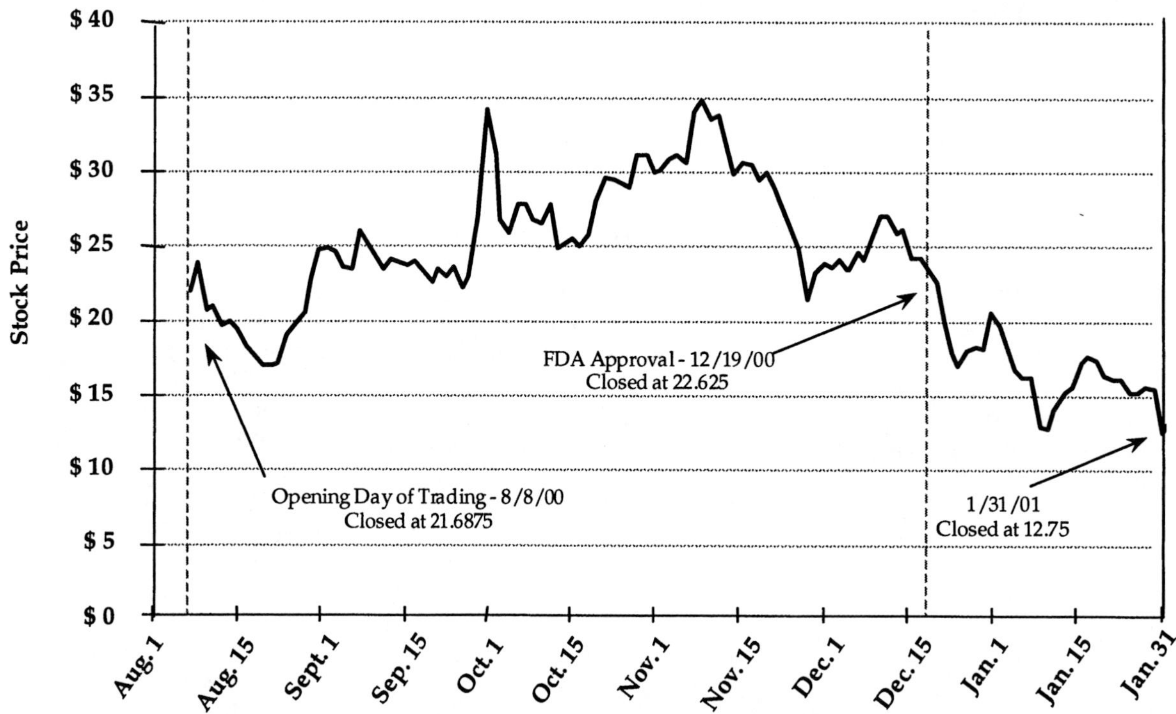

Source: Adapted from Web site, http://finance.yahoo.com.

Exhibit 3 Leading Pharmaceutical Companies, Ranked by U.S. Sales (in millions)[a]

Company (Headquarters)	U.S. Sales
Pfizer/Warner-Lambert (U.S.)	$ 14,607
Glaxo Wellcome/SmithKline (U.K.)[b]	12,490
Merck (U.S.)	10,486
Bristol-Myers Squibb (U.S.)	8,778
Astra/Zeneca (U.K.)	8,304
Johnson & Johnson (U.S.)	7,636
Eli Lilly (U.S.)	6,173
Pharmacia (U.S.)	6,055
American Home Products (U.S.)	5,832
Schering Plough (U.S.)	5,716

Source: Standard & Poor's industry survey, "Healthcare: Pharmaceuticals," December 21, 2000.

[a] For 12 months ending September 30, 2000.

[b] Merger pending.

Exhibit 4 The Allocation of $26 Billion in Research and Development in 2000

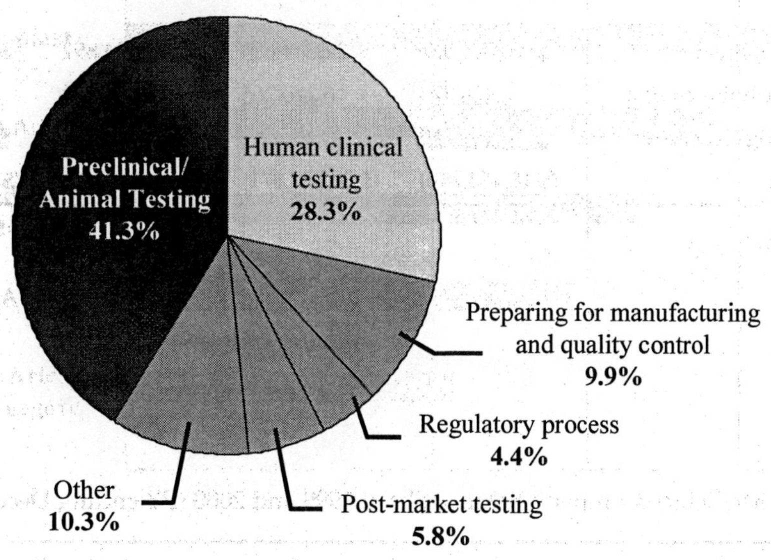

Source: "Health's Price Tag," *The Boston Globe,* March 28, 2001, p. D4.

Exhibit 5 Best-Selling Prescription Drugs in the United States in 1999

Drug (Company)	Use	Retail Sales (in millions)
Prilosec (Astra/Zeneca)	Anti-Ulcer	$ 4,187
Lipitor (Warner Lambert)	Cholesterol Reducer	3,002
Prozac (Eli Lilly)	Antidepressant	2,571
Prevacid (TAP)	Anti-Ulcer	2,364
Zocor (Merck)	Cholesterol Reducer	2,301
Epogen (Amgen)	Red Blood Cell Stimulant	1,842
Zoloft (Pfizer)	Antidepressant	1,737
Claritin (Schering Plough)	Antihistamine	1,534
Paxil (SmithKline Beecham)	Antidepressant	1,516
Zyprexa (Eli Lilly)	Antipsychotic	1,495

Source: Standard & Poor's industry survey, "Healthcare: Pharmaceuticals," December 21, 2000.

Exhibit 6 The Medicines Company Operating Income: 1997 to 2000

	1997	1998	1999	2000
Revenue from Operations:	$ 0	$ 0	$ 0	$ 0
Operating Expenses:				
Research & Development	$ 16,044,367	$ 24,004,606	$ 30,344,892	$ 39,572,297
Sales, General & Administrative	2,420,373	6,248,265	5,008,387	15,033,585
Total Operating Expenses:	$ 18,464,740	$ 30,252,871	$ 35,353,279	$ 54,605,882
Loss From Operations:	($ 18,464,740)	($ 30,252,871)	($ 35,353,279)	($ 54,605,882)

Source: Company records.

Exhibit 7 The Medicines Company Balance Sheet: 1999 and 2000 (FY ending December 31)

	1999	2000
Assets:		
Cash, Cash Equivalents, and		
Marketable Securities	$ 7,237,765	$ 80,718.013
Inventory	0	1,963,491
Fixed Assets (Net)	430,061	965,832
Other Assets	323,572	715,794
Total Assets:	$ 7,991,398	$ 84,363,130
Liabilities and Stockholders' Equity:		
Current Liabilities	$ 11,495,321	$ 15,124,147
Long-Term Liabilities	91,053,732	0
Stockholders' Equity (Deficit)	(94,557,655)	69,238,983
Total Liabilities and Stockholders' Equity:	$ 7,991,398	$ 84,363,130

Source: Company records.

Exhibit 8 Status of Angiomax Clinical Trials

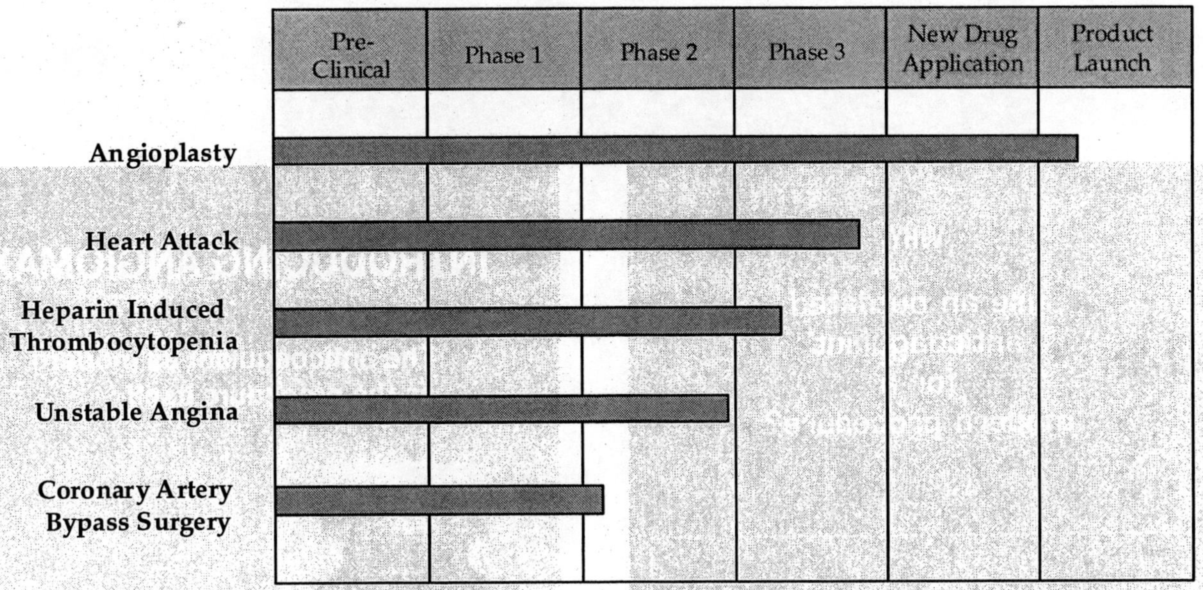

Pre-Clinical
Phase 1
Phase 2
Phase 3
New Drug Application
Product Launch

Angioplasty
Heart Attack
Heparin Induced Thrombocytopenia
Unstable Angina
Coronary Artery Bypass Surgery

Source: The Medicines Company 2000 Annual Report.

Exhibit 9 An Example of a Two-Page Angiomax Ad—January 2001

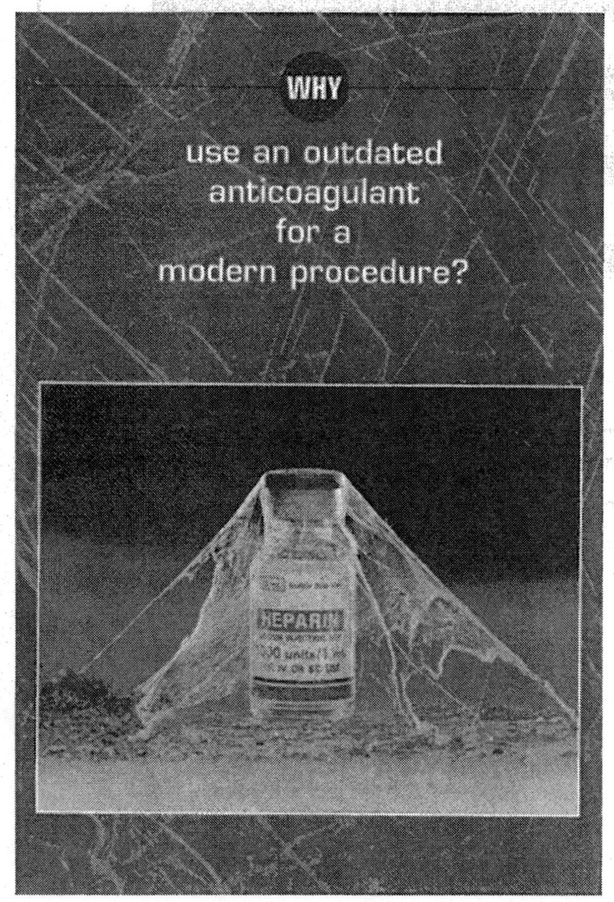

Page 1

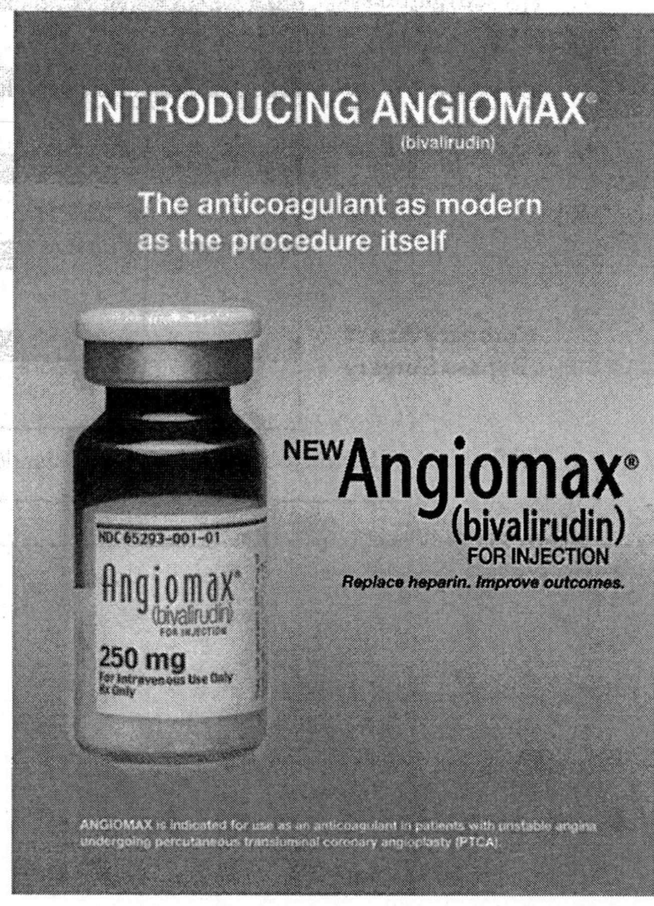

Page 2

Source: Company documents.

Richard Ivey School of Business
The University of Western Ontario

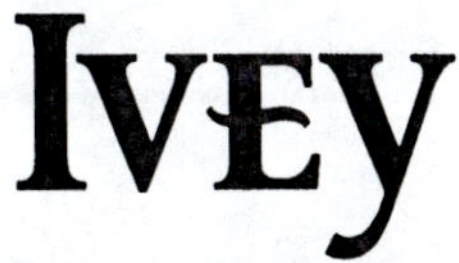

9B03A005

FORD WINDSTAR

Satish Jha prepared this case under the supervision of Professors Robert Fisher and David Sharp solely to provide material for class discussion. The authors do not intend to illustrate either effective or ineffective handling of a managerial situation. The authors may have disguised certain names and other identifying information to protect confidentiality.

INTRODUCTION

By the third quarter of 2001, it was clear to Brian Tafler, the brand manager of the Windstar in Canada that the Windstar — Ford of Canada's only brand in the minivan category — was not going to meet its annual sales targets. The latest market data showed that Windstar's share of the minivan category had fallen from 21.7 per cent in December 1999 to 16.9 per cent by August 2001. The minivan category itself was shrinking, and the category had become intensely competitive. A looming recession was expected to put the brakes on consumer spending. Added to these dismal market conditions were Windstar's nagging quality problems that had resulted in several product recalls. Ford's brand image too had been seriously affected by the controversies surrounding Firestone tires on Ford's Explorer SUVs. Also, a large number of Windstars were expected to come off-lease in Canada in 2002, and this would exert a downward pressure on Windstar resale values. Tafler's challenge was to develop a viable marketing plan that would reverse the decline and put Windstar on the path to regaining market share and restoring its brand image.

MINIVAN HISTORY AND DEVELOPMENT

Minivans were designed for families, for people with two or more children and who were tired of cramming into sedans for long and short-haul trips. Chrysler invented the category with the launch of the Dodge Caravan in 1983. The new type of vehicle rapidly unseated the station wagon as the staple family car and prompted other major automakers like General Motors and Ford to follow suit with their own brands in 1984 and 1985, respectively. By the early 1990s, the appeal of the roominess and comfort of the minivan had extended to include empty nesters and commercial users. The minivan category evolved to include two categories based on wheelbase. Long-wheel base (LWB) minivans, such as the Dodge Grand Caravan and Ford Windstar, were about 13 inches longer than the short-wheel base (SWB) minivans such as the Dodge Caravan. LWB minivans offered more roominess and comfort, whereas the SWB minivans were less expensive and offered more manoeuvrability.

The minivan category was dominated by the Big Three automakers (Daimler-Chrysler, General Motors and Ford) that accounted for over 80 per cent of the market. Daimler-Chrysler's Dodge Caravan was the market leader with 45 per cent market share until 1995. General Motors' strategy was to fragment the category based on buyers' needs and offer the potential minivan customer a wide choice. Therefore, it had five more or less distinctive brands in the category (Chevrolet Venture and Astro, Pontiac Montana, GM Safari and Oldsmobile Silhouette) and offered its customers several choices in both the LWB and SWB versions. Ford, in 1994, had three brands in the minivan category, with the LWB Windstar, and the SWB Aerostar and Mercury Villager. Nissan with Quest and Toyota with Previa were the other significant brands up until the mid-1990s.

The second half of the 1990s saw the dominance of the American automakers strongly challenged by Japanese players, led by Honda and Toyota. Honda entered the market with its Odyssey brand in late 1995, and Toyota replaced its Previa with the entirely redesigned Sienna in late 1997. Both brands were based on the very popular sedan platforms (Honda Accord and Toyota Camry) that were among the best-selling cars in North America. Both brands were LWB minivans targeted at customers who preferred imports to domestics. Both brands rode the reputation of superior quality associated with Honda and Toyota, and by the late 1999, both had increased their market share in the minivan category. Mazda (a subsidiary of Ford Motor Company) entered the market in 1999 with a revamp of its MPV brand, and it too had started gaining market share by late 1999. By the end of the 1990s, Chrysler's market share had eroded by almost eight percentage points. General Motors found itself introducing newer models and increasing incentives to maintain its share, while Ford had withdrawn both its Aerostar (in 1997) and Mercury Villager (in 1999) due to shrinking sales and high variable costs. By 1999, Ford's presence in this category was limited to the Windstar. In late 2001, the Korean manufacturer, Kia, entered the market with its Sedona brand. Kia adopted a low entry price strategy that it had successfully tried in entering other categories. Kia Sedona, which looked remarkably similar to the Windstar, was expected to win market share at the Ford's expense.

By the start of 2000, every major automobile manufacturer had at least one brand entry in this category, and the new entrants were increasingly fragmenting the minivan category. Also, the minivan category itself was shrinking (Exhibit 1) due to the popularity of sports utility vehicles (SUVs) such as the Ford Explorer and Dodge Durango, compact SUVs such as the Honda CRV and Ford Escape, and multi-activity vehicles (MAVs) such as the Chrysler's PT Cruiser and Pontiac Aztec. The minivan category's profitability had declined because of a dramatic rise in marketing spending, sales incentives in particular, especially by American automakers.

FORD WINDSTAR

The first Windstar was introduced in Canada in 1991. It quickly became one of the largest selling auto brands in Canada and an important member of Ford of Canada's brand portfolio. As the minivan was synonymous with family travel, safety was an important consideration in the purchase decision. Hence, safety was an important element in the design of the Windstar. It was the first to be given a five-star rating by NHTSA — the highway safety regulatory body within the industry — and led the industry in introducing safety features. The latest-generation Windstar had an innovative feature called the Personal Safety System, or PSS, that protected occupants in an accident. As a result, Windstar was consistently ranked by several industry publications as one of the best minivans in terms of safety and in meeting the needs of the family.

But Windstar fell short when it came to introducing product innovations. For instance, in 1995, Dodge Caravan introduced the sliding fourth door. Windstar did not follow suit because Ford's market research showed that minivan buyers did not want a fourth door. The fourth door went on to become a huge success and became a standard for all minivans. Windstar got its fourth door two years after the Dodge Caravan introduced the feature.

Honda Odyssey introduced the third row 'flip-fold' seat in 2001, which enhanced cargo space if needed and became one of the key purchase criteria for minivan buyers. Windstar did not have a third row flip-fold seat at the time of this case. To compound its problems, Windstar's image was adversely affected by nagging quality problems and several product recalls during the late 1990s. While major competitors like GM and Chrysler had both LWB and SWB versions, the Windstar offered its customers limited choice by persisting with only the LWB version. This was an issue because 40 per cent of all minivans sold in Canada were SWB. To make the LWB Windstar attractive to the price-sensitive SWB buyers, Ford of Canada priced the base Windstar lower than comparable LWB minivans.

A third of all Windstar buyers were in the 35 to 49 age group. This age group was also one of the prime targets for brands being launched in newer categories like SUVs. Another third of Windstar buyers were retired and hence expected a low-maintenance vehicle. A significant number of Windstar buyers had limited education, lived in rural areas and sought proof of safety and market success. They also considered themselves old-fashioned but not conservative.

All these problems notwithstanding, the two millionth Windstar was scheduled to be produced in December 2001 in Oakville, Ontario, where all Windstars sold in 32 countries around the world were assembled.

COMPETITION

The competition in the minivan category was intense, with eight products in the LWB segment and nine vehicles in the SWB segment. Ford competed in both segments with the LWB Windstar. In the LWB segment, Windstar's market share had fallen from 44 per cent at the end of 1998 to just under 30 per cent in August 2001. In the same period, Pontiac Montana had increased its share of the segment from nine per cent to 14.1 per cent during the same period, and Chrysler's Grand Caravan had increased its share of the LWB segment from 19 per cent to 27.4 per cent. The charge of the imports was led by Honda Odyssey, which had almost tripled its share of the LWB segment during the same period from 3.3 per cent to just over 11 per cent. As the LWB segment itself had shrunk marginally from 1998 levels, the winners in the LWB segment had captured market share primarily from Ford Windstar and Toyota Sienna. Exhibit 2 provides sales data for all the minivan brands in Canada.

General Motors

The world's largest automaker had five brands competing in the minivan category, led by Chevrolet Venture and Pontiac Montana. GM always believed in being the leader in every category of the market. It usually adopted a strategy of introducing several brands built upon the same platform, and then offering strong incentives to push sales. GM held 31 per cent market share in the minivan category in May 2001.

Chevrolet Venture

Sold in both SWB and LWB forms, this model had just over 11 per cent market share in the minivan category. Thirty-seven per cent of minivan buyers were familiar with the Chevrolet Venture brand.

Buyer profile

Fifty-eight per cent of its buyers were under 50 years old with 75 per cent males. They were highly pro-Canadian, most likely to see vehicle as just transportation and seek the cheapest solution. They did not consider vehicle safety and roominess as critical and were more likely to accept style over engineering.

Pontiac Montana

Sold both SWB and LWB forms and had increased its market share by almost 40 per cent from 1998 levels. It had 10.2 per cent share of the segment in 1998 but by August 2001, its share had gone up to 14.1 per cent. It offered an optional 4-Wheel drive and adopted a fully independent rear suspension similar to the Honda Odyssey. Thirty-one per cent of minivan buyers were familiar with the Pontiac Montana brand. GM positioned Montana similar to other Pontiac models — "built for drivers." Montana owners felt that their minivan was closer to an SUV than competitive vans.

Buyer profile

Almost 60 per cent of its buyers were under 50 years of age, had the lowest education, and were more likely to live in rural areas. Thirty-seven per cent were safety-minded, least likely to see themselves as conservative and most likely to believe that the vehicle reflected the driver. Its buyers were also less apt to seek safety/success validation before purchase.

Daimler-Chrysler

Despite financial and quality problems in the 1990s, Daimler-Chrysler was still the undisputed leader in the minivan category with Dodge Caravan. Its LWB minivan was called the Grand Caravan. Daimler-Chrysler had a luxury minivan brand called the Town & Country, but its volumes were quite low. Daimler-Chrysler had 36.5 per cent market share as of August 2001.

Dodge Caravan

The Caravan had many firsts to its name including the first in the minivan category and the first to introduce the sliding fourth door. It had the highest brand awareness[1] with 77 per cent of minivan buyers familiar with the Dodge Caravan brand. For the past few years, Dodge has relied heavily on the claim that Caravan is the top-selling nameplate in Canada.

---

[1] *Brand awareness was measured as some knowledge about the product and its key attributes.*

Buyer profile

Forty per cent of Caravan buyers were 60 years or older and 37 per cent of its buyers were retired. Over 65 per cent had no kids in the household. A major proportion of its buyers had limited education and the brand was becoming increasingly popular amongst lower-income households. Thirty-nine per cent of its buyers were safety minded and would pay more for safety features. They were least likely to seek uniqueness and least apt to see vehicle as a reflection of the driver. They considered passenger room extremely important.

The Imports

Honda Odyssey, Toyota Sienna and Mazda MPV have led the charge of the imports after entering the minivan category in Canada. Together they account for 14.8 per cent of the minivan category. While the Odyssey and Sienna offered a LWB version only, the MPV sold only in the short-wheel base segment.

Honda Odyssey

Introduced in 1997, the Odyssey did not live up to the Honda reputation for manufacturing quality on launch. However, it recovered quickly. The 2002 Odysseys had adjustable middle seats and third-row seats that folded flat into the floor, creating additional room for cargo. It had about 6.6 per cent of the market share in the minivan category in 2001. Twenty-nine per cent of minivan buyers were aware of the Honda Odyssey brand.

Buyer profile

Fifty-seven per cent of its buyers were in the 35 to 49 age group with 96 per cent of its buyers married. Forty-four per cent of its buyers had one to two children living in household. Its buyers were well educated with 52 per cent going to university and had the highest income amongst minivan buyers. The Odyssey was a popular choice with professionals. Its buyers sought easy-to-maintain vehicles that they could keep for a long time. They also sought product uniqueness and didn't value styling over engineering. Thirty-four per cent of its buyers were safety-minded.

Toyota Sienna

Introduced in 1996 and built on the best-selling Camry platform, the Toyota Sienna didn't do as well as the Honda. However, Toyota was planning to introduce both short-wheel and LWB versions in 2003. The Sienna had several safety features and an excellent reliability history. Its Camry platform provided for a smoother ride. Toyota also introduced the dual power sliding doors in its 2002 models and a newer model was to be launched in 2003. The Sienna has about 4.3 per cent market share. Nineteen per cent of minivan buyers are familiar with the Toyota Sienna brand.

Buyer profile

The Sienna is a popular choice amongst buyers in the 35 to 39 and 60 to 69 age groups. Its buyers were well educated (57 per cent with at least some university), highly apt to look at safety tests and sought market success but were less likely to consider roominess as critical. Like the Odyssey buyers, they too sought an easy-to-maintain vehicle that they could keep for a long time.

Mazda MPV

The MPV had fallen short of market expectation ever since it hit the market in 1996; however, MPV offered many segment-leading interior features. Its second-row seats could be configured as captain's chairs or pushed together to form a bench, and the third-row seats could tumble flat into the floor. Its most novel feature was the roll-down windows in its sliding doors, which made passengers feel less claustrophobic. MPV was also the only minivan that offered a moonroof. The MPV had about 3.9 per cent market share. Twenty-four per cent of minivan buyers were familiar with the Mazda MPV brand.

The Others

Nissan Quest (a twin to Ford's Mercury Villager), Volkswagen Eurovan and Kia Sedona completed the minivan competitive landscape. Together they accounted for less than 0.5 per cent of the category. The Kia Sedona that was introduced in 2001 was selling well and expected to gain market share over the next few years.

CONSUMER BEHAVIOR

The average age of minivan buyers was increasing. Whereas the 35 to 49 age group accounted for 47 per cent of minivan sales in 1998, they made 40 per cent of category purchases in 2001. In contrast, the 65-plus age group accounted for just 12 per cent of minivans sales in 1998, but now was responsible for 19 per cent of purchases. The changing demographic profile of minivan buyers was having a major impact on the sales of several minivan brands. First, older buyers seemed to buy and use minivans for different reasons than younger buyers. Second, the 35 to 49 age group was more than twice as large as the 59 to 74 age groups, and hence some analysts attributed the decline in the minivan sales to this changing demographics (see Exhibit 3).

Research revealed that the typical minivan buyer considered 14 attributes when making a purchase decision. Of these 14 attributes (see Exhibit 4), nine had a strong correlation with purchase intent. 'Proud to own' brand imagery had the biggest association with purchase, while luxurious interior finish had the lowest association. As new players introduced innovative options into their products, these attributes would change over time. Ford Windstar led the competition in eight out of those 14 attributes, twice as many as Chrysler's Dodge Caravan (see Exhibit 5). However, this had not translated into a higher share for Ford's Windstar. See Exhibits 6 through 8 for important research findings on the importance of various product benefits and features on minivan brand choices.

The process of purchasing a minivan was driven by many factors and ranged in duration from a few months to three or more years. However, Ford found it useful to describe the process in terms of three phases: the consideration phase, the active shopping phase, and buying phase. The key attributes sought in a minivan changed depending on which phase of the purchase process a buyer was in (see Exhibit 9).

A typical minivan buyer used a variety of information sources before making a decision. These sources ranged from informal channels that could not be controlled (like immediate family and advice of friends and relatives) to more formal marketing channels (like dealer advice, dealer/manufacturer sales information, and media exposures through advertising). See Exhibit 10 for differences across minivan alternatives in the sources of information used in the purchase decision.

FORD'S ACTION PLAN

Brian Tafler had developed a set of marketing programs to consider for use over the next 12 months. His immediate goal was to stabilize Windstar's market share, while maintaining at least a positive overall contribution per unit. His strategy was based on the knowledge that an all-new Windstar was under development, but it would not enter the market until the 2004 model year (September 2003). Of paramount importance was the need to maintain the Windstar brand, and its position in the overall Ford portfolio, until the new model was ready.

Tafler knew the market was very competitive and margins were tight. He knew his variable production and allocated overhead costs per unit were approximately 80 per cent of the selling price (for more information on industry margins see Exhibit 11).

Tafler also knew that Ford was currently spending $5,204 per vehicle in marketing incentives, and this would not change. Similar to other domestic manufacturers, Ford spent approximately $1,500 per vehicle on factory-to-dealer credits. These credits allow dealers to advertise a lower price without cutting into their gross margins. The balance of the average incentive was made up of subvented (i.e., subsidized by the manufacturer) interest rates on leases and purchases. Although the factory-to-dealer incentives would definitely not be changed, longer subvented lease rates were under consideration, along with several other alternatives.

Direct Mail Campaign

Tafler was considering one or both of the following direct mail campaigns.

Lease Renewal Customers

Approximately 20,000 Windstars were coming off lease over the next year. One option was to develop a targeted renewal campaign directed specifically at these customers. This would involve a branded mailing that highlighted new features on the current Windstar (such as the Personal Safety System and Family Entertainment System). The estimated development and production cost for each full color, high gloss mailer was $20. The campaign would run for three months and approximately 5,000 renewal customers would be targeted. The current Windstar lease renewal rate was 40 per cent. Hence, 40 per cent of existing Windstar lease customers would normally lease another Windstar. By creating a highly focused direct mailer campaign that offered a $500 loyalty discount, Ford expected that it could retain 45 per cent to 50 per cent of its returning lease customers.

Potential New Customers

An alternative program would focus on consumers who currently leased a minivan from another domestic manufacturer. Based on marketing research about the type of customer who leased each brand (i.e., demographic profiles, attitudes, satisfaction levels, etc.) Ford would create a targeted direct mail piece to go along with a $500 switching incentive. The cost of a direct mail piece was the same as for the previous alternative, but there would be an additional $10 cost per customer to purchase a customer database. Tafler expected that the direct mail program would convert two per cent to three per cent of those contacted. As the typical lease period average around 30 months, 1999 year-end sales volume would be used to determine the number of customers to be targeted. Approximately 50 per cent of all minivans in 1999 were leased.

Repositioning Through Advertising

The automotive industry used a three-tiered structure advertising structure.

Tier 1

The manufacturer paid for and controlled all the advertising. The advertising in this tier was focused on building brand image, and the impact on sales was seen only after a few years of sustained advertising. An example of a Tier 1 and can be found in Exhibit 12.

Tier 2

The dealer associations, which include the manufacturer and its dealers, paid for the advertising costs. At this level, the advertising usually focused on promoting a particular brand within a region for a brief period.

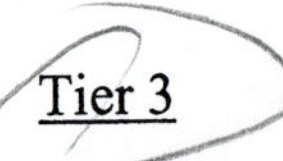

Tier 3

The dealer paid for and produced dealer-specific advertising. At the dealership level, most advertising had a short-term focus and hence focused on price promotions and incentives to attract customers.

Co-ordination among the three tiers was not easy because manufacturers put a premium on building brands while dealers were more interested in immediate sales. Since 1998, the total spending on minivan advertising and promotions in Canada had increased by over 10 per cent. Domestic automakers had increased their share of voice[2] (SOV) from just below 62 per cent in 1998 to over 64 per cent in 2001. Chrysler's SOV had dropped, but the company still led the advertising spend within the minivan category. General Motors had increased its advertising spend. It had also realigned its advertising strategy: instead of spending advertising dollars on promoting all five of its products in the minivan category, it now was focusing on promoting only the Pontiac Montana and Chevy Venture. Ford Windstar's share of advertising spend had dropped significantly from 1998 levels. Even in absolute terms, Windstar was spending $3 million less on advertising in 2001 than it did in 1998. Among the imports, Honda and Toyota had reduced their share of advertising. Mazda MPV and Kia Sedona together accounted for less than 15 per cent of the advertising spent. See Exhibit 13 for advertising spending by brand for Tier 1 and Tier 2 advertising.

---

[2] *SOV is the advertising dollars spent by a manufacturer as a percentage of total industry or category expenditures.*

Tafler considered Tier 2 print advertising that focused on the price of the base LX model to fight the SWB market directly. The idea was to "get customers to the dealers" and then count on the dealers and the salespeople to convert the customer to a higher priced model. Tafler knew this approach would pull down the prices of the other Windstar models, significantly reducing revenue. In a best-case scenario, Ford could expect to increase unit sales over the next three months by five per cent, but it would reduce prices of the other sales it made by five per cent. The cost of a 52-week national campaign — a full page ad, once a week, in all major newspapers — would be approximately $2 million.

If he didn't go with a price-oriented strategy, Tafler knew he would have to keep the Windstar brand in front of target consumers with image advertising. As a general rule of thumb, SOV should be equal to market share over the long run. Currently, advertising per unit for the Windstar was $598 per unit (this figure includes an allocated portion from corporate advertising and all Tier 1 and Tier 2 media) and this would be a baseline level that would continue for the next year. Tafler believed that in the long-run, image advertising would be necessary to maintain and enhance the Windstar brand. He wondered about which key attributes or benefits should be emphasized in Windstar Tier 1 advertising.

Value Pricing

One way to create excitement at retail would be to create value packages that bundled attractive features and value priced them. Ford was considering including a Family Entertainment System (a combination TV and VCR) at no charge in its mid to high-end models (Sport, SEL and Limited). This was usually a $1,500 option. The competition offered this type of feature on only their top-of-the-line models, so this was a potential selling feature. This strategy was designed to slow the sales decline and improve the vehicle mix by selling higher end models that had higher margins. This strategy was also attractive as it was relatively easy to build a Tier 1 advertising campaign around it. A one per cent to two per cent increase in unit sales was expected over the next three months. The variable cost of this option for Ford was approximately $1,100. Traditionally about five per cent of customers bought this item.

Sales Incentives

Incentives were an important sales tool and usually included benefits to a buyer like subvented lease or financing rates, cash-backs and other discounts. Since 1998, most manufacturers were increasingly using incentives to trigger a purchase decision. Incentives offered by domestic manufacturers were significantly higher than those offered by imports.

Leasing

In 2002, approximately 55 per cent of Ford Windstar sales in Canada were leases. At the present time, Ford offered 24- and 36-month subvented lease rates on the Windstar (48- and 60-month leases were possible, but not at reduced rates). GM and Chrysler were currently offering excellent rates on 24-, 36-, and 48-month terms whereas the imports did not offer subvented lease rates. The average lease length for the industry was approximately 30 months.

Most leasing and financing for manufacturers were done by their captive finance companies. Hence finance companies like General Motors Acceptance Credit and Ford Credit provided attractive lease and financing options to their customers. Even though the cost of funds for these companies was estimated to be between four per cent to five per cent in 2001, the interest rate charged to the customer was approximately zero per cent to two per cent. As most of these finance companies had independent operations, they recovered the difference from the manufacturers.

Longer lease terms allowed customers to lower their monthly outlay of cash, but they were very costly for the manufacturer. A longer lease term also meant that customers would not be back in the showroom for an additional 12 to 24 months. Furthermore, customer satisfaction was lower after three or four years, as many vehicles would need servicing such as brakes and tires at that point. The current cost per year of a lease rate that is reduced by 2.5 per cent was $865. By offering longer lease terms, it was expected that the sales mix would have a larger proportion of vehicles leased. It was also expected that the unit volume over the next three months would increase by two per cent.

Cash Offers

As an alternative to longer subvented leasing, Tafler considered making cash discounts available to a buyer or salesperson if an outright purchase was made. All of the following alternatives were combinable with subvented leasing rates except the purchase cash alternative (if a customer was leasing, they would not also be able to get a purchase cash discount). Of course, every dollar spent on sales incentives was a dollar less to the bottom-line. The alternatives were:

1. Purchase cash: $2,000 on all Windstar purchases.
2. Red Carpet Lease Cash: $500 on all Windstar leases.
3. Renewal Offer: $1,000 cash on returning leases.
4. Christmas Bonus: $500 cash to purchases and leases in December.
5. Salesperson Incentive: $100 for every vehicle sold in a 30-day period, plus a golf vacation (worth approximately $4,000) for the top salesperson in each of six sales regions.

Tafler believed that each $1,000 in sales incentives would produce an additional two per cent increase in volume over the next three months. It was estimated that 70 per cent of all non-leased vehicles were financed.

Brian Tafler knew the incentives on Windstar were already at an all-time high of $5,204 per vehicle, and significant increases were not desirable because the Windstar was operating at close to break-even levels. Any marketing plan that was implemented would, at minimum, have to address not just sales volume and contribution effects, but also the brand image of Windstar. Beginning in September 2001, the next 12 months would be crucial for Ford of Canada and Windstar.

Exhibit 1

MINIVAN SEGMENT

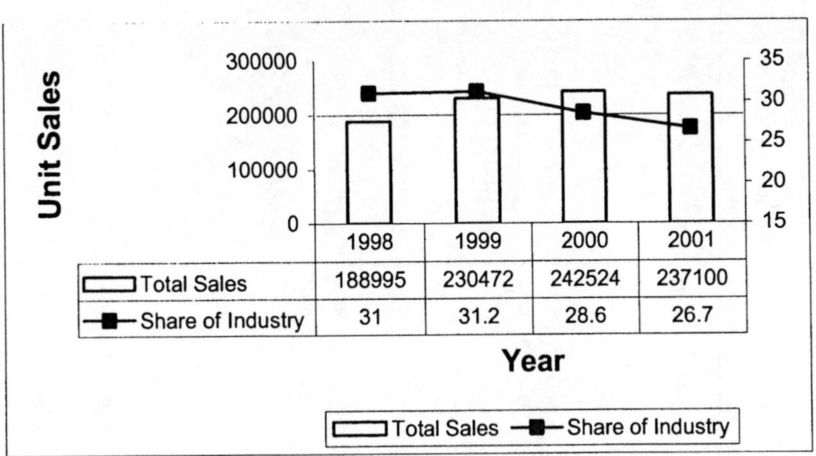

	1998	1999	2000	2001
Total Sales	188995	230472	242524	237100
Share of Industry	31	31.2	28.6	26.7

Source: Ford of Canada.

Exhibit 2

MARKET SHARES OF MAJOR MINIVAN BRANDS

	1998			1999			2000			2001 August*		
Brands	**Long-wheel base**	**Short-wheel base**	**Total**	**Long-wheel base**	**Short-wheel base**	**Total**	**Long-wheel base**	**Short-wheel base**	**Total**	**Long-wheel base**	**Short-wheel base**	**Total**
Aerostar	626	104	730	36	16	52	5	5	10	-	-	-
Windstar	50,530	-	50,530	54,847	-	54,847	49,059	-	49,059	29,682	-	29,682
Total Ford	**51,156**	**104**	**51,260**	**54,883**	**16**	**54,899**	**49,064**	**5**	**49,069**	**29,682**	**-**	**29,682**
Venture	8,072	9,836	17,908	9,818	12,669	22,487	11,724	12,903	24,627	9,687	9,891	19,578
Montana	10,530	8,819	19,349	14,782	8,084	22,866	14,589	12,289	26,878	14,449	10,340	24,789
Silhouette	3,027	-	3,027	3,876	-	3,876	3,780	-	3,780	2,450	-	2,450
Astro	-	10,039	10,039	-	8,622	8,622	-	7,272	7,272	-	4,043	4,043
Safari	-	10,335	10,335	-	8,955	8,955	-	7,191	7,191	-	3,978	3,978
Total GM	**21,629**	**39,029**	**60,658**	**28,476**	**38,330**	**66,806**	**30,093**	**39,655**	**69,748**	**26,586**	**28,252**	**54,838**
Caravan	22,223	28,956	51,179	30,494	41,671	72,165	40,246	47,215	87,461	29,070	33,716	62,786
Town & Country	2,484	-	2,484	3,647	-	3,647	2,418	-	2,418	1,351	-	1,351
Total Chrysler	**24,707**	**28,956**	**53,663**	**34,141**	**41,671**	**75,812**	**42,664**	**47,215**	**89,879**	**30,421**	**33,716**	**64,137**
Toyota Sienna	14,788	-	14,788	15,020	-	15,020	11,092	-	11,092	7,612	-	7,612
Honda Odyssey	3,881	-	3,881	12,146	-	12,146	13,240	-	13,240	11,658	-	11,658
Mazda MPV	-	2,085	2,085	-	4,690	4,690	-	8,936	8,936	-	6,923	6,923
Nissan Quest	-	1,927	1,927	-	953	953	-	479	479	-	150	150
Kia Sedona	-	-	-	-	-	-	-	-	-	-	601	601
VW	-	733	733	-	146	146	-	81	81	-	30	30
Total	**116,161**	**72,834**	**188,995**	**144,666**	**85,806**	**230,472**	**146,153**	**96,371**	**242,524**	**105,959**	**69,672**	**175,631**

* *Annual sales for 2001 were expected to be 1.35 times total sales until August 2001.*
Source: *Ford of Canada.*

Exhibit 3

CANADIAN POPULATION AND GROWTH RATES BY AGE GROUPS

Census 2001			Growth rates
Age Groups	**Population in millions**	**% share**	**Projected growth from 2001 to 2006**
0-14	5.8	18.8	-5.1%
15-24	4.2	13.5	3.5%
25-35	4.4	14.1	1.0%
35-39	2.7	8.5	-11.9%
40-44	2.7	8.5	1.0%
45-49	2.4	7.7	11.7%
50-59	3.7	12.0	18.6%
60-69	2.4	7.9	15.3%
> 69	2.8	9.0	10.1%

Target

Male to female ratio is not expected to change at 1.02:1

Source: Statistics Canada, www.statcan.ca/English/gdb/demo23a, November 2003.

49%

Growing/aging market
focus on value through Tier 3 incentives
if possible, introduce novel feature (reason for Dodge success)

Exhibit 4

CORRELATION OF IMAGERY WITH PURCHASE CONSIDERATION

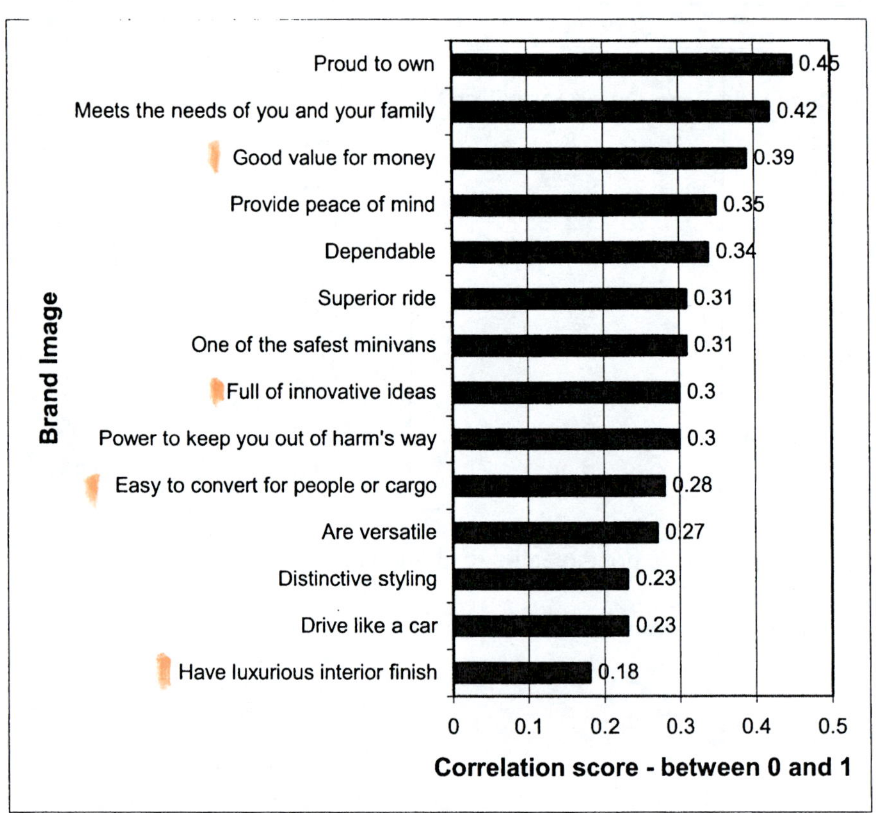

Source: Ford of Canada Brand Study.

Exhibit 5

PERFORMANCE OF WINDSTAR ON THE 14 ATTRIBUTES

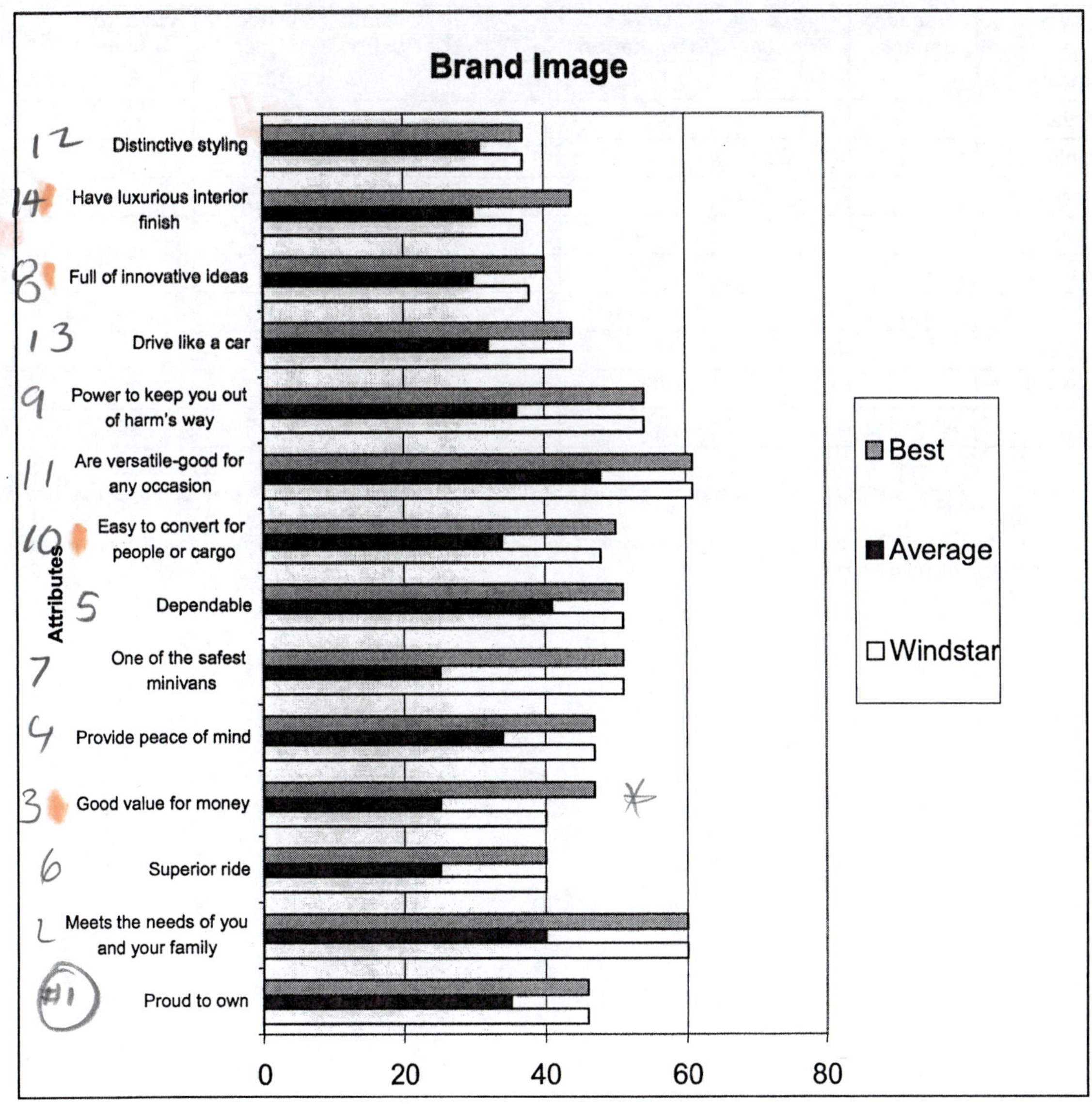

Scale in percentages

Source: Ford of Canada Brand Study

Note: The above bars lists, from least important (distinctive styling) to most important (proud to own), some of the key attributes that a buyer seeks from a brand within the minivan category. The first top bar indicates the leader's score in the category, the middle bar indicates the average score for all brands on this attribute and the bottom bar indicates Windstar's score. Hence on the 'Proud to own' attribute, Dodge Caravan and Ford Windstar lead the category.

Exhibit 6

TOP THREE REASONS FOR PURCHASE

	Seating Capacity	Fuel Economy	OEM's Reputation	Safety	Overall Quality	Price/ deal	Value for money	Reliability
Windstar						*34%	25%	28%
Venture	23%					42%		30%
Montana		22%				29%		28%
Caravan						27%	28%	28%
Odyssey			39%		21%			50%
Sienna			33%	28%				44%
MPV	30%			30%		32%		
Sedona**	X					X	X	
Domestic	20	14	11	17	11	32	23	29
Imports	14	6	33	18	19	15	19	43

* *Read as "Thirty-four per cent of Windstar buyers mentioned price/deal offered as one of three reasons for their purchase."*

** *Sedona was newly launched in 2001, hence inadequate data are available. 'X' represents case writer's opinion on what consumer's response might be.*

Exhibit 7

MINIVAN PURCHASE REASONS

	% Mentioned as one of top-three purchase reasons									
	1998					2001				
	Total	<35	35-49	50-64	65+	Total	<35	35-49	50-64	65+
Price/Deal/Value	48	55	* 49	44	40	50	57	51	47	43
Reliability/Durability/Overall Quality	50	49	49	51	50	47	42	48	51	46
Performance/Fun to Drive	39	36	36	43	48	38	38	36	40	43
Fuel Economy/Service-Repairs/Trade-in/Warranty	34	37	33	34	33	37	38	36	37	38
Comfort & Roominess	24	22	28	23	22	22	21	25	21	22
Manufacturer's Reputation	18	14	18	21	22	18	17	16	19	18
Safety	15	14	16	14	15	17	17	19	16	16
Styling	17	22	16	13	12	15	20	15	13	9

** Read as — "Fifty-five per cent of buyers under the age of 35 mentioned price, deal or value as one of their top three reasons for puchase."*

Source: Maritz New Vehicle Buyer Study.

Goals

(1) Maintain share → 16.4% / 20.8%

(2) Maintain brand image

(3) Maintain profitability → $586/car

Options

Direct Mail

+

↑ awareness

reminder to renew

low cost

Quick & easy

−

junk mail

low conversion rate

Max = 5k

to 500/purchase

easy to imitate

Ad.

+

Brand image

Shared cost

SUV ↓ than market

can't imitate

−

long term

high cost

Exhibit 8

FORD WINDSTAR AND OTHER MAJOR MINIVAN BRANDS
Sector Demographics and Regional Trends
(%)

(A) Media Awareness — Influenced by Tier 1 and Tier 2 Advertising

Brands	16-34	35-54	55+	Male	Female	Quebec	Rest of Country
Ford Windstar	61	50	52	60	45	58	52
Chevrolet Venture	56	47	44	54	42	50	48
Dodge Caravan	79	68	60	76	60	73	68
Chrysler Town & Country	23	27	32	33	21	22	29
Honda Odyssey	31	33	29	38	25	23	34
Toyota Sienna	20	26	18	25	21	27	23

(B) Purchase Consideration — Influenced by media awareness, shows what percentage of potential minivan buyers in that age group considered a particular brand.

Brands	16-34	35-54	55+	Male	Female	Quebec	Rest of Country
Ford Windstar	55	41	52	45	46	43	46
Chevrolet Venture	47	44	51	45	47	46	45
Dodge Caravan	64	64	61	68	59	64	64
Chrysler Town & Country	33	36	38	41	32	31	38
Honda Odyssey	45	42	49	45	41	44	43
Toyota Sienna	37	35	40	35	37	36	36

(C) Overall Opinion — Influenced by many factors such as advertising, corporate image, vehicle quality, dealers, past experience, etc.

Brands	16-34	35-54	55+	Male	Female	Quebec	Rest of Country
Ford Windstar	55	54	55	54	53	53	53
Chevrolet Venture	52	48	47	49	49	54	48
Dodge Caravan	66	63	72	68	63	63	67
Chrysler Town & Country	33	49	56	52	42	46	48
Honda Odyssey	55	57	53	61	48	52	56
Toyota Sienna	41	51	48	54	41	49	47

(D) Key images associated with the Windstar

Brands	16-34	35-54	55+	Male	Female	Quebec	Rest of Country
Proud to own	32	39	53	39	41	42	39
Meets the needs of you and your family	43	49	57	51	48	47	50
Good value for money	35	32	35	31	35	33	32
Peace of Mind	35	42	40	34	45	42	39
Dependable	40	41	38	34	46	38	40
One of the safest minivans	43	46	53	49	45	55	45
Easy to convert	38	41	37	38	41	33	41

Source: Ford of Canada Research

Exhibit 9

ATTRIBUTES SOUGHT IN A MINIVAN BY PHASE OF BUYING PROCESS

	Key Attributes sought in a minivan	
Consideration Phase (56% of potential minivan buyers were in this phase)	• I can be proud to own • Meets the need of my family • Is good value for money • Gives me peace of mind • Is dependable	Image and brand perception (1 to 3 years before purchase)
Active Shopping Phase (38% of potential minivan buyers were in this phase)	• I can be proud to own • Is versatile • Is dependable • Meets the needs of my family	Image and features (4 to 12 months before purchase)
Decision Phase (6% of potential minivan buyers were in this phase)	• Reliability • Price or deal offered • Value for money • Passenger seating capacity	Features and price (0 to 3 months before purchase)

Source: Ford of Canada Brand Study.

Exhibit 10

SOURCES OF INFORMATION WHEN PURCHASING A MINIVAN (%)

Sources of information	Windstar	Caravan	Montana	Venture	Odyssey	Mazda MPV	Sienna	All domestic	All imports
Immediate family	32	34	38	28	14	25	28	34	20
Consumer guides	12	14	8	13	41	22	35	12	34
Dealer's verbal advice	12	10	9	10	7	10	5	10	8
Dealer's/manufacturer's sales info	7	9	7	9	9	4	6	8	7
Friend's relatives info	7	4	10	10	10	6	9	7	8
Newspaper advertising	7	8	7	9	0	8	1	8	2
Special private viewing	6	6	6	7	3	5	3	6	4
Internet	3	2	4	3	3	7	3	3	4
Television advertising	2	4	4	1	0	3	1	3	1
Magazine article	1	2	1	2	3	3	3	1	3
Auto shows	2	1	1	1	3	0	2	1	2
Magazine advertising	2	2	1	1	0	1	0	1	0
Newspaper article	1	0	1	1	1	2	1	0	2
Radio advertising	1	0	1	0	0	0	0	0	0
Direct mail	0	0	0	0	0	0	0	0	0
Other	7	5	3	6	7	4	3	5	6

Exhibit 11

AVERAGE INDUSTRY MARGINS

	Aggregate Domestic			Aggregate Imports		
	Low end	**Middle**	**High end**	**Low end**	**Middle**	**High end**
Volume Mix	10%	70%	20%	20%	60%	20%
MSRP*	$ 26,000	$ 32,000	$ 40,000	$ 30,000	$ 35,000	$ 40,000
Dealer margin	12%	12%	12%	10%	10%	10%
OEM Margins**	15%	20%	25%	15%	20%	25%
Option margin	Varies from 15% to 30%			Varies from 15% to 30%		

45

* *Does not include tax, or delivery charges.*
** *Does not include per vehicle marketing incentives.*

Source: Ford of Canada

Exhibit 12

TIER 1 ADVERTISEMENT

Source: Company files.

Exhibit 13

MINIVAN — SHARE OF ADVERTISING (MANUFACTURER + DEALER)

	Share of advertising (%)			
Minivan Brands	**1998**	**1999**	**2000**	**2001**
Caravan/Voyager	33.2	31.6	35.0	29.2
Windstar	19.0	18.2	21.0	14.2
Pontiac Montana	0.0	6.1	12.3	9.3
Chevy Venture	9.7	14.2	11.7	11.5
Honda Odyssey	6.0	6.5	2.3	1.8
Toyota Sienna	10.3	4.5	5.7	10.3
Mazda MPV	4.2	7.9	8.5	11.3
Chevy Astro	3.5	0.4	0.4	0.2
GMC Safari	4.0	0.5	0.5	0.2
Olds Silhouette	0.1	0.1	0.1	0.0
Nissan Quest	0.6	0.1	0.0	0.0
Kia Sedona	0.0	0.0	0.0	3.1
Others	9.4	9.9	2.5	8.9
Total	100.0	100.0	100.0	100.0
Total Expenditure	$93.5 million	$96.8 million	$107.6 million	$103.7 million

HARVARD | BUSINESS | SCHOOL

9-509-049
REV: MAY 28, 2009

THOMAS STEENBURGH
JILL AVERY
NASEEM DAHOD

HubSpot: Inbound Marketing and Web 2.0

None of [the old rules of marketing] are true anymore. The Web has transformed the rules, and you must transform your marketing to make the most of the Web-enabled marketplace of ideas.

—David Meerman Scott, author of *The New Rules of Marketing and PR*

Business was good at HubSpot. Founders Brian Halligan and Dharmesh Shah were thrilled with the progress their young company had made in the two years since they began their journey to convince corporate America that the rules of marketing had changed. To be successful in the marketplace, HubSpot needed to be much more than just a software company. Its founders had to become evangelists, preaching a new way of doing business that would fundamentally change the way marketers reached their customers. To their great pleasure, Halligan and Shah were finding a willing audience for their ideas. HubSpot was now considered a thought leader in the Web 2.0 space, coining the term "inbound marketing" to describe marketing strategies and practices that *pulled* prospective customers towards a business and its products, through the use of Web 2.0 tools and applications like blogging, search engine optimization (SEO), and social media.

Halligan and Shah realized that their business was at a crucial juncture. They had just reached the noteworthy milestone of 1,000 customers, attaining this level of critical mass by practicing what they preached. HubSpot had built its business by turning its back on traditional marketing methods and was solely using innovative inbound techniques to acquire customers. Looking ahead, the founders wanted to accelerate their growth rate and increase profitability. Ironically, they were grappling with many of the same issues that their customers faced when implementing inbound marketing practices.

Halligan and Shah realized that they would need to work through these issues in order to achieve their goals for the company. First, they would need to decide which customers to serve, pulling the best opportunities from the diverse pool of customers who were contacting them. Second, they would need to make some decisions about their current pricing model to entice new customers to the company and to maximize the profitability of existing customers. Third, they would need to assess whether they could achieve enough scale through inbound marketing efforts, or whether they needed to supplement their inbound programs with traditional, interruptive outbound programs. This was more than a test of HubSpot as a company; it was a test of the inbound marketing business philosophy. If HubSpot couldn't scale its own business using inbound marketing, then how could it convince its customers that inbound marketing would work for them?

Professor Thomas Steenburgh and Professor Jill Avery (Simmons School of Management) and Naseem Dahod (MBA 2009) prepared this case. HBS cases are developed solely as the basis for class discussion. Cases are not intended to serve as endorsements, sources of primary data, or illustrations of effective or ineffective management.

Founding HubSpot

The two HubSpot founders met at MIT. As early and eager students of Web 2.0, Halligan and Shah recognized the transformative power the Internet possessed for changing the way small businesses operated. After graduation, Halligan joined Longworth Ventures, a venture capital firm with an expertise in technology. As he worked with start-up companies, he recognized an issue with which they all struggled—how to harness the Internet to build a business. Halligan, like many of his clients, came from a traditional sales and marketing background, working for high tech companies Groove Networks and Parametric Technology Corporation. However, at Longworth, he began to realize that the traditional marketing and sales methods he had previously employed were losing their effectiveness in the new Web 2.0 world. Shah also grew up in the technology sector, holding a number of management and development positions in technology companies. Prior to HubSpot, Shah was founder and chief executive officer of Pyramid Digital Solutions, an enterprise software company and the winner of three Inc. 500 awards, which was acquired by SunGard Data Systems. Shah also authored OnStartups.com, a top ranking blog and online community for entrepreneurs.

Halligan and Shah founded HubSpot in 2006. Combining Halligan's marketing, sales, and venture capital expertise with Shah's technological knowledge and experience as a successful entrepreneur, the two were a winning combination. Halligan became the chief executive officer and served as HubSpot's evangelizing front man. Shah became the chief software architect and focused on product development. On the strength of their business plan, Halligan and Shah attracted premier financial partners. After initially self-funding the business, Halligan and Shah raised $5 million from General Catalyst, a Cambridge-based venture capital firm in 2007. Less than a year later, the team raised an additional $12 million from Matrix Partners, a venture capital firm with offices in Boston and Silicon Valley. For a young start-up, HubSpot had a solid financial foundation.

Halligan and Shah strove to create a distinct culture at HubSpot. They headquartered the company near MIT in Cambridge, Massachusetts, a hotbed of activity for high tech start-ups, and they staffed up with young, eager MIT graduates who were immersed in Web 2.0 culture. The HubSpot office buzzed with energy. The sleek, minimalist architecture contrasted with the animated and passionate young team, who craved a fast-pace. The team battled over business with the same gusto that they battled over the last slice of pizza.

Inbound Marketing

HubSpot built software products that helped companies execute inbound marketing programs to supplement or replace their traditional outbound programs. In the current environment, outbound marketing's effectiveness was diminishing as consumers, feeling bombarded by the daily deluge of commercial messages, began tuning out. Increasingly, direct mail, trade shows, and telemarketing were yielding less new business. In contrast, companies were finding that search engines, blogs, and social media were generating new business at higher rates. These communication programs were more consistent with the inbound marketing approach. As HubSpot explains on their corporate blog:

> Outbound marketing is about pulling people away from their dinner, or family, or TV and interrupting their lives. Do you really think you are important or interesting enough for them to want to talk to you instead of doing whatever they were doing when you interrupted them? They have not invited you into their home, and they certainly do not happen to enjoy being interrupted. Instead of spending your whole day interrupting people and hoping they pay attention, try setting up a blog and writing interesting content, so that people want to hear what you have to say and come find you when they're interested in your products.

Inbound marketing is a collection of marketing strategies and techniques focused on pulling relevant prospects and customers towards a business and its products. Inbound marketers offered useful information, tools and/or resources designed to attract prospective customers to the company during the time when prospects are actively engaged in a search for a particular product or service. The informative content that the inbound marketer produced was used to entice prospects to interact with the company and begin a relationship with it. As HubSpot vice president of marketing Mike Volpe explains, "Instead of interrupting people that don't care, why not help those who want what you're offering to find you? We have found that building interesting tools is a more effective marketing tool than doing advertising. Things like this get people curious and draw them in." This new approach to marketing complemented the way consumers were actually making purchasing decisions today, by using Internet search, online blogs, and social networking sites like Facebook and Twitter to learn about products and services before they bought them. HubSpot preached this new way of marketing:

> Instead of interrupting people with television ads, inbound marketers create videos that potential customers want to see. Instead of buying display ads in print publications, they create their own blog that people subscribe to and look forward to reading. Instead of cold calling, they create useful content and tools so that people call them looking for more information. Instead of driving their message into a crowd over and over again like a sledgehammer, they attract highly qualified customers to their business like a magnet.

To be maximized, inbound marketing required three distinct skills. The first was the ability to write compelling content that would attract customers to the business. Importantly, this content had to be useful to customers and not just a promotional message, according to HubSpot:

> Whole Foods publishes recipes, profiles of their vendors, forums and a lot more. Across all of these mediums they use the right tone. Their content is useful first, and promotional second, not the other way around. This means that their customers find them when they want to know how to make oatmeal cookies, when they want to learn more about where their apples come from or when they want to watch a cooking show.

The second was the ability to distribute that content so that it was easily found by prospective customers using search engines, which required a sophisticated understanding of search engine optimization. The third was the ability to attract and engage a community of followers who interacted with the content, added their thoughts to it in an ongoing dialogue, and disseminated it to others. Firms who nurtured an active audience gained credibility in the marketplace, as it was the support of an audience that conferred expertise in a particular area.

One of the benefits of inbound marketing was, in contrast to traditional outbound marketing where a business' message was pushed to a mass audience which contained many who were not in the market for the product, that it was designed to create content that pulled in only those customers who were interested in the product. This created marketing efficiencies. According to Mark Roberge, vice president of sales for HubSpot, inbound marketing blended marketing and sales together: "One of our salespeople calls it "smarketing"—we really blend it together so much more." Volpe explained this concept further in an interview with RainToday.com: "Our sales people hear things like 'Oh, HubSpot. I've been meaning to talk to you guys,' or 'Oh, I just watched your webinar yesterday. I had a couple of questions.' So it's the opposite of a cold call. It's like getting a call from one of your friends because we've already built a relationship. We really don't do any cold calling."

Volpe estimated that the cost of a lead generated using inbound marketing was 5–7 times less than a lead generated by outbound marketing. Businesses had increased the portion of their marketing budgets dedicated to inbound marketing, particularly in business-to-business (B2B) industries, where, 37% was spent on inbound marketing and 30% was spent on outbound marketing. Given its lower costs and increased efficiencies, inbound marketing allowed small businesses to compete with larger firms in a way that had never been possible in the pre-Internet world dominated by mass media. Small business had realized that inbound marketing helped level the playing field and were more aggressively allocating their budgets to inbound marketing techniques.

The HubSpot Product

Embodying the philosophy of Web 2.0, the HubSpot web-based software product was a complete inbound marketing system, designed to help businesses attract prospects, qualify their potential, and convert them into paying customers. The goal was to enable a firm to generate more qualified leads, to generate these leads more efficiently, and to convert them into sales. HubSpot's user-friendly product allowed even those who were not familiar with Web 2.0 to build and manage a thriving inbound marketing program. The software included templates to design content for websites, blogs, and social networking sites, tools to help customers optimize their exposure on the Internet, tools to help customers solicit and engage the right customers, and tools to analyze their results.

Content Design

HubSpot offered its customers a content management system (CMS), software that made creating and editing online content easy. Further, HubSpot's CMS allowed small businesses to add interactivity, the hallmark of Web 2.0, to their old, "brochureware" websites. Pre-designed templates helped customers create their corporate websites, providing guidelines for creating web pages, blogs, online forms, and landing pages. The templates were designed to be turn-key so that customers without HTML programming knowledge could easily publish content online and have that content be search engine friendly. HubSpot's "Keyword Grader" scanned the Internet and returned an analysis of the key words relevant to the company's business that were driving online search results. Including these key words in their content, companies could improve their organic search results, making it more likely that their content would be found by potential customers. Steve Douglas, president and creative director for The Logo Factory, explained how it worked for customers:

> I had been doing SEO all wrong when I came to HubSpot, trying to optimize my site for the wrong keywords. With HubSpot, I'm now able to see the words people are actually using to find my products and services. I'm able to see which words have the greatest search volume in search engines, helping me choose the right words to optimize my site. HubSpot has helped me be a lot smarter about how I optimize my site and track my progress. (HubSpot, Customer Quotes, 2009)

Exposure Optimization

The HubSpot product contained a series of tools designed to help customers make their published content more visible on the Internet. These included search optimization tools that graded the firm's content based on its likelihood to be included early in the search results that are returned when a potential customer searches through Google, Yahoo, or other search engines. The optimization tools graded the company's website, its key landing pages, and its blogs, and made suggestions for improving them to increase exposure. HubSpot's "Link Grader" analyzed the links a firm had on its website to see which ones were generating the most inbound traffic. The Link Grader also analyzed links to competitors' websites to see which ones were driving customers to them instead of to the firm. Customer, Noel Huelsenbeck, president of Vocio expense management software, gushed:

> I love the HubSpot software. With just a little page optimization I've already gotten great results and my traffic and keyword rankings continue to improve steadily. I'm about to sign a deal from a company that typed in one of our top keywords for which we are now the #1 organic result, thanks to HubSpot! That one deal will pay for all the money spent with HubSpot three times over. On top of that, the support is incredible. The HubSpot team had dedicated their time, even at off hours, to get my site up and optimized. The application is great, but it's the people that make this company stellar. (HubSpot, Customer Quotes, 2009)

Lead Tracking and Intelligence

The HubSpot software had marketing intelligence analytics for tracking the interactions customers have with the firm's content. This enabled firms to analyze which of their inbound marketing programs were working to generate qualified leads, by telling them where potential customers were coming from and how they were engaging with the company. Firms could generate an interaction profile for each customer by tracking the pages they viewed and the types of forms they completed. Firms could use this information to qualify prospective customers according to their potential. For example, HubSpot itself used the lead tracking software to construct its sales funnel (see **Exhibit 1**). Information about each customer allowed HubSpot to qualify some of its "visitors" as "prospects," and then "leads", and then "opportunities" based on the behaviors they exhibited while on the site.

Team Jodi, a real estate firm, had seen a significant increase in business, claimed owner Jodi Bakst:

> The traffic to my site increased by 97% in November, by an additional 62% in December, by an additional 31% in January and we're on track for another big increase in February. In real estate, the absolute number of leads is way down. But what I'm looking at is the percentage of good leads. The percentage of good leads is actually going up right now and I attribute it to all of the hard work I am doing, 90% of which I learned from HubSpot. (HubSpot, Marketing Case Study, 2009)

HubSpot used a software-as-a-service (SaaS) pricing strategy for its product. Rather than paying a large upfront fee, customers paid a smaller monthly fee (between $250-500 per month), much like a gym membership. HubSpot's low cost and ease of use for Web 2.0 novices were its competitive advantages. Volpe explained the difference between HubSpot and one of its competitors, Eloqua:

> Eloqua is really expensive and complicated. It is awesome for larger enterprises. Everyone we talk to that uses Eloqua says, "if you can get it to work, it's super powerful, but you have to give up your first born child to pay for it and you need to hire a full-time employee to run it because they have all these scripting languages and all this really, really difficult stuff."

HubSpot's customers were required to purchase a $500 onboarding package, which bought them four hours of HubSpot consulting. During this time, a consultant helped them through a process designed to kickstart their inbound marketing program: 1.) setting up the software, 2.) using the SEO features to get found, 3.) converting prospects to leads to customers, 4.) analyzing their results, and, 5.) institutionalizing the process so that it could be repeated. Once the original consulting hours were depleted, customers were on their own, unless they purchased additional consulting time at a cost of $500 for four hours. Customers were also given access to "Success.HubSpot" which provided Internet marketing training and resources. Halligan described the HubSpot product as much more than a piece of software; it was a system of tools and training (see **Exhibit 2** for product release timeline):

> HubSpot is a complete inbound marketing system that will help you get found by more prospects and convert more of them into paying customers. We use the word "system" intentionally. HubSpot is more than software. We have a complete inbound marketing

methodology comprised of best practice guides, training materials, software tools, a community and support. Plus, HubSpot is hosted on demand software, meaning that you don't need any IT staff to get started. We don't just give you a new marketing tool. We teach you to be an expert in how to use it.

HubSpot's products had garnered acclaim which drove buzz for the company. In 2008, HubSpot received the W3 Silver Winner Award in branding and marketing and the MITX Impact Award for innovative business strategy. HubSpot's "Website Grader" was an official honoree for the best websites in the IT hardware/software category in the 12th Annual Webby Awards. In February 2009, HubSpot was named in the top ten of PromotionWorld's "Best SEO Companies" ranking.

HubSpot's Marketplace

Halligan and Shah envisioned that HubSpot would become the market leader of the industry space carved out by software companies and consulting firms focused on helping businesses fill and manage their customer funnel. The customer funnel metaphorically described the critical processes firms undertook to attract prospective customers to their business, qualify these prospects to determine which ones have the highest probability of converting to paying customers, and, finally, close the sale. The customer funnel is divided into three main activity areas. Most of HubSpot's competitors chose to play in only one of these areas, although some offered integrated services that spanned across. **Exhibits 3** and **4** summarize the increasingly crowded competitive field.

Creating Traffic

The goal in the top part of the funnel was to attract large numbers of prospective customers. Firms used marketing programs to capture attention and interest to feed prospects into the funnel. Firms offered information, contests/sweepstakes, or free consulting on their websites to entice prospective customers. To receive the information or to participate, prospects filled out an online form which asked them their contact information and other information that was valuable to the firm, such as budget available for the purchase and estimated purchase timing. HubSpot's competitors in this area included consultants who built online advertising, websites, blogs, and social media presence, for companies, as well as software companies with SEO products which helped companies maximize their likelihood of getting found by consumers using search engines.

Analyzing and Qualifying Leads

The goal in the middle of the funnel was to assess the potential of different prospective customers brought in by the lead generation programs. Selling a customer required an investment of human and financial resources and firms wanted to ensure that they were targeting these resources to prospects who were most likely to convert to customers. Many prospects brought in through lead generation had a low probability of becoming a customer, and firms could save substantial money if they could identify those customers early and weed them out. The lead qualification process focused on finding customers with potential to pass along to the sales force. HubSpot's competitors in this area included consultants and software companies with proprietary methods for rating and ranking prospects based on historical analysis of the company's current customers and conversion rates.

Closing the Sale

The goal in the bottom of the customer funnel was to convert prospects into customers. One player, Salesforce.com, dominated this segment, providing easy to use, customizable software which helped firms create a database of their prospects and track their conversion progress in real time. Salesforce.com's software had become the industry standard for managing and tracking sales efforts.

Halligan and Shah hoped that HubSpot could dominate the lead generation and analysis/ qualification stages of the customer funnel, just as Salesforce.com dominated the stage devoted to closing the sale, claiming "HubSpot could be to marketing what Salesforce.com is to sales."

Filling HubSpot's Customer Funnel

By 2009, HubSpot had 1,000 very diverse customers. HubSpot attracted these customers through inbound marketing, practicing what they preached by using their own software. HubSpot used several different tactics to drive prospects into the funnel. First, the company had a robust website which attracted over 300,000 unique visitors in 2008. The website featured whitepapers, webinars, podcasts, and a blog which provided information about Web 2.0 and inbound marketing strategies. HubSpot created and managed an 8,000 member LinkedIn group called Pro-Marketers, dedicated to marketing professionals who were interested in learning about Web 2.0 and inbound marketing. Employees came together every Friday to host their own television show, "HubSpot TV," a live streaming podcast also available on iTunes which featured interactive commentary on topical events. HubSpot also produced YouTube video spoofs which changed the lyrics of popular songs like "You Oughta Know" by Alanis Morissette to sell the inbound marketing concept, the most popular of which was viewed over 50,000 times. Another video, entitled "Cold Calling is for Losers" was viewed over 35,000 times and humorously showed the futility of outbound marketing techniques.

The HubSpot team was encouraged to build their own Web 2.0 presence to supplement corporate activities. Many employees blogged, tweeted, and participated on social media sites to promote HubSpot. Inbound marketing was a passion for the HubSpot team and they used every avenue they could to evangelize it to whoever would listen. As the website claimed, "At HubSpot, we live and breathe inbound marketing. We know a lot about it. We love to teach. We'll make you an expert."

HubSpot's most successful inbound marketing program was its freeware, small software programs that were available for free and accessible on the Internet. Three commonly used programs were the Website Grader, Twitter Grader, and Facebook Grader. All were designed to provide useful information to prospective customers and introduce them to HubSpot. The graders allowed users to evaluate how well their websites, Twitter accounts, and Facebook presence were performing. For example, Website Grader analyzed a company's website, rated it versus other sites on the Internet, and offered suggestions for improvements. Users who accessed the free web tools often completed a lead form expressing interest in other offerings, which fed them into HubSpot's customer funnel. By 2009, over 650,000 websites, 22,000 Facebook profiles, and 2 million Twitter accounts had been graded by the free tools. The freeware had also generated a lot of positive press and online buzz.

Volpe explained how all these activities fed HubSpot's funnel: "We think about the size of the community we've built. It includes people on our email list, people that subscribe to our feed in iTunes, people that subscribe to our blog, people that follow one of our accounts on Twitter, people that are fans of our page on Facebook. It's sort of how many fans we have cultivated in the world."

When HubSpot was just getting started, the sales force called on all leads coming into the funnel. HubSpot sold to any customer who was interested in buying its products. This helped achieve the critical mass the fledgling venture needed to survive. However, as the number of prospective customers grew, HubSpot began carefully qualifying leads before turning them over to the sales force. HubSpot constantly updated its lead rating algorithm based on their success with converting different types of prospects, and the varying customer retention rates experienced post-sale.

By 2009, the company was weeding out almost 50% of the leads in its funnel. Low quality leads were given no further attention. The remaining 50% were rated on a scale of 1 (low probability of conversion) to 10 (high probability of conversion). 63% of the rated leads were graded with scores ranging from 7 to 10, making them a high priority for the sales force's attention. The selling process was fairly involved and focused on a sales person guiding a prospect through an online product demonstration; closing a sale took between 30-45 days from the point of initial contact to final sale.

Since HubSpot's inbound marketing did not target a specific type of customer, HubSpot found itself attracting a diverse set. HubSpot's customers came from many different industries, including professional services, health care, software, real estate, and construction materials. They included businesses selling to other businesses (B2B), as well as businesses selling directly to consumers (B2C). **Exhibits 5** and **6** show the composition of HubSpot's customer portfolio. Two different types of customers were visible: small business owners and marketing professionals working in larger firms. HubSpot affectionately dubbed these two personas "Owner Ollie" and "Marketer Mary."

"Owner Ollie" The Small Business Owner Customer

Owner Ollies made up 68% of HubSpot's customer portfolio. Owner Ollies owned small businesses with 1–25 employees. Owner Ollies were busy, as they were simultaneously managing the human resources, marketing, sales, operations, and finance areas of their companies. Given their small size, they did not have a dedicated marketing professional on their staff and, thus, they did most of the marketing themselves. Owner Ollies were curious about Web 2.0 and inbound marketing, but had not made investments in consulting, software, or programs in this area. Their primary objective was to generate more leads for their businesses; Owner Ollies were focused on feeding the tops of their customer funnels. Time and resources were scarce and Owner Ollies wanted quick, simple solutions to help them generate leads, because leads were the lifeblood of their small businesses. Owner Ollies were fairly easy to sell; the cost to acquire this type of customer was around $1,000. As Volpe explained, "Ollie doesn't even think about marketing most of the time. He's thinking about finance and HR and there is a leak in the pipes in the office. He's got all kinds of stuff to worry about. He typically doesn't shop around and try to find any other software competitive to HubSpot. He gets on the phone, he decides if he likes it, he gives you his credit card number and he's like, 'Great, let's do it.'"

"Marketer Mary" The Marketing Professional Customer

Marketer Marys made up 31% of HubSpot's customer portfolio. Marketer Marys were marketing professionals working in companies which ranged from 26 to 100 people. Unlike Owner Ollies who tended to work on marketing alone, Marketer Marys were supported by a marketing team. As marketing professionals, Marketer Marys were more educated than Owner Ollies about Web 2.0 and were looking for assistance with running their programs, evaluating their results, and justifying their return on investment to senior management. Marketer Marys often had web consultants who designed online websites and programs. Hence, Marketer Marys were more interested in the analytics and reports that HubSpot provided. Marketer Marys ran many more inbound marketing programs than Owner Ollies, and needed more robust and sophisticated tools to design them and measure their results. Marketer Marys had more money to spend on products like HubSpot, but were harder to reach and had a longer selling cycle as they often had to get approval from managers higher up in their organizations. The cost to acquire this type of customer was $5,000.

As these two customer segments emerged in the customer base, HubSpot tweaked its product, developing two different versions, each with features designed to better serve the needs of either Owner Ollies or Marketer Marys. (The differences between the two are summarized in **Exhibit 7**.)

HubSpot took good care of its customers. Jonah Lopin headed up the HubSpot services group, known as the "customer happiness department." Lopin and his team quickly realized that the customers HubSpot was serving were very diverse, making it difficult to standardize processes across customers. Different customers had different familiarity and comfort with Web 2.0 tools. B2C companies were much more sophisticated Web 2.0 users than B2B companies and many found that HubSpot's content templates were too rudimentary for their needs. Most B2C companies already had highly performing websites and social media presence and had engaged Web 2.0 consultants and agencies to work with them prior to coming to HubSpot. In contrast, most B2B customers had little to no experience with Web 2.0 and no other agencies or consultants supporting their efforts. They required more attention from Lopin and his team during start-up and during their lives as customers.

The second difference was that B2B customers seem to derive greater value from inbound marketing than B2C customers. Many of the B2B customers sold products or services that were complex, which required buyers to undergo in-depth learning prior to purchase. Blogs, podcasts, webinars, and other Web 2.0 programs that explained the product served as valuable inputs into a customer's decision making process and were effective feeders of B2B customer funnels. The buying processes associated with the B2B businesses were much more complex than those associated with B2C businesses, due to a longer decision making cycle involving multiple stakeholders at the buying firm. Because of this, B2B customers were more selective about whom they focused their sales forces' attentions on and derived great value from the lead qualification analysis that HubSpot provided.

The third difference was that Owner Ollies were less knowledgeable and sophisticated than Marketer Marys. Owner Ollies also derived greater initial value than Marketer Marys, as Volpe explained, "The great part about Ollie is that we can actually have a much larger impact on his overall business than we can with Mary. It saves him a ton of money and he is getting a much better customer flow. It has fundamentally changed his business."

Lopin also saw differences in the customer retention data, as the churn rates (the rate at which customers cancelled their HubSpot subscriptions) varied across segments. The results of his analysis are listed in **Table A** and in **Exhibit 8**. Although Marketer Marys were a harder sell up front, they stayed longer than Owner Ollies. Lopin speculated that usage of the monthly analytics and reporting was driving her longer customer life. Owner Ollies were focused on using SEO to increase visitors to their websites. They derived much of their value in the first few months as a customer. Once Owner Ollies thought they were "done" optimizing, they would cancel their HubSpot subscription.

Table A Churn Rates by Segment

	Average Churn Rate (cancellations per month)
Owner Ollies	4.3%
Marketer Marys	3.2%
Total B2B	3.3%
Total B2C	6.0%
CMS	2.1%
Non-CMS	5.5%
Total	**4.1%**

Source: Company reports.

Investigating further, Lopin realized that customers who hosted their websites on HubSpot's content management system had lower churn rates than customers who hosted with other companies. Lopin urged the sales force to push the content management system hosting service to new customers. As a result, an increasing number of Owner Ollies were migrating their websites to HubSpot. In 2009, 13% of Owner Ollies selected HubSpot to host their site, paying an initial fee of $500 which covered twelve hours of HubSpot consulting designed to make the migration process painless. In contrast, only 2% of Marketer Marys hosted their websites with HubSpot.

Lastly, Lopin saw differences in the amount of time different types of customers were willing to put into using the HubSpot software. To derive meaningful results from the software, customers needed to consistently invest ten hours per week to it. This was a significant time investment, particularly for Owner Ollies. Customer Geoff Alexander, president of Geoff Alexander & Company, a telesales training company, explained: "It took a couple of hours to mash through all the training, but the key to HubSpot is putting the time into it. Without HubSpot, I just would have winged it. The investment required for HubSpot is actually a lot like paying for web intelligence school. I was ignorant of the nuts & bolts of SEO and online lead generation for years. Now I'm making up for it." (HubSpot, Marketing Case Study, 2009)

Some of HubSpot's current customers were not putting in the time, as shown in **Table B**. Fifteen percent of current customers had not logged in to the HubSpot software over the past 12 weeks.

Table B Customer Usage

	Percent of Customers
Logged into HubSpot system > 50% of weeks	45%
Logged into HubSpot system <50% of weeks	55%
Logged into HubSpot system 12/12 of weeks	23%
Logged into HubSpot system 0/12 of weeks	15%

Source: Company reports.

When customers complained that HubSpot was not working for them, the first thing the customer service team looked at was the amount of time the customer was spending on HubSpot. As Lopin explained, "It's like saying that your gym isn't working. People say 'I joined a gym six months ago and I'm still kind of out of shape and it's not working.' No, it's like, you're not working out. There's no question that inbound marketing is effective, it's just that you've got to do the work."

HubSpot customers who were using the software were seeing results. Dedicated users experienced a burst of increased leads in the first six months after using the software, a result of the creation of inbound marketing programs. Over time, the growth rate in leads diminished, but customers continued to gain value by focusing on efficiently rating and following up on the leads with the most potential. **Exhibit 9** shows the increased leads generated by HubSpot for its customers.

Scaling Up

While their employees were celebrating breaking the 1,000 customer mark, Halligan and Shah were not resting on their laurels, realizing that they still had a lot of work to do. The founders realized that they needed to quickly scale up the HubSpot business. Their venture partners saw huge market potential for HubSpot and looked for the company to make significant inroads into small and medium size businesses. **Table C** lists the number of small and medium size businesses in the United States that formed HubSpot's market potential.

Table C Market Potential: Small- and Medium-Sized Businesses[a]

Category	Number of Employees	Number of Businesses
Large	100 to 499	86,538
Medium	20 to 99	526,355
Small	10 to 19	632,682
Very Small	5 to 9	1,043,448
Total	-	**2,289,023**

Source: Company reports.

[a]Roughly half of all businesses are B2B, half are B2C.

Volpe was excited about the opportunity:

> We're growing fast, there's a market there. We're trying to get as big as we can as fast as we can. We have this gigantic vision for what the product should do and it is relatively broad. And I think it's why we think that the market we are going after is potentially very, very large and today, our product is a small, small fraction of what it needs to be. The company is still small. We've got only so many engineers and we can only build things so fast and that whole process in matching the product to the market and building the right features at the right time is difficult. Sales and marketing have been ahead of the product and we just need to continue to focus on the product and hope that it will catch up more.

As they looked back at their achievements, Halligan and Shah realized that the inbound marketing that built their business presented them with challenges that they would have to overcome to reach the next level. While traditional marketers prospected for new customers based upon a predetermined target market which was strategic, inbound marketers fished for customers, took what they caught, and then figured out who their actual market was. This left HubSpot with a very diverse customer base and made strategic planning more difficult. Different types of customers valued different features, and prioritizing items in the long list of potential software updates proved challenging. A mix of customers also added layers of complexity and cost to the sales and customer service areas of HubSpot. Halligan and Shah wondered if they should continue to throw a wide net to attract all different types of customers or if they should narrow their focus to a particular target market. Roberge believed that HubSpot needed to refine its focus:

> If we picked one type of customer to focus on, we would likely get to success faster. Ollie and Mary speak different languages, have different needs. Now, we are choosing between them and dividing our development resources. There are certain applications that are specific to Ollie and they would be designed and implemented differently. And then it affects customer support and how well we really get to know our customer, understand them, and then ace the product.

Halligan and Shah debated which segments were the best customer segments to cater to. Was it the B2C or B2B market? Was it Owner Ollies or Marketer Marys? Employees disagreed about who was more profitable long term. Roberge placed his bets on Marketer Marys, "I think there are more Ollies out there, but I think we can get more money out of Mary. There's a lot of macroeconomic risk associated with Ollie because there are a lot of small businesses that are just bad business models, they are risky during recessions." Others argued that Ollies were likely to stick around longer, especially when they were using the content management system. Narrowing the target market presented challenges for an inbound marketing company. HubSpot was already ignoring 50% of the leads brought in by their inbound marketing programs. This selectivity seemed at odds with their desire to grow quickly. Shouldn't they sell to anyone who wanted to buy the product?

Halligan and Shah also wondered if their current pricing strategy was effective. While the software-as-a-service (SaaS) monthly pricing model seemed to be the right way to capture maximum value from customers and provide a reliable income stream for HubSpot when it started, the patterns in customer churn rates were showing that some customers were obtaining the initial burst of value from the software and then canceling it within the first several months. Halligan and Shah wondered whether they were leaving money on the table by not charging more for the HubSpot software up front or locking in customers for longer periods of time. The diverse customer base also presented opportunities and challenges for pricing and made Halligan and Shah consider if the two products and price points they had developed to address the Owner Ollie and the Marketer Mary market segments were adequate, given their different business needs and sensitivity to price.

Finally, an internal debate raged within HubSpot about the role of outbound marketing programs going forward. Looking at aggressive growth targets, some employees, including Roberge, were itching to supplement the inbound marketing tactics with traditional outbound marketing programs, including targeted telemarketing and traditional advertising. Roberge lamented:

> Most sales organizations are responsible for doing their own lead generation for prospects. We have to wait for the inbound marketing programs to bring leads to us. I'm not allowed to cold call prospective customers because HubSpot's been preaching inbound marketing and publishing these videos and webinars about how cold calling is "for losers." If someone then gets a cold call from someone on my team, that can hurt our brand. So I am actually restricted from doing outbound prospecting which makes things more challenging for me, because I own the sales number and I have to sit back and be dependent on what marketing brings to me. So yeah, I think we are hindering scale a little bit by not creating outbound marketing programs.

Looking at their growth rates, see **Exhibit 10**, Halligan and Shah realized that they would have to push things up a notch to achieve their long term goals. However, the founders were as committed to inbound marketing for their own company as they were for their customers'. Volpe, in an interview with RainToday.com explained, "If we couldn't make inbound marketing work for our own company, then we shouldn't be selling software that helps other companies do it." Though the founders' vision was centered around inbound marketing, the reality was that most businesses—including HubSpot customers—would likely have a mix of inbound and outbound marketing.

Exhibit 1 The HubSpot Customer Funnel

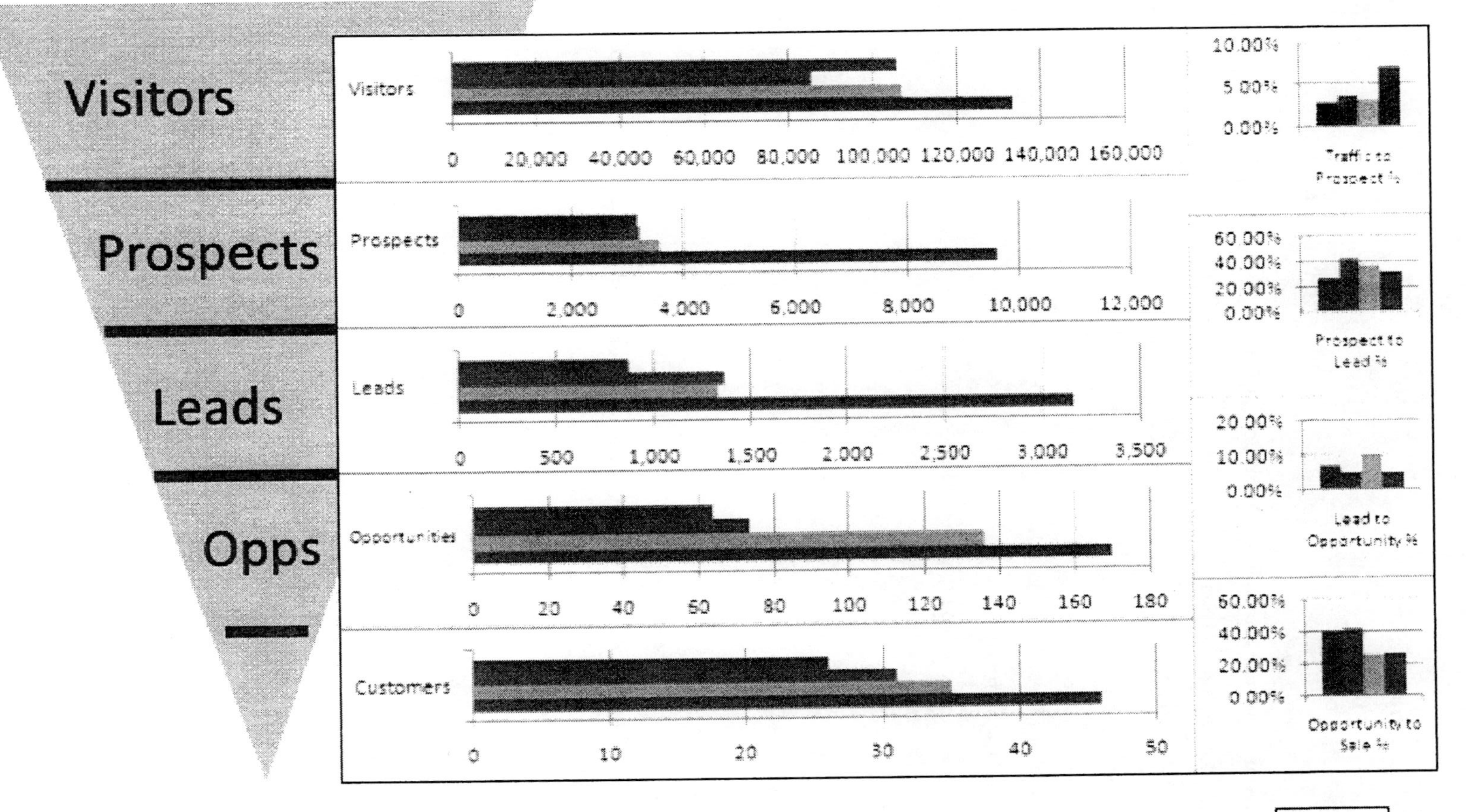

Source: Company reports.

Exhibit 2 HubSpot Product Timeline

2006

Q1: Content Management System, Blog, Analytics (alpha).

Q2: Search Marketing tools (alpha)

Q3: First paying customers

2007

Q1: Public launch of WebsiteGrader.com

Q2: Series A VC round funding

Q4: v1.0 Product Launch, 100 paying customers.

2008

Q1: Started using "the cloud" on Amazon EC2. 100 million page views served

Q2: Series B VC round funding. Introduction of two separate products ($250/month and $500/month)

Q3: PageGrader aka The Crawler, HubFeed (entry into social media),
Single Sign-On, Salesforce.com Integration, HubSpot Express + Trials

Q4: Changed products to HubSpot Owner and HubSpot Marketer. Launch Grader.com, TwitterGrader, Facebook Grader.

2009

Q1: 1,000 customers, 500 million page views served, Free Trials for main product

Source: Company reports.

Exhibit 3 HubSpot's Competitive Field

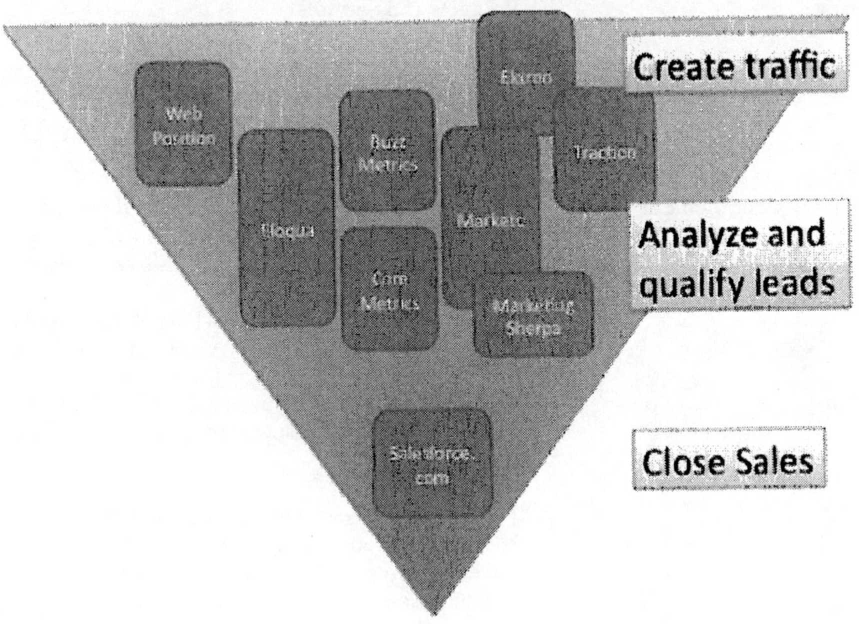

Source: Casewriters.

Exhibit 4 The Marketplace

Company	Products and Services
Web Position	Offered tools to improve a web site's search engine rankings. The software included a summary dashboard, trend graphs, several metrics (link popularity and search engine saturation reporting) and many search engines.
Nielsen's BuzzMetrics Services	Provided tools to help clients understand how consumers perceived their brand, monitor trends that may be influencing their industry, monitor how marketing campaigns are resonating with consumers.
Ektron	Provided a software platform with all of the tools that were needed to create, deploy, and manage a company's web site.
Traction	Provided business and government organizations with enterprise weblog software that allowed groups and teams to communicate more effectively.
Marketo	Provided SaaS solutions that helped marketing and sales teams collaborate throughout the sales cycle, from demand generation to the close of a sale. Their solution included email marketing, lead nurturing, lead scoring, and sales effectiveness tools and was tightly integrated with salesforce.com.
Eloqua	Provided software to automate a broad range of marketing functions. Their solution could help clients build databases, create email campaigns, capture leads and measure their marketing effectiveness.
Coremetrics	Provided on-demand web analytics and precision marketing solutions. Their platform could capture and store all customer and visitor clickstream activity to build a "Lifetime Individual Visitor Experience" or LIVE Profile.
Marketing Sherpa	Is a research firm specializing in tracking what works and what doesn't in all aspects of marketing.

Source: Casewriters.

Exhibit 5 New Customer Acquisitions

	Number of Customers				Percent of Customers			
	Sep-08	Oct-08	Nov-08	Dec-08	Sep-08	Oct-08	Nov-08	Dec-08
New Owner Ollies	**24**	**31**	**27**	**34**				
B2B>25	2	3	3	2	8%	10%	11%	6%
B2B<25	11	11	13	19	46%	35%	48%	56%
B2C>25	1	0	0	2	4%	0%	0%	6%
B2C<25	10	17	11	11	42%	55%	41%	32%
New Marketer Marys	**41**	**60**	**68**	**74**				
B2B>25	9	18	21	30	22%	30%	31%	41%
B2B<25	12	24	22	19	29%	40%	32%	26%
B2C>25	4	9	7	13	10%	15%	10%	18%
B2C<25	16	9	18	12	39%	15%	26%	16%
Total B2B	**34**	**56**	**59**	**70**	**52%**	**62%**	**62%**	**65%**
Total B2C	**31**	**35**	**36**	**38**	**48%**	**38%**	**38%**	**35%**
Total >25	**16**	**30**	**31**	**47**	**25%**	**33%**	**33%**	**44%**
Total <25	**49**	**61**	**64**	**61**	**75%**	**67%**	**67%**	**56%**
Total	**65**	**91**	**95**	**108**	**100%**	**100%**	**100%**	**100%**

Source: Company reports.

Exhibit 6 Customer Portfolio in December 2008

	Number of Customers	Percent of Customers
Owner Ollies	694	73%
Marketer Marys	255	27%
Total B2B	647	68%
Total B2C	302	32%
Total >25 CMS	21	2%
Total <25 CMS	122	13%
Non-CMS	806	85%
Total	**949**	**100%**

Source: Company reports.

Exhibit 7 HubSpot's Product Portfolio

HubSpot Owner	HubSpot Marketer
For business owners who need a simple system to generate more qualified leads and convert those leads into sales.	For marketing professionals who require flexible, sophisticated inbound marketing tools, including closed loop marketing reports.
Includes:	Includes:
• Search Engine Optimization (500 Keywords)	• Search Engine Optimization (2,000 Keywords)
• Business Blogging	• Business Blogging
• Business Blog Analytics	• Business Blog Analytics
• Competitor Analysis (Up to 5)	• Competitor Analysis (Up to 20)
• Marketing Analytics	• Closed-Loop Marketing Analytics
• Website Editor (Required)	• Website Editor (Optional)
• Lead Tracking & Intelligence	• Lead Tracking & Intelligence
• Landing Page Wizard	• Lead Grader
• Marketing Intelligence	• Lead Visit Alerts
• Social Media	• Landing Page Wizard
• Inbound Marketing Advice	• Marketing Intelligence
	• Social Media
	• Inbound Marketing Advice
	• Salesforce.com Integration
$500 consulting fee at start-up	$500 consulting fee at start-up
$250/month ongoing fee	$500/month ongoing fee

Source: Company reports.

Exhibit 8 Churn Rate Detail

Churn Rate by Age of Customer

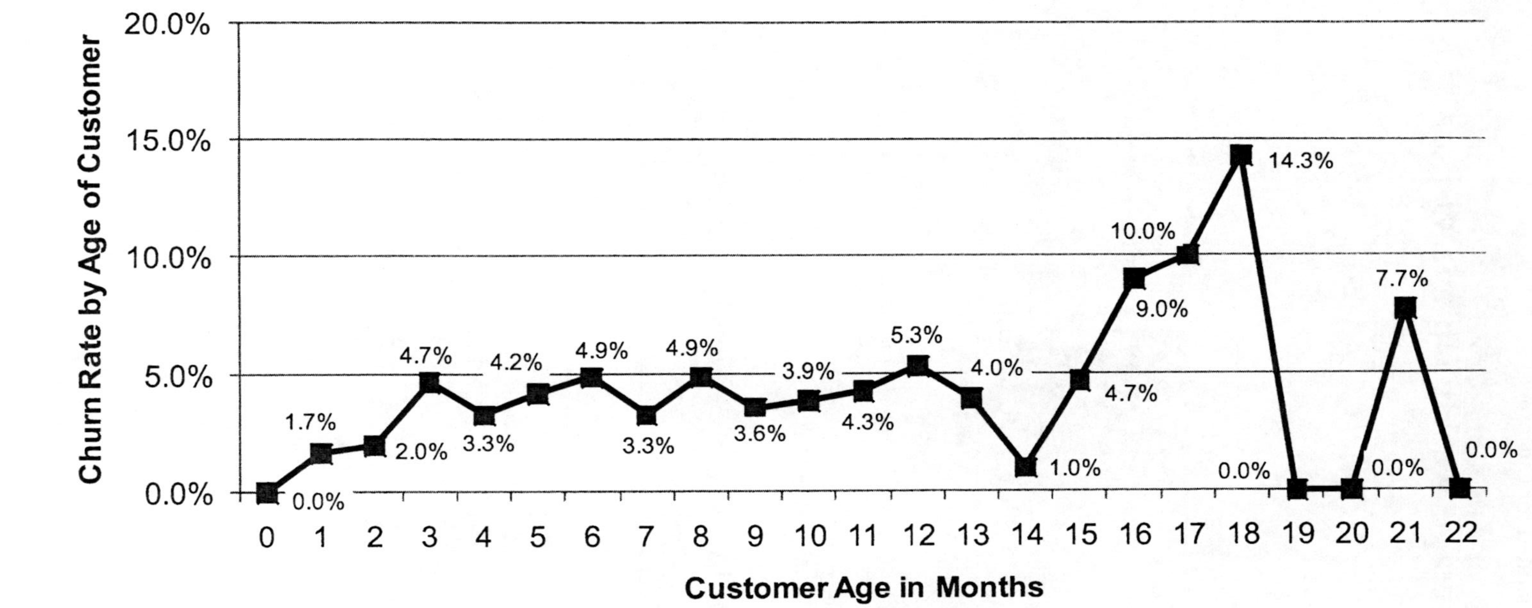

Source: Company reports.

BUSINESS TYPE VS. BUSINESS SIZE

Average Churn Rate (cancellations per month)

	Very Small Businesses	Small Businesses
B2B	7.3%	1.4%
B2C	7.8%	4.1%

Source: Company reports.

Exhibit 9 Visitors and Leads Generated for Customers

M/M Growth in Average Weekly Unique Visitors

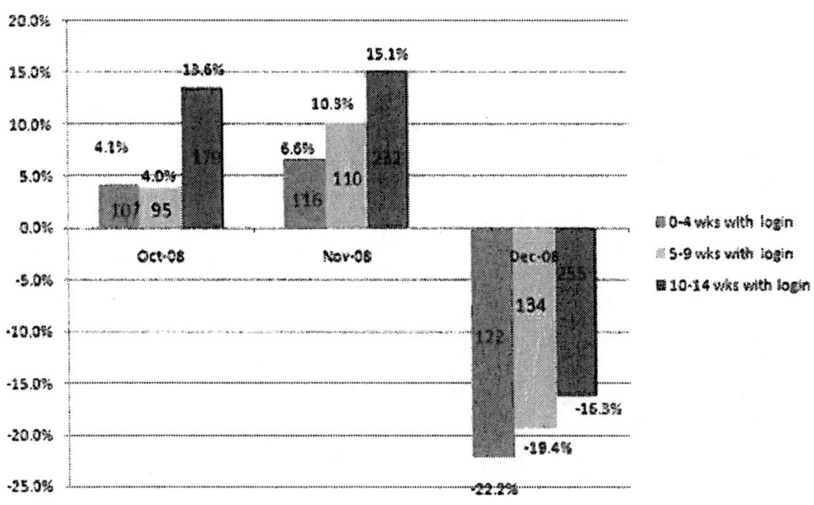

Customers included in analysis: (381 for Oct, 458 for Nov, 511 for Dec)

- Accounts must be over 3 weeks entering the lift period
- All weeks in lift period must have >10 unique visitors

M/M Growth in Average Weekly Leads

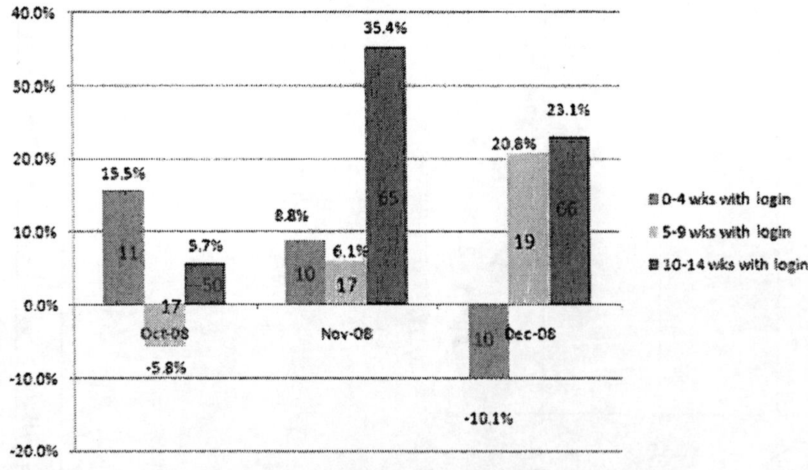

Customers included in analysis: (78 for Oct, 92 for Nov, 95 for Dec)

- Accounts must be over 3 weeks old entering the lift period
- All weeks in lift period must have >1 lead

Source: Company reports.

Exhibit 10 HubSpot's Growth Rate

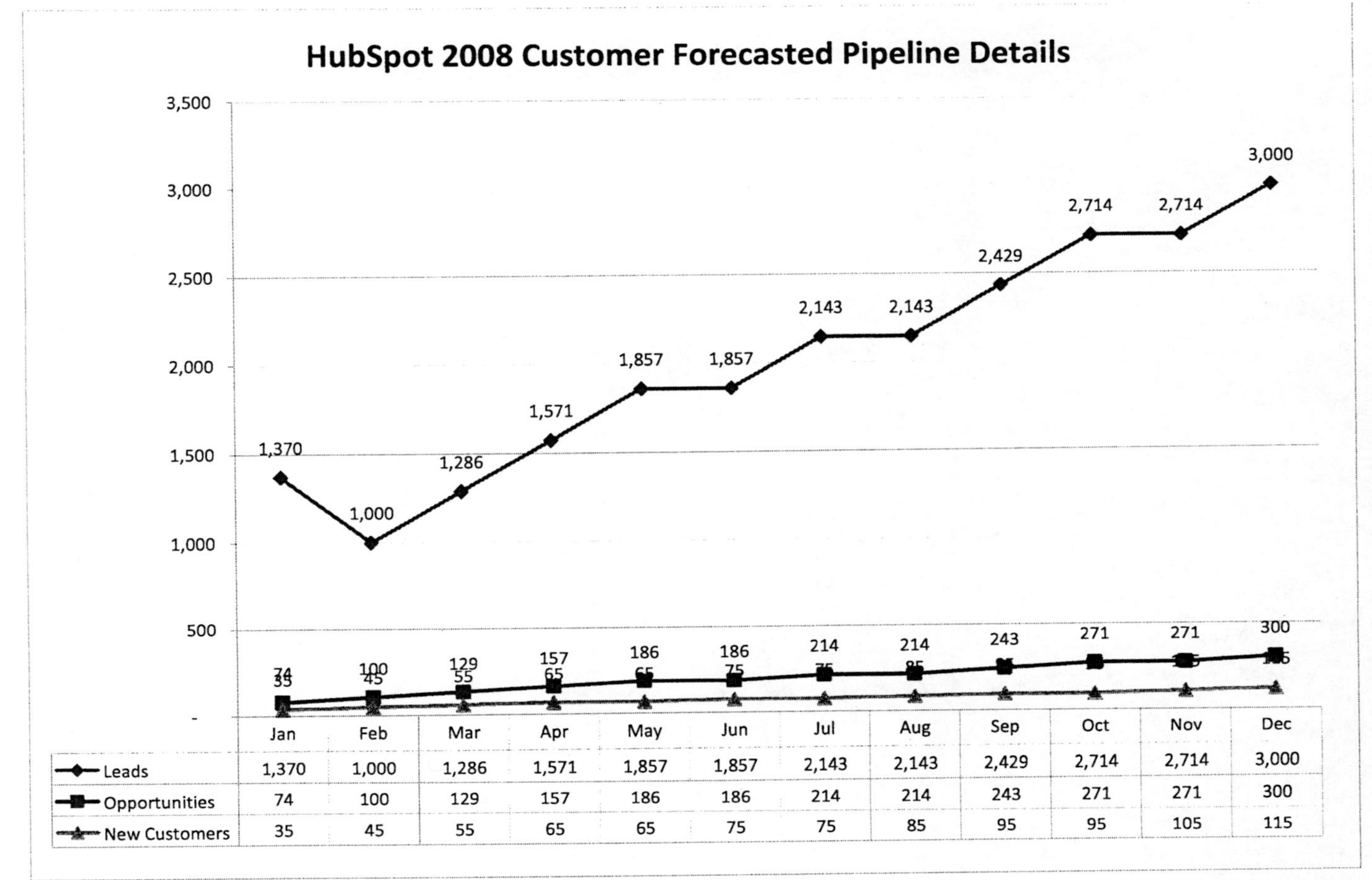

	Jan	Feb	Mar	Apr	May	Jun	Jul	Aug	Sep	Oct	Nov	Dec
Leads	1,370	1,000	1,286	1,571	1,857	1,857	2,143	2,143	2,429	2,714	2,714	3,000
Opportunities	74	100	129	157	186	186	214	214	243	271	271	300
New Customers	35	45	55	65	65	75	75	85	95	95	105	115

Source: Company reports.

Nestlé Refrigerated Foods: Contadina Pasta & Pizza (A)

In 1990, the Nestlé Refrigerated Food Company (NRFC) contemplated the introduction of a refrigerated pizza product to the U.S. market. In 1987, Nestlé had entered the refrigerated food market with Contadina Pasta and Sauces. The product had been very successful, with sales of $50 million in its first year, growing to over $100 million in sales by 1990. However, it was recognized that Nestle's rapid growth in the refrigerated pasta market must taper off, as new competitors entered the market niche. In the past year, Contadina's marketing management had been working on extending the Contadina product line into pizza. Stephen Cunliffe, president of the Nestlé Refrigerated Food Company, remarked,

> Nestlé Refrigerated Foods entered the U.S. market with Contadina pasta and sauces. We took risks. We acquired a small company at a premium in order to be the first company to bring refrigerated pasta to market on a national basis. We invested heavily in distribution to get the product to market without high spoilage rates. We broke away from the traditional sales force and used brokers to sell our product. These risks paid off and Contadina became the market leader in refrigerated pasta and sauces, but to continue our rapid growth, we need other new product opportunities.

Cunliffe sought to further opportunities for Nestlé's growth in refrigerated pasta. Prior to launching a pizza product, however, he knew he had to take a hard look at the numbers to ensure its business viability.

Nestlé Refrigerated Foods

NRFC, located in Glendale, California, was a wholly owned subsidiary of Nestlé, S.A. In 1993, Nestlé, S. A., was one of the world's largest food companies with sales of over $37 billion. Its 500 plants operated in 60 countries employing over 195,000 people producing a wide range of food and beverage products ranging from Perrier mineral water to Stouffer's frozen foods. The original business, founded in 1866 by Henri Nestlé, was based on milk and infant formula products for children. Over time, numerous other food products were added including chocolate, instant coffee, culinary, refrigerated and frozen products, ice cream, mineral water, and pet foods. Nestlé's financial statements, major markets, and product lines are outlined in **Exhibit 1**. Throughout its

---

Research Associate Marie Bell prepared this case under the supervision of Professor V. Kasturi Rangan as the basis for class discussion rather than to illustrate either effective or ineffective handling of an administrative situation.

history Nestlé had been committed to research and development for its new products, quality improvements, manufacturing advances, and, most important, adaptation of products to meet the specific taste of varied cultures and markets. Nestlé maintained a long-term focus, making strategic investments and developing experimental processes to ensure its position as one of the world's premier food companies. Always a major player in the United States in specialized markets such as confectionery (chocolate, candy), coffee, and frozen foods, Nestlé became a major food force in 1985 with its $3 billion purchase of Carnation Co. which owned brands such as Coffee-mate creamer and Friskies pet foods. In addition to entrenching Nestlé more firmly in the U.S. market, Nestlé planned to use the Carnation acquisition to spearhead the development of other food businesses such as refrigerated or "chilled" foods.

In 1991 Nestlé combined its existing operations with those of Carnation to form Nestlé USA, composed of five operating units. The NRFC became a part of the Nestlé Frozen, Refrigerated and Ice Cream Company. (**Exhibit 2** details the organizational structure at Nestlé USA and NRFC.) Prior to that date NRFC was a relatively autonomous subsidiary of Carnation Company, and after the reorganization NRFC still retained its exclusive focus on building a refrigerated business.

New Product Development Process

Marketing departments within Nestlé's operating companies were responsible for new product development. The market research department (MRD), a separate entity within Nestlé USA, supported operating companies within Nestlé USA, and was especially active in new product development. By the late 1980s NRFC had established a seven-step process for taking a new product idea to market. The steps were guidelines rather than mandates, and each new product champion or the new product development team had considerable flexibility to add steps or skip steps when appropriate and necessary. The seven steps were:

- *Idea generation.* Ideas for new products came to product marketing from several sources: individual ideas, product management brainstorming, Nestle's international business, successes, the salesforce, distribution channels, and customers. MRD conducted focus groups and referred to secondary research sources (demographic trends, category overviews, market trends, etc.) to refine the idea into a preliminary concept.

- *Concept Screening/Idea Refinement.* Once ideas had been generated, MRD conducted a survey to identify those with the highest potential. Components of the survey included an indication of volume potential with key measures such as purchase interest, purchase frequency, price/value rating, and overall liking. In addition, the concept screening provided diagnostic information on product design, positioning, and target market selection.

- *Product Development.* Prototype products were developed by R&D, in conjunction with marketing, and production staff. The products were tested either at a central location or in homes. The in-home testing by the consumer had the advantage of capturing product preparation and use issues as well as family member opinions on the product. The number of product tests were variable, usually one or two, and the test was either done "blind" where the respondent was unaware of the brands tested, or where the brand affiliation was disclosed to the consumer.

- *Quantification of Volume.* Depending on the level of risk involved, MRD recommended one of three types of studies by BASES, a market research firm, to estimate potential sales volume. A Pre-BASES was a concept test only with rough volume estimates. A BASES I was a concept test with volume estimates generally thought to be within a 25% accuracy range. A BASES II test involved a concept test in combination with a product taste test and was reliable within 20%.

While a number of factors contributed to the reliability of the BASES estimates, the major factors were the sample size used, the in-home product usage, the similarity of the estimated marketing plan to the actual plan used to launch the product, and BASES experience with similar product categories. Even if volume estimates for Year One were positive, weakness on key after-use measures, particularly price/value, would be an indication of poor prospects for ongoing success. Additionally there was a special BASES II Line Extension test for new products that were part of a pre-existing product line. If a product proved financially viable, a detailed marketing plan was developed, production decisions made, and the product was prepared for launch.

- *Test market.* A test market might be recommended instead of a BASES study when little capital investment was required but there was a perceived high risk in the product itself or its marketing. Both a test market and a BASES study were conducted in very high risk situations, or when the BASES study uncovered potential problems. Test markets might not be conducted if there was moderate to low investment requirements, few negatives in the BASES study, and a high risk of being beaten to a national rollout by competitors learning about the product in a test market.

- *Commercial Evaluation.* Almost all of Nestlé's new products were supported by television advertising. Prior to the launch, MRD became involved in evaluating an ad's ability to create awareness for the brand as well as purchase interest.

- *Introductory Tracking.* Subsequent to rollout, performance was tracked through awareness, attitude, and usage studies, and household panel data.

Refrigerated Foods: Background

Food products are either fresh or processed. Fresh foods in U.S. grocery stores consist mostly of meat, vegetables, fruit, and dairy products such as eggs and milk. Processed foods are food products that have been prepared and then packaged for sale. Processed food is available in three major forms: frozen, refrigerated or chilled, and shelf stable. Frozen foods usually have to be reheated or cooked from the frozen state. Stored at temperatures of 0° Fahrenheit frozen foods (e.g., ice cream, frozen vegetables) have long shelf lives often running into months. Refrigerated foods are kept cool but not frozen, which allows rapid cooking or reheating by the consumer. Stored at temperatures of 33°-40° Fahrenheit degrees, they have shorter shelf lives of 12-90 days (e.g., yogurt, frankfurters, cream cheese). Shelf stable foods can either be ready-to-eat or require additional preparation. They need no special storage temperature, either because they have been sterilized or due to the nature of the food itself. Shelf lives are relatively long (e.g. cereal, canned food).

Convenience and perceived quality attract consumers to refrigerated food. Refrigerated foods require little planning and preparation. The consumer does not have to defrost the product, but merely remove it from the refrigerator and eat or cook it. The refrigerated form, however, makes the product a manufacturing and distribution challenge relative to other types of food products. For example, refrigerated products need to meet higher microbial (bacteria) standards than their frozen counterparts. The freezing process stops microbial growth, whereas refrigeration only slows it. Additionally, as the manufacturer cannot assume "perfect" refrigeration practices across the distribution system, high quality manufacturing is required to ensure that the customer purchases a safe product.

A relatively undeveloped category in the United States in 1987, non-commodity refrigerated foods (both desserts and entrees) were a fixture in European grocery stores. Indeed in 1987, refrigerated foods were responsible for approximately 7% of Nestlé's global sales despite little contribution from the potentially large U.S. market. Refrigerated food products had been especially successful in the United Kingdom with the Marks & Spencer chain of retail stores offering a wide range of products from soups to entrees and desserts. Many in the food industry believed that a similar success could be created in the United States based on the latent customer demand for convenient, good tasting, fresh products that were both quick and easy to prepare. Both General Foods and Kraft had tried to replicate the U.K. experience in the United States in the 1980s but had floundered due to distribution limitations. The direct store distribution system used successfully in the British market was less effective and more expensive in the United States with its larger number of urban areas and dispersed geographies. The British market was characterized by a fewer number of stores in more densely populated, urban centers.

Based on its U.S. strength in the confectionery category (e.g., chocolate, and chocolate bars such as Crunch), Nestlé initially considered entering the refrigerated food category with a pudding dessert product. It was pre-empted, however, by Jell-O's very successful Jell-O brand pudding. Nestlé was able to counter this setback with its parallel development in the rapidly growing ethnic food category. Italian foods, especially pasta and sauces, were the largest of the rapidly growing consumer trend toward ethnic foods. Indeed, according to the *Restaurant & Institutions* annual survey, pasta was one of the Top 20 foods on menus. There was a clearly communicable message of the superiority of "fresh pasta" already understood by the customer, and although many of Nestlé's major competitors were investigating this market opportunity, none were close to bringing a product to market.

Believing in the viability of the refrigerated food category in the United States and the strong growth in the Italian food segment, Nestlé considered the benefits of in-house development versus purchase of an existing business. Internal development required an estimated two years of product development, test marketing, and capital investment before a product could reach store shelves. Nestlé reasoned that if its major competitors were going through the same cycle, all products would reach the market simultaneously without any one product or company capturing any significant first-mover gains. Not wanting to be pre-empted as it had been in the pudding market, Nestlé sought to purchase an established regional player in the refrigerated pasta and sauces category, thereby leapfrogging its competition to market.

Nestlé Buys Lambert's Pasta & Cheeses

In 1987, Nestlé outbid one of its international rivals, Kraft (now part of Phillip Morris's Kraft General Foods subsidiary), for the purchase of a small New York-based pasta company called Lambert's Pasta & Cheese. Lambert's Pasta & Cheese had been established in the early 1980s by a real estate developer with a passion for food. He founded gourmet stores in New York City selling freshly made pasta and imported cheeses. When local supermarkets asked to stock the product, Lambert's developed a process which extended the shelf life from the usual 2-3 days to 40 days by a series of technical innovations which included replacing the residual oxygen in the pasta package with nitrogen. The 38-day extension allowed for the creation of a feasible distribution system. It piggybacked existing industry distribution systems, shipping from a plant to a warehouse to grocery stores. The key was that this extended product life was accomplished without impairing product quality. Capitalizing on its product breakthrough, Lambert's had gone public in 1986, achieving distribution in New York, Atlanta, Boston, Washington, D.C., and California. Lambert's owned and operated two small U.S. factories and had sales of $15 million. With its $56 million purchase price, Nestlé paid a very high multiple of earnings for the small firm which would soon become known as Contadina Fresh.

The Contadina Experience

Soon after the purchase of Lambert's Pasta & Cheese, Nestlé hired Stephen Cunliffe as president of the Nestlé Refrigerated Food Company. Atypically, Cunliffe was not a lifelong Nestlé or Carnation employee, having worked in North America for Jacobs Suchard, AG, a Swiss-based coffee and confectionery company. His charter was to establish a beachhead for Nestlé in the refrigerated foods category, beginning with pasta and sauces. With a goal of profitability within three years, he focused on marketing, while simultaneously addressing issues of manufacturing, distribution, and sales.

Branding

In 1987, pasta was available in two forms in the United States. Fresh pasta was available in gourmet stores and restaurants, but was not widely sold in grocery stores. Dry pasta, however, was a staple item in grocery stores located in either the "ethnic food aisle," or the dry prepared foods aisle with rice, Kraft dinner, etc. Macaroni was the leading type of dry pasta sold, followed by spaghetti, and extruded shapes such as rigatoni and lasagna noodles. Other ingredients needed to make the pasta dishes were located nearby, including tomato paste and tomato sauce, as well as pre-made jarred sauces. Fresh pasta was considered to be of superior quality. It invariably sold at a price premium, needed to be cooked within 2 days of purchase, and required a trip to a specialty store.

In developing a national pasta product line, NFRC needed to identify a brand name for its product that would be accepted in all regions of the United States. Carnation's Contadina brand seemed an ideal candidate. Traditionally Contadina products had been shelf stable, commodity tomato-based products (tomato paste, tomato sauce, etc.) which established the brand within the food category of ingredients used in the preparation of Italian foods. Earlier focus groups conducted in 1985 found that the Contadina name strongly communicated an image of authentic Italian cooking, and was associated with "old fashioned," traditional foods rather than convenience products. This research also suggested that more contemporary products under the Contadina brand name could be made to fit with the traditional values and image, and could communicate specific benefits, with support from packaging and positioning. Given the Contadina brand name, research was commissioned to develop the optimal product name for the pastas and sauces. Using mall intercepts of 200 potential purchasers in three geographically dispersed cities, Nestlé Refrigerated Foods found that Contadina Fresh Classics was a strong candidate with 70% of respondents ranking it first or second among eight potential names. In the final outcome the word "classics" was dropped, and the product range was branded "Contadina Fresh."[1]

Market Potential

Prior to acquiring Lambert's Pasta & Cheese, Nestlé had ascertained that the potential market size for pasta and sauces could be attractive. Now Nestlé retained BASES to conduct a BASES I study, with the objective of assessing the current level of awareness and usage of fresh pasta and fresh pasta sauces, and understanding customer perception of three possible Contadina positioning statements with respect to competitive brands. Additionally NRFC wanted to estimate first year trial volume for pasta and sauces, simulate total Year 1 sales volume, and understand the likely sales effects of alternate positionings.

[1]In later years, revised interpretation of labeling regulations by the F.D.A. obliged Nestlé and other food manufacturers to discontinue use of the word "Fresh" in association with processed refrigerated foods.

BASES used the market forecasting methodology outlined in **Exhibit 3**. The firm conducted primary market research to assess the concept appeal and the level of product satisfaction both with the concept and its substitutes. Research findings were compared with industry composites for similar products to determine overall market strength. Adjustments were made to forecast key market data such as trial rate, repeat purchase, transaction size, and purchase frequency. Additionally the BASES model used marketing plan components such as media selection, consumer and trade promotion, and distribution to further refine key market data, ultimately building Year 1 sales forecasts.

In conducting its study, BASES completed approximately 300 concept tests in six different cities with about one-third of the completed interviews encompassing an alternate positioning: Homemade, Pasta Dinner, and Superior. The positioning statements for each were:

- ***Homemade.*** *"A complete line of fresh pastas and sauces with the taste and quality of authentic homemade recipes."*
- ***Pasta Dinner.*** *"Fresh pasta dinners so good they'll make a meat and potatoes man smile."*
- ***Superior.*** *"A complete line of fresh pastas and sauces that are superior to any pasta or sauce you've tried before."*

All respondents were 18+ females, living within 100 miles of the interview city site, had not been interviewed by a market research firm within the previous three months, and were the primary grocery shopper. The key findings from the 300 concept tests are outlined in **Exhibits 4** to **6**. The results of the same 300 concept tests broken down by positioning are outlined in **Exhibits 7** and **8**. Although there was little material difference between the three positionings, Superior was the favored alternative.

The concept test confirmed many of the beliefs at NRFC. The concept received high intent to purchase, with about 75% of the 301 surveyed likely to purchase the product.[2] There were few fresh pasta brands purchased in the marketplace, with 77% of those in favor of the concept never having purchased fresh pasta before. Despite the low incidence of fresh pasta purchase, pasta appeared to be a staple item, with about 90% of the total sample usually purchasing some brand of dry pasta, and 17% usually purchasing frozen pasta. These findings also indicated that no one brand was overwhelmingly preferred. Findings in the sauce category were similar to that of pasta. Approximately 62% of those surveyed displayed a favorable purchase intent, with over 90% indicating that they had never purchased fresh pasta sauce. Over 75% of the respondents prepared "homemade" sauce, with over half of homemade sauce makers preparing sauce more than once a month. Jarred and bottle sauces were purchased most often (71% of the time) with infrequent purchase of dry packages (6%) and frozen (3%). Of the jarred sauces Ragu was the survey leader with 40%, followed by Prego with 20%.

Using the market research findings and marketing plan data, the market research firm used its model (**Exhibit 3**) to estimate first year trial volume and repeat purchase volume. A simplified version of these calculations is shown in **Exhibit 9**. A key determinant of the trial volumes was the trial rate forecast. The research results indicated a 75% positive purchase intent. Although BASES' model is proprietory, an industry rule of thumb is that 80% of those who said they "definitely would buy" and 30% of those who said that they "probably would buy," would actually buy; resulting in an adjusted trial rate of 34.5%. BASES further refined the adjusted trial rate based on NRFC's marketing plan for pasta which called for $25 million in expenditures

[2]In this instance, "likely to purchase" is Top Two Box with respondents stating either they "definitely would buy" or "probably would buy."

comprising $13 million in advertising (85% television, 15% magazine), $6.2 million in consumer promotion (1 million direct mail coupons per month for the first three months with a 10% expected redemption rate, followed by 2.15 million $.50 coupons dropped six months after the initial rollout with a 5% expected redemption rate), and $4.8 million in trade promotion. NRFC estimated that its $13 million advertising expenditure would secure approximately 2,300 GRP's,[3] which BASES estimated would generate 48% awareness among the general population. Additionally NRFC anticipated that the combination of its advertising and consumer and trade promotion would result in 70% ACV[4] distribution. Further modification of the trial rate for these factors yielded an expected trial rate of 11.6%. BASES had also estimated from its research that 1.0 unit of pasta would be purchased at trial.

The next component of first year volume was repeat purchase. As no actual product had been used in the concept test, BASES used consumer reaction to the concept and its prior experience with dry pasta to forecast repeat purchase. As the actual perception of product quality was unknown, three scenarios were forecast, one each for a mediocre product, an average product, and an excellent product. The purchase cycle was derived from the claimed frequency of purchase, while the average units per purchase were derived from the claimed transaction amount. Because refrigerated pasta had a shorter shelf life it was assumed that it would have a 6-week purchase cycle, rather than the 7.8-week purchase cycle observed for dry pasta. The number of repeat purchase occasions per repeat customer was estimated to be 2-3 on average in the first year. The total forecasted volume is outlined in **Table A**:

Table A Total Forecasted Units of Pasta (000s)

	Mediocre Product	Average Product	Excellent Product
Trial volume	9,000	9,000	9,000
Repeat purchase volume	8,500	12,300	13,900
Total estimated volume	17,500	21,300	22,900
Minimum business requirements based on Nestlé's projected investment and return criteria	20,000	20,000	20,000

With minimum business requirements of 20 million units, the market research firm recommended that NRFC proceed with the introduction of refrigerated pasta, assuming that it would be able to pre-empt the competition in all major metropolitan markets. It recommended a product launch with high quality, yet broad appeal/positioning. It was also thought necessary to communicate product location within the store. As seen in **Table B**, a similar analysis of the sauce market indicated that it was about two-thirds the size of the pasta market and, like pasta, also above NRFC's minimum business requirements. Each 9-oz. package of pasta was expected to serve two people as a main course and sell for approximately $2.50 retail, resulting in a $43 million-$57 million market. The 15-oz. sauce package was designed to serve three to four people and sell for an average $2.50 retail price, resulting in a $25 million-$35 million retail market.

[3]GRPs (gross rating points) are a measure of advertising impact. It is calculated as percent of target market reached multiplied by exposure frequency (e.g., 30% x 4 times = 120 GRP).

[4]ACV (all commodity volume) is a measure of distribution reach. 70% ACV, for example, means that a product is distributed in stores which represent 70% of sales volume of all food products sold in that area.

Table B Total Forecasted Units of Sauce (000s)

	Mediocre Product	Average Product	Excellent Product
Trial volume	6,000	6,000	6,000
Repeat purchase volume	4,200	7,000	8,200
Total estimated volume	10,200	13,000	14,200
Minimum business requirements based on Nestlé's projected investment and return criteria	12,000	12,000	12,000

Positioning

BASES also used a technique it called PASS (positioning analysis and segmentation summary) to help NRFC better understand brand positioning issues: the major criteria consumers perceived in a brand, the criteria that have the greatest influence on brand preference, brand fit in the marketplace *vis-à-vis* competitors, and appeal among a particular market segment. NRFC supplied BASES with 27 attribute statements (**Exhibit 10**) used by consumers when describing the difference between brands of pasta. These attribute statements had been drawn from earlier qualitative research. During PASS, each respondent was asked to name the brands of pasta they usually purchased. The respondent then indicated the degree to which the 27 attribute statements described each of the brands in their usage set.

A multivariate research technique, called Factor Analysis, was used to reduce the 27 attributes to the major criteria which customers used to differentiate brands of pasta. Although five major criteria emerged which represented the consumer's macro view of the pasta category, three explained almost all of the variance in the brand ratings data as collected on the 27 attribute statements. These major criteria were ordinary main meal (41%), quality (39%), and a light meal/side dish (20%). Two other criteria, convenience and pasta as a staple food, explained less than 1% of the variance respectively. The next step was to plot the positioning of pasta competitors, including the three Contadina positionings. Based on this analysis the high quality positioning as a light meal/side dish was the clear winner (**Exhibit 11**). Further analysis indicated that the relative importance of the brand positioning did not differ across light versus heavy pasta users. It did not differ across the following four psychographic segments either. (These segments were also identified by the self-reported survey data.)

The Shopper
I like to try out new products or recipes.
I regularly use coupons when grocery shopping.

The Gourmet Cook
I seldom cook dishes that are quick and easy to make.
I regularly buy gourmet/specialty foods.
I enjoy cooking and consider it a creative outlet.

I enjoy eating ethnic foods.

The Health Activist
I am cutting back on red meat.
The number of calories in food is important to me.
I exercise regularly to stay fit and healthy.

The Uninvolved

I seldom plan meals more than one or two days ahead.

Manufacturing and Distribution

Review of existing manufacturing facilities at Lambert's Pasta & Cheese made it clear that considerable change was required. As Cunliffe explained, "The existing facilities were not top-class. The factory lacked the sanitation standards required of a national company, and the existing retail outlets were not part of our strategy for the future. Additionally, management lacked the sophistication needed to excel in a large organization." Having made the decision to establish a new manufacturing facility, the next question was how many facilities would be required and their optimal location and capacity. Given the short shelf life of refrigerated foods, conventional wisdom dictated many small manufacturing plants located close to major markets. However, NRFC believed that considerable efficiencies could be created by using just one manufacturing location. Cunliffe opted to build a single factory in Danville, Virginia, capable of producing 60 million units at $.87 per unit, with fixed costs of $0.15 and variable costs of $0.72. The decision to source a perishable product nationally from a single location clearly demanded a highly efficient system of distribution.

George Carney, vice president of Distribution for Nestlé Food Company, remarked,

> To an outsider, a 40 day shelf life seems like an eternity. What most people do not understand is that our customers, large grocery stores and grocery wholesalers, demand delivery of the product to their facilities with 30 days of shelf life remaining. They need these 30 days to rotate stock in their warehouses, distribute to individual stores, and allow for "real" shelf time of three to four weeks at the store prior to sale to the end consumer. That leaves us with 10 days to produce, ship, and deliver our product throughout the United States.

Working with 10 days' delivery time, NRFC devised a simple but highly effective distribution system. An order placed with Nestlé's customer service line was forwarded to the factory in Danville for production. It took approximately three days to fill the order, after which orders were placed on freight trucks for delivery to six pooling locations. At the pooling stations, the trucks were unloaded and cross-docked with other Nestlé products to optimize the weight- and volume-carrying capacity of the trucks. For example, a truck filled with Contadina pasta carried only about half of its capacity in terms of weight because pasta was light in weight compared to its package volume. On the other hand, a truck filled with 60% pasta and 40% of another product, such as Liquid Coffeemate (high weight/volume ratio), resulted in a truck filled to 100% capacity. The efficient weight-to-volume allocation on the freight trucks was effective, bringing distribution costs down from $.65/case to $.38/case, yielding an important cost savings for both products.

Sales

Traditionally the sales function for all of Carnation's businesses was the responsibility of Carnation's 700-person direct sales force which called on both head offices and individual grocery stores. Despite the professionalism and experience of Carnation's sales force, Cunliffe was concerned with the "share of voice" that Contadina would receive from the sales force given its limited experience in the new refrigerated foods category. Additionally, the fixed charge allocation for the direct sales force to the fledgling unit would have been a substantial one at

$3 million-$4 million. The other option was to utilize food brokers who acted as sales agents earning a 3%-5% commission, selling to both field and headquarters locations. Although brokers sold multiple products, Contadina thought it could get a "larger share of sales time" from the broker organization because dollar values were high on Contadina's products and could potentially represent a sizable revenue stream to the broker. Additionally, there were good brokers available in major markets who already had significant experience in perishable/refrigerated foods. As a result, Cunliffe opted to develop the broker organization in order to build a smaller, more focused organization to gain a larger "share of sales time," develop specialization with refrigerated foods, and have "greater numbers of people on the street monitoring the product." Contadina initially set up 12 Contadina sales managers, all drawn from the Carnation sales organization, to manage the broker network, responsible for managing over 50 brokers who had 1,200 salespeople calling on food retailers.

Contadina Is Launched

Lambert's major assets were its high quality product recipes and packaging technology. NRFC's strategy was to capitalize on these assets and distribute the first nationally branded refrigerated pasta and sauce product. The product would be stocked in grocery store refrigerated sections predominantly near the deli or the dairy case. Each item would be freshness- dated with an expiration date to accentuate product quality and freshness. The pasta product line included both white and spinach varieties in strand and filled forms. The sauce line included tomato, cream, and pesto varieties. The full product line and retail prices are shown below (see also **Exhibit 12**):

Pasta Varieties (each 9-oz. package makes two main courses or four side dishes)	Price
Strand pasta (linguine, fettucine, angel's hair)	$1.99
Filled pastas (ravioli, tortellini, tortelloni, agnolotti)	2.99

Sauce Varieties (each container of sauce makes four main courses or eight side dishes)	Price
Plum tomato: with a touch of parmesan (15 oz.)	$1.99
Bolognese: tomato with meat (15 oz.)	2.49
Alfredo: cream, butter, parmesan, romano (15 oz.)	2.49
White clam: cream, white wine, clams, garlic (11 oz.)	2.79
Pesto: fresh basil, cheese, olive oil, herbs, nuts and spices (7 oz.)	2.79

Assuming standard margins, NRFC projected that its ex-factory prices would be approximately 66% of suggested retail prices.

NRFC supported its product launch with a $7 million advertising campaign, 85% of which was in television advertising and 15% in print media. An additional $5 million was allocated to consumer promotion and $4 million to trade promotions.

NRFC opted to sell its products using a "component" approach with pasta items packaged and sold separately from sauces rather than packaged together in a single unit. Stephen Cunliffe commented on the advantages of this approach,

> The component marketing of pasta and sauces proved very successful. We achieved better quality as flavor did not migrate from one product to another. Moreover, because each component is processed separately we were able to utilize the most appropriate technology for that component, thereby ensuring higher quality over the product's shelf life. Additionally, we found that the component strategy made consumers feel less guilty about their purchase. As meals were assembled in the kitchen, consumers felt they had a home cooking element. The component approach was useful in reducing sticker shock—for example, to serve two people, consumers were more willing to pay $4.00 for sauce[5] and $2.50 for pasta than $6-7 for a complete meal.

Contadina Fresh Pasta and Sauces were rolled out nationally in the second half of 1988 and quickly became the established market leader, with $75 million in retail sales in 1988 and $150 million by 1990. The pasta line accounted for nearly 80% of the sales volume. Nestlé had beaten its competitors to market with a high quality refrigerated food entry.

Di Giorno Enters

Contadina's early success was threatened in 1989 with Kraft's Di Giorno pasta and sauce product. After an earlier investigation of other acquisition opportunities, Kraft acquired a factory in Birmingham, Alabama, retooled it, and was ready to rollout its product. Rather than using a 40-day shelf life technology, Kraft had developed a 90-day product in order to fit the pasta product into Kraft's established cheese distribution system. NRFC was very concerned about Kraft's entry into the refrigerated pasta and sauce market. A serious competitor, Kraft General Foods, Inc., was a subsidiary of Phillip Morris Companies, Inc., with operating revenue of approximately $25 billion. The General Foods USA division of Kraft General Foods was one of the largest processors and marketers of packaged grocery products in the United States, in addition to its manufacture and marketing of frozen food products. Its principal brands included Maxwell House and Yuban coffees, Jell-O desserts and novelties, Post cereal, Tombstone and Jack's frozen pizza, and Entenmann's bakery products. Kraft USA's principal products in 1987 included cheese and related products such as salad dressings, margarine and vegetable spreads, jellies and preserves, and packaged pasta dinners. In addition to its Kraft brand, other brands included Philadelphia Cream Cheese, Miracle Whip, Cheez Whiz, and Budget Gourmet frozen entrees. Cunliffe recalled the DiGiorno threat:

> Nestlé, Kraft, and Unilever compete against each other on a global basis. For Nestlé, and the future of Contadina, it was strategically important that we win the competitive battle against Kraft in the United States with this product.

Given this strategic direction, Contadina set a goal of maintaining a 2:1 share ratio nationally, and a higher ratio in such priority markets as Boston, New York, Miami, San Francisco, Washington, D. C., and Los Angeles. When DiGiorno entered these markets with high value coupons hoping to induce trial, Contadina responded with lower value coupons sufficient to reward loyal buyers and attract frequent category buyers. DiGiorno coupon values ranged from $.50 to $1.80. Contadina responded with its own coupons in priority markets of $.20 to $.90. DiGiorno also used deeper trade deal levels, resulting in lower consumer price promotions and higher levels of advertising than Contadina.

Rather than threatening Contadina, the DiGiorno entry resulted in considerable growth in the refrigerated pasta category. Both Contadina pasta and sauce volume increased in priority

---

[5]The cost of manufacturing the sauce was significantly higher than originally projected, and the price was therefore subsequently adjusted upwards from $2.50 to $4.00.

markets along with DiGiorno, with pasta increasing 30% and sauce increasing 11%. Further, the percent of households buying refrigerated pasta grew 20%, with Contadina's penetration up 5%. Cunliffe continued,

> NRFC learned important lessons from the DiGiorno attack. We had the advantage of being the first mover in a new product category. If we had waited, we could not have sustained the DiGiorno entry.

Contadina Pizza

With a goal of building the refrigerated food category, NRFC had begun working on its next product while still fine-tuning the pasta and sauces business plan. Before its purchase by Nestlé, Pasta & Cheese had started to develop a pizza product. While the product was carried on a limited basis in New York, it had not yet been "converted" to a refrigerated food product with a longer shelf life. Given Contadina's success, NRFC began a product development process for a refrigerated pizza concept.

The product line extension into pizza was a logical one. Pizza was a part of the large Italian ethnic food category, with pizza available in three forms: frozen, deli-made, or freshly prepared in restaurants for eat-in dining, home delivery, or takeout. The $18.4 billion pizza market was dominated by restaurants (also called pizzerias), with 88% of all pizza sold by restaurants even though an estimated 60% of pizzas were eaten at home. Estimates were that 76% of all U.S. families had eaten at a pizza restaurant within the previous six months (including takeout and delivery). Pizza consumption was strongest in the northern and eastern parts of the United States. Nestlé's research of at-home pizza consumption indicated that delivered/takeout pizza accounted for 75% of the last 10 incidences of pizza consumption, with frozen pizzas from supermarkets accounting for 16%, fresh pizza from a grocery store 5%, and homemade pizza 4%. In 1990, the delivered/takeout market was served by large national franchisors such as Pizza Hut and Domino's, each with hundreds of retail outlets as well as numerous regional and local competitors. The total number of franchised pizza restaurants in the United States was estimated to be upwards of 10,000, without counting another 25,000 or so outlets that also served pizza. The average selling price of a 12" pizza was approximately $8 to $10. The frozen pizza market was more fragmented without a clear market leader, with an average 6" to 8" frozen pizza selling for $2-$3.

By the end of 1988, NRFC developed two new pizza concepts: a pizza "kit" and a pre-assembled, heat-and-eat pizza. Both products were intended to serve two to three people. The kit was refrigerated and consisted of a crust packaged together with separate packets of cheese and sauce. The sauce was available in either tomato or pesto. The product development group expected the 12" crust, sauce, and cheese to sell for approximately $6.40. Additional toppings were also developed which were expected to be sold separately for about $1.30 per topping. The varieties of topping included pepperoni, sausage, vegetable, and extra cheese. The second pizza concept was a refrigerated, pre-assembled pizza available in four varieties: Italian pepperoni, Italian sausage, Italian three-cheese, and Italian mushroom and bell pepper. The expected selling price of the 12" pre-assembled pizza was $7.60. Initially both products were to be available in two sizes: small (8") or large (12".) Customer research, however, indicated that 77% of consumers would buy the 12" pizza, serving two-three people. As a result NRFC proceeded with a single-size, 12" pizza product.

The next step in the product development process was to test the two concepts (pizza kit and pre-assembled) with potential consumers. NRFC asked its MRD to conduct a preliminary concept test. Unlike a BASES study, this concept test was not used to project potential product volume, but rather to assess market interest in its new offerings and obtain diagnostics for refinement of its concept. Four hundred mall intercept concept interviews were conducted in four cities (New York, Atlanta, Chicago, and Los Angeles). Two hundred people were interviewed for each concept, with equal representation of males and females. To qualify for the survey, respondents had to be the primary grocery shopper for the household or alternatively have input into the pizza purchase decision. Findings from the study were promising. Positive purchase intent for the kit was about 58% overall (49% among males and 66% among females). For the pre-assembled option positive purchase intent was approximately 52% (50% among males, and 54% among females). Further findings from the study are outlined in **Exhibits 13 through 15.**

With the favorable concept test feedback, NRFC continued its product development process. Further investigation by the R&D group indicated that the refrigerated pre-assembled concept was infeasible from a production standpoint. Not only did the flavors of the sauce and toppings migrate into one another, but also the sauce and toppings infiltrated the crust resulting in a poor quality product. The kit product, consistent with NRFC's component approach, however, was feasible. Moreover, national distribution was a possibility, and given the state of the art robotics that could be installed in a pizza line at the Danville factory, there was considerable support for a uniform, high-volume pizza product.

In early 1990, NRFC commissioned another market research study on its pizza product. This time the product concepts tested were the Pizza Kit with the option of available toppings sold separately (referred to as **Pizza and Toppings** in Exhibits), and the Pizza Kit (i.e. , the crust, cheese and sauce) with no additional toppings sold separately (referred to as **Pizza Only** in Exhibits). The objectives of the study were to determine the impact on trial of the kit by the availability of the separate toppings and to analyze the strengths and weaknesses of both concepts. NRFC commissioned a BASES II Line Extension Study, involving both a concept and an in-home product use test. The sampling frame for the study is shown in **Table C.**

Table C BASES II Line Extension Study

	Pizza Kit & Toppings			Pizza Kit Only—No Toppings		
	General Population (Random Sample) Contadina		Contadina Pasta Users (Quota Sample)	General Population (Random Sample) Contadina		Contadina Pasta Users (Quota Sample)
	Nonusers	Users		Nonusers	Users	
Concept test	318	81	100	155	43	35
In-home test	142	44	48	-	-	-

BASES conducted mall intercept interviews in seven cities (New York, Baltimore, Orlando, Pittsburgh, Milwaukee, Denver, and Los Angeles) for the study. They interviewed women over age 18, who lived within a 45-minute drive of the mall interview site, and were the principal grocery shopper.[6] For the pizza kit and toppings option, 399 randomly selected women from the general population reviewed a concept board (**Exhibit 16)** and completed a concept interview. Of these women, 81 were Contadina pasta users. For the pizza kit only option, 198 randomly selected women reviewed the concept board (**Exhibit 17**) and completed a concept interview. Of these women, 43 were Contadina users. An additional quota of respondents who had purchased Contadina pasta in the past year were interviewed in order to have a large enough sample of Contadina pasta users to analyze. A quota sample of 100 Contadina pasta users participated in the pizza kit and toppings

[6]Respondents were also disqualified if they were employed in an advertising agency, market research firm, and food retailing (including pizzerias). Recent participation in a market research survey was also grounds for disqualification.

option, while 35 Contadina pasta users participated in the pizza only concept test. Results from the survey were used in the BASES forecasting methodology. Those respondents likely to purchase the product after viewing the concept board were given the product to try at home. After a 7-10 day in-home usage period, participants were called back to get their after-use impressions of the product, with a little more than half of the starting sample completing this portion of the survey. As the pizza product was in the same ethnic food category as the pasta and carried the same brand name, Contadina pizza was treated as a brand extension. The product pricing remained consistent with the earlier concept test, the Pizza Kit and Toppings option was priced at $6.39 for the kit and $1.29 for the toppings. The Pizza Only was priced at $6.39. Similar to its Contadina Pasta line, NRFC expected its factory pricing to be two-thirds of retail prices. The results of the study are seen in **Exhibits 18** to **24.**

NRFC marketing staff believed that the Contadina pasta users would represent approximately 24% of the 95.5 million[7] target households. Initial responses from the Northeast region indicated approximately 25% penetration. Additionally, the BASES random sample **(Tabl C)** was consistent with this finding with approximately 21% of the general population stating that they had used Contadina Pasta within the past year. MRD, however, urged caution in interpreting this data, because the BASES study had been conducted only in high potential markets. Based on MRD's experience in other product categories, it felt that the parent brand penetration could range between 5%-25%, and recommended that volume projections be sensitive to this range.

With a launch decision imminent, NRFC marketing staff compiled the data in **Table D,** drawn from their own estimates as well as those of BASES. NRFC's intention was to support either the Pizza and Toppings or the Pizza Only option, with $18 million in market support comprising $9 million in advertising, $5 million in consumer promotion, and $4 million in trade promotion. Based on this plan NRFC projected a 37% overall awareness. However, as Contadina pasta and sauce users (called "parent brand users") were likely to be more aware of the Contadina name, NRFC expected that awareness of Contadina pizza would be twice as high among Contadina users as compared with nonusers (60% awareness for users, 30% awareness for nonusers).

Table D

	Pizza Kit & Toppings	Pizza Only
Awareness:		
Contadina Pasta & Sauces Users	60%	60%
Nonusers	30	30
Overall Awareness	37	37
ACV[a]	58	58
Purchase Assumptions:		
Units purchased at Trial	1.2 kits	1.1 kits
Repeat rate	22%	22%
Repeat purchase units	1.0 kits	1.0 kits
Repeat purchase occasions	2.0	2.0

[a]AVC adjustments for parent brand users versus nonusers were also made, but an overall 58% ACV penetration in this case was considered an acceptable assumption.

[7]The pasta launch had targeted only 77.4 million households, which represented 89% of U.S. households.

Additionally, NRFC recognized that toppings would not be sold with every pizza kit if the Pizza and Toppings option was launched. The BASES research indicated that 50% of those favorable to the Pizza and Toppings options would buy toppings at every pizza kit purchase and that an additional 25% would purchase toppings half the time. If toppings were purchased, BASES estimated that 1.5 topping units would be purchased during a trial purchase occasion and 1.0 topping units would be purchased on repeat purchase occasions.

Stephen Cunliffe, when contemplating with senior marketing staff on whether to launch Contadina pizza immediately, offered his view:

> We have established the Contadina brand name in pasta, and pizza is a natural next step. We've used our technology to develop a good product at a reasonable price point, in a new food category. Our models indicate that our basic business requirements for pizza is $45 million [factory dollar sales]. With our projected investment costs of $12 million we only need to capture a .3% share of the retail pizza market. We can't delay. Kraft test-marketed a refrigerated pizza product when they were testing DiGiorno pasta and sauces. If NRFC doesn't get its product to market, we will lose our first-mover advantage and never get the market share we deserve.

As Stephen Cunliffe pored through the numerous exhibits from his market research staff, he pondered if he should launch a pizza product, if so which option, how large a market he would find, and what market share he could achieve. Kraft had indeed test-marketed a refrigerated pizza product at the time of its pasta test markets. Results from the test market were unclear, but many within Nestlé expected a Kraft pizza product within the next six months.

Exhibit 1 Nestlé, S.A. Selected Statistics, Product Lines

Millions of Swiss francs	1992	1991
Sales by Product Line		
Beverages	13,521	11,917
Milk product & dietetics	14,890	13,924
Prepared dishes & cooking aids (& miscellaneous activities)	15,718	14,956
Chocolate & confectionery	8,598	8,077
Pharmaceuticals	1,773	1,612
Total	54,500	50,486
Sales by Geographic Region		
Europe	26,632	24,350
North & South America	19,214	18,098
Rest of the world	8,654	8,038
Total	54,500	50,486
Trading Profit by Product Line		
Beverages	2,415	2,136
Milk products & dietetics	1,394	1,192
Prepared dishes & cooking aids (& miscellaneous dishes)	806	782
Chocolate & confectionery	658	685
Pharmaceuticals	364	291
Total	5,637	5,086
Trading Profit by Geographic Region		
Europe	2,359	2,276
North & South America	2,158	1,861
Rest of the world	1,120	949
Total	5,637	5,086

Definition of Product Lines

Beverages: Soluble coffee, roast and ground coffees, chocolate and malt-based drinks, mineral waters, fruit juices and fruit drinks, and tea-and coffee-based ready-to-drink beverages.

Milk products & dietetics: Milks (powdered, condensed, evaporated), soya milk, coffee creamer, infant milks, infant cereals, dietetic foods, milk-based refrigerated products (yogurts, desserts, and cheeses), ice-cream, breakfast cereals, and clinical nutrition.

Prepared dishes & cooking aids (& miscellaneous activities): Culinary products (bouillon, soups, sauces, canned or dehydrated prepared dishes), pasta, frozen foods, chilled pasta and sauces, cold meat products, pet care, ingredients for the food industry and hotels.

Chocolate & confectionery: Chocolate, sugar confectionery, biscuits, and pastry.

Pharmaceuticals: Ophthalmic products (Alcon), and infant cosmetic products.

Source: Annual Reports

Exhibit 2 Nestlé USA Organization Chart

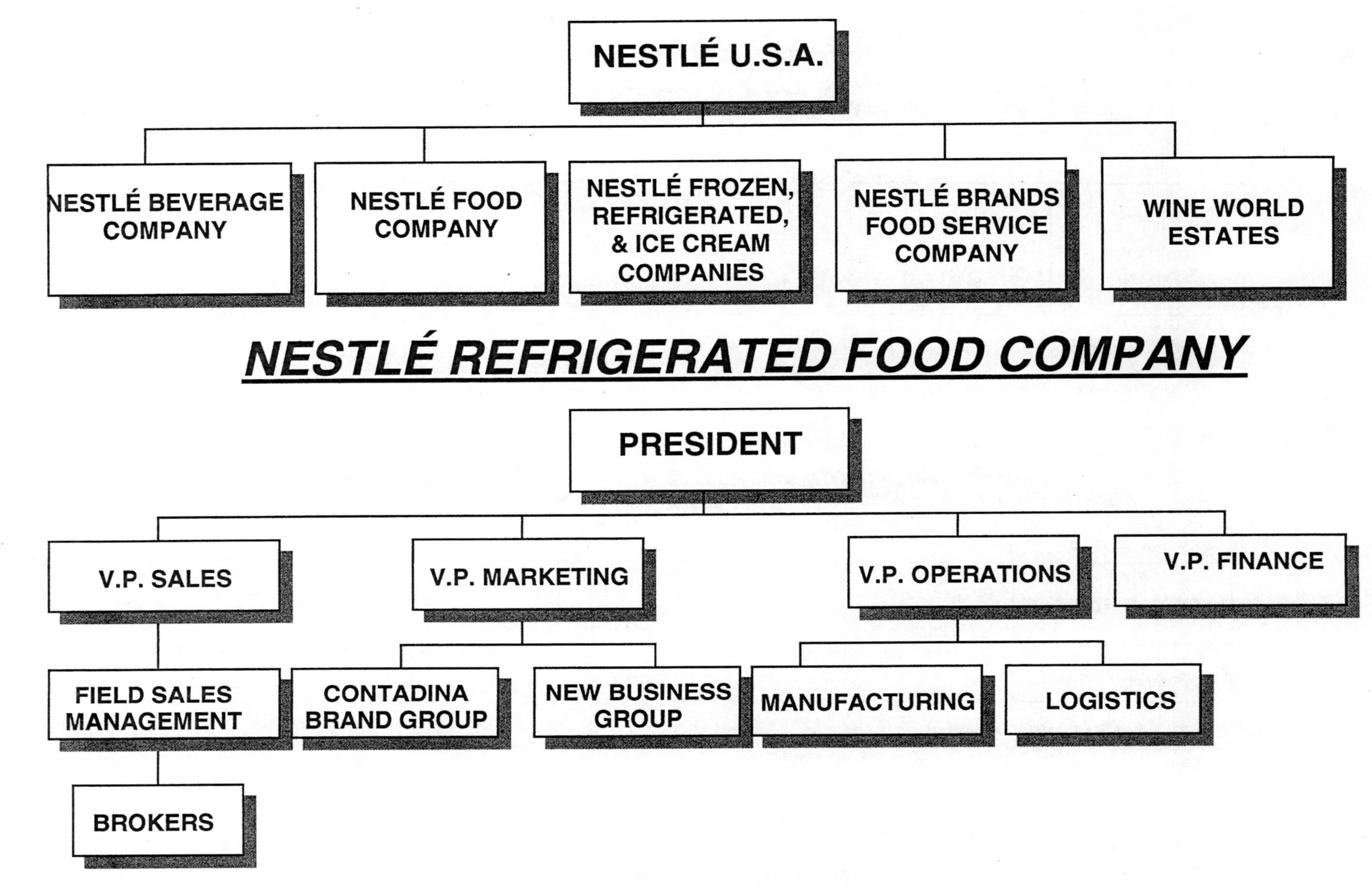

Exhibit 3 Market Forecasting Methodology—Overview of the BASES System

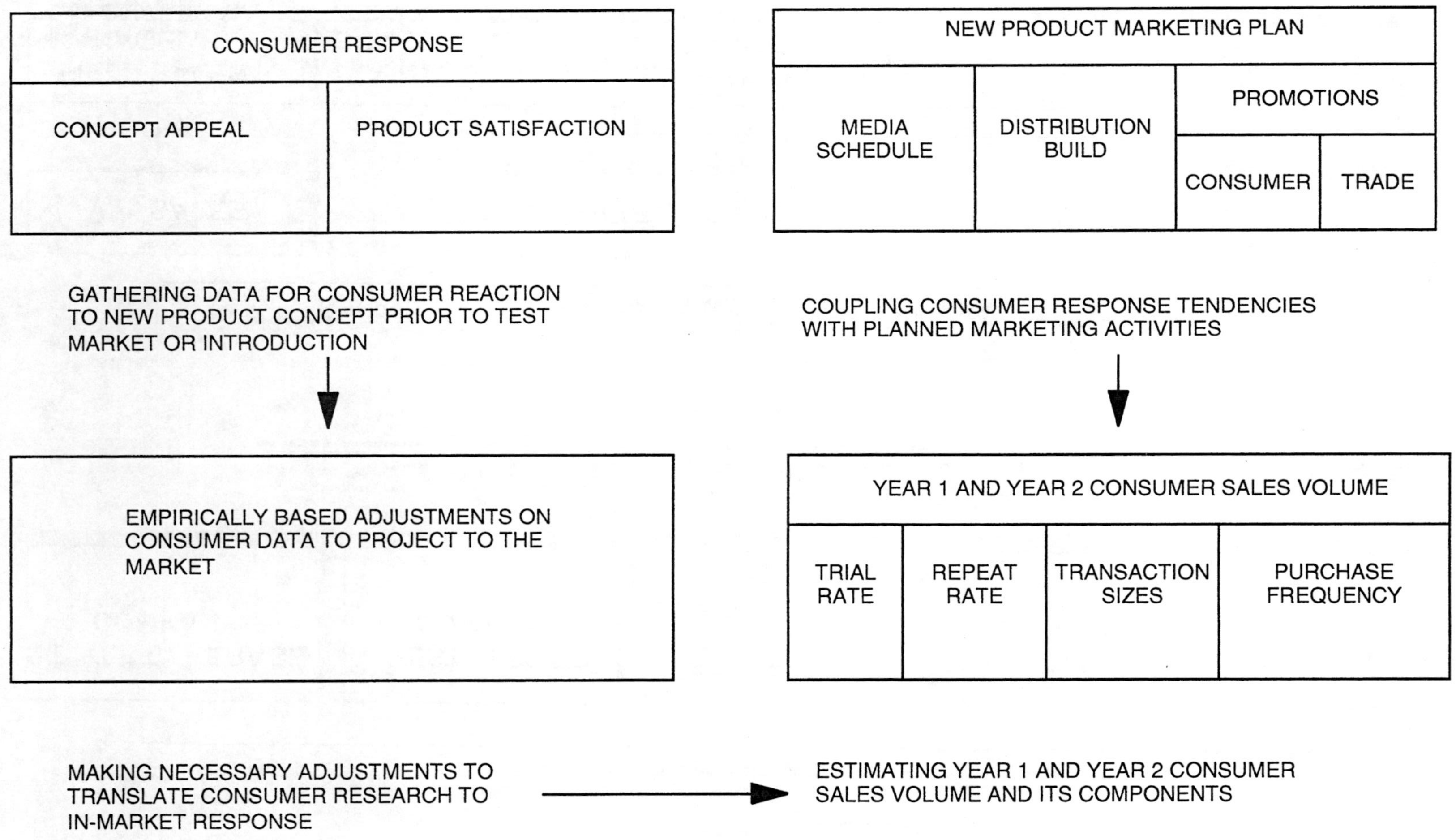

CONSUMER RESPONSE

CONCEPT APPEAL | PRODUCT SATISFACTION

GATHERING DATA FOR CONSUMER REACTION TO NEW PRODUCT CONCEPT PRIOR TO TEST MARKET OR INTRODUCTION

EMPIRICALLY BASED ADJUSTMENTS ON CONSUMER DATA TO PROJECT TO THE MARKET

MAKING NECESSARY ADJUSTMENTS TO TRANSLATE CONSUMER RESEARCH TO IN-MARKET RESPONSE

NEW PRODUCT MARKETING PLAN

MEDIA SCHEDULE | DISTRIBUTION BUILD | PROMOTIONS (CONSUMER, TRADE)

COUPLING CONSUMER RESPONSE TENDENCIES WITH PLANNED MARKETING ACTIVITIES

YEAR 1 AND YEAR 2 CONSUMER SALES VOLUME

TRIAL RATE | REPEAT RATE | TRANSACTION SIZES | PURCHASE FREQUENCY

ESTIMATING YEAR 1 AND YEAR 2 CONSUMER SALES VOLUME AND ITS COMPONENTS

Exhibit 4 Key Concept Measures—Pasta

Measure	Contadina (N = 301)	Industry Median[a]
Definitely would buy	24%	20%
Probably would buy	51	41
Top Two Box	75%	61%
Mean likability[b]	4.3	3.8
Mean Price/Value rating[c]	3.6	3.8

[a]Industry median is based on shelf stable rice and pasta products which may or may not be relevant for comparison to a fresh product.

[b]Six-point scale with 6 being like extremely.

[c]Five-point scale with 5 being very good value.

Exhibit 5 Demographics—Pasta

Demographic	Total (301)	Unfavorable[a] 7 7)	Total Favorable[b] (224)	Definitely Buy (71)	Probably Buy (153)
Mean household size	3.0	2.8	3.0	2.8	3.1
Household composition					
Children 13-18	17%	15%	18%	20%	17%
Children 6-12	21	24	20	11	24
Children Under 6	24	20	25	15	31
% Married	62	55	64	59	66
Respondent age					
24 and under	21%	23%	20%	18%	21%
25-34	30	30	30	24	33
35-44	21	28	18	10	22
45-54	13	8	15	25	10
55+	15	10	17	25	13
% Employed	63	62	63		
Mean family income (000)	$30.1	$29.7	$30.2	$29.3	$30.7
% College Educated	68	77	64	62	67
Race:					
White	91%	92%	90%	87%	90%
Black	6	5	6	9	5
Other	3	3	4	4	5

[a]Unfavorable is Bottom Three Boxes; May or may not buy, probably would not buy, and definitely will not buy
[b]Favorable is Top Two Boxes; Probably would buy, definitely would buy

Exhibit 6 Key Concept Likes, Dislikes, Uniqueness

Item	Total (301) %	Favorable (224) %	Unfavorable (77) %
Likes			
General variety	28	28	28
Filled variety	16	16	16
Natural/not artificial	28	30	23
Quick/fast/saves time	20	22	16
Easy to prepare/already prepared	17	20	11
Packed fresh/packed then refrigerated	6	8	1
Like small size	5	7	1
Clear package/can see what's inside	5	5	4
Like the shapes	5	5	5
Looks appetizing	4	5	1
Good/reasonable price	8	9	4
Fresh/made fresh & dated	26	27	21
Like/eat pasta	13	16	4
Like Contadina/good name	9	11	4
Good meal/dinner	7	8	4
New/different	7	8	3
Dislikes			
Too expensive	8	3	23
Not like green/spinach color	6	5	11
Not like spinach taste	3	2	5
Not like pasta/rarely buy/eat	2	1	7
Not use this type of pasta	2	-	7
Nothing disliked	61	74	24
Concept Uniqueness			
Extremely new and different	15	17	8
Very new and different	38	41	32
Somewhat new and different	35	32	41
Slightly new and different	8	7	11
Not at all new and different	4	3	8
Mean Uniqueness (5-point scale)	3.5	3.6	3.2

Exhibit 7 Key Concept Likes, Dislikes by Alternate Positioning

Item	Homemade (97) (%)	Pasta Dinner (102) (%)	Superior (102) (%)
Likes			
General variety	29	24	31
Filled variety	18	17	15
Natural/not artificial	31	30	28
Quick/fast/saves time	9	30	21
Easy to prepare/already prepared	18	25	10
Packed fresh/packed then refrig.	5	6	2
Like small size	8	4	4
Like the shapes	4	2	10
Looks appetizing	5	5	3
Good/reasonable price	7	9	8
Good price for amount	--	4	--
Light/not gummy/sticky	1	--	8
Fresh/made fresh & dated	26	31	20
Like/eat pasta	13	16	9
Like Contadina/good name	10	8	9
Good meal/dinner	2	12	8
New/different	4	9	7
Dislikes			
Too expensive	14	4	6
Not like green/spinach color	7	7	5

Exhibit 8 Key Concept Measures—Alternate Positionings

	Homemade n=97	Pasta Dinner n=102	Superior n=102	Industry Median[a]
Purchase Intent				
Definitely would buy	27%	19%	24%	20%
Probably would buy	43	56	54	41
Top Two Box	**70%**	**75%**	**78%**	**61%**
Might or might not buy	22%	20%	14%	
Probably/definitely would not buy	8	5	8	
Mean likability[b]	4.2	4.2	4.3	3.8
Mean price/Value rating[b]	3.6	3.6	3.7	3.8

[a]Industry median is based on shelf stable rice and pasta products which may or may not be relevant for comparison to a fresh product.

[b]Six-point scale with 6 being like extremely.

[c]Five-point scale with 5 being very good value.

Exhibit 9 Volume Estimate—Year 1, Pasta

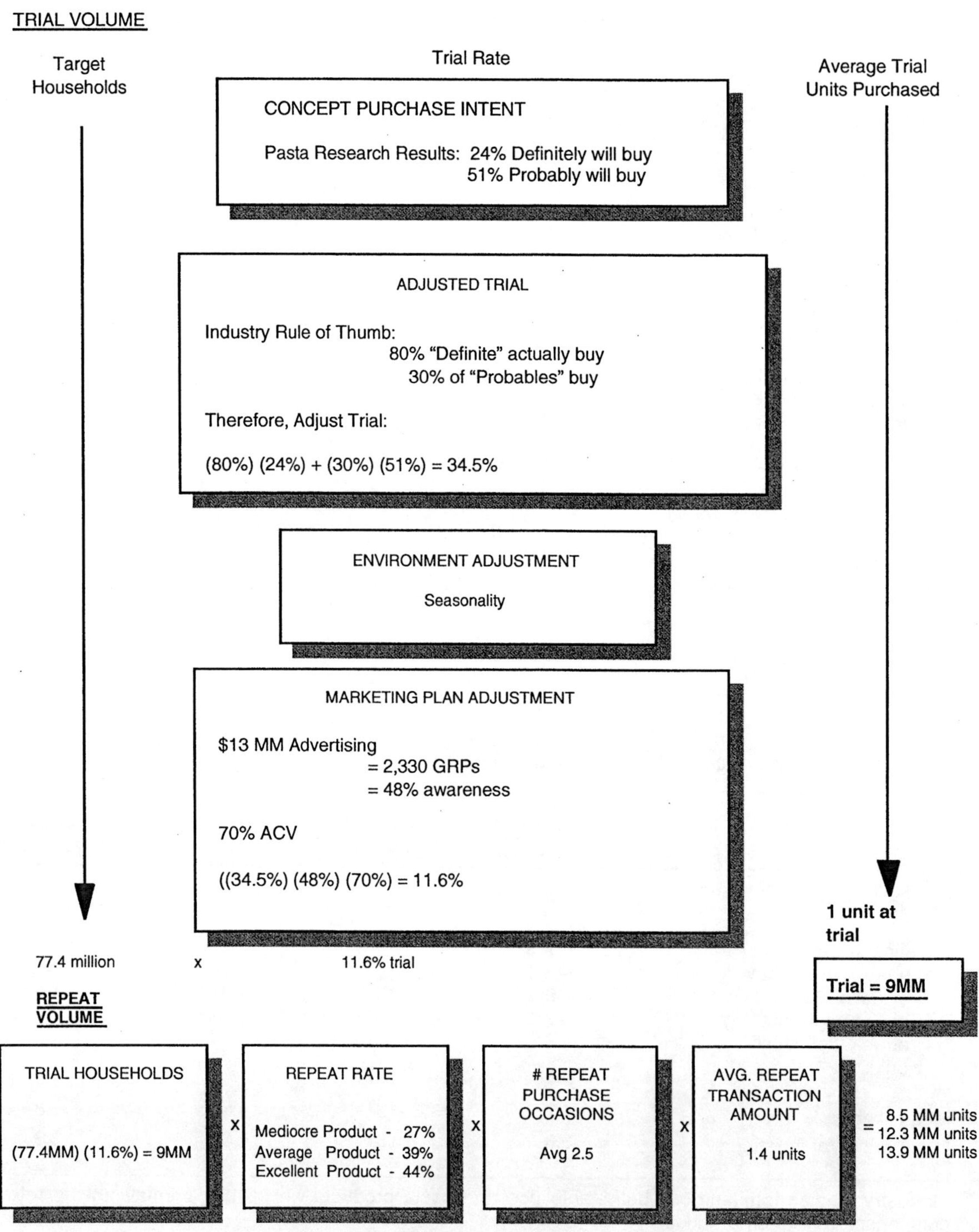
TRIAL VOLUME
Target Households
Trial Rate
Average Trial Units Purchased
CONCEPT PURCHASE INTENT
Pasta Research Results: 24% Definitely will buy
51% Probably will buy
ADJUSTED TRIAL
Industry Rule of Thumb:
80% "Definite" actually buy
30% of "Probables" buy
Therefore, Adjust Trial:
(80%) (24%) + (30%) (51%) = 34.5%
ENVIRONMENT ADJUSTMENT
Seasonality
MARKETING PLAN ADJUSTMENT
$13 MM Advertising
= 2,330 GRPs
= 48% awareness
70% ACV
((34.5%) (48%) (70%) = 11.6%
1 unit at trial
77.4 million
x
11.6% trial
Trial = 9MM
REPEAT VOLUME
TRIAL HOUSEHOLDS
(77.4MM) (11.6%) = 9MM
x
REPEAT RATE
Mediocre Product - 27%
Average Product - 39%
Excellent Product - 44%
x
REPEAT PURCHASE OCCASIONS
Avg 2.5
x
AVG. REPEAT TRANSACTION AMOUNT
1.4 units
=
8.5 MM units
12.3 MM units
13.9 MM units

Exhibit 10 Attribute Statements

1. Appetizing appearance
2. Doesn't stick
3. Don't have time to cook
4. Easy to prepare
5. For the whole family
6. Informal meal
7. Instead of takeout
8. Light meal
9. Light taste
10. Manufacturer you can trust
11. Meal by yourself
12. Meal with adults
13. No artificial ingredients
14. Nutritious pasta
15. On hand
16. Quality ingredients
17. Quality pasta
18. Quick to prepare
19. Recipe taste
20. Regular meal
21. Side dish
22. Special meals
23. Stays fresh
24. Tastes fresh
25. Treat for family
26. Value for money
27. Would doctor up

MAJOR CRITERIA USING FACTOR ANALYSIS AND PROPORTION OF VARIANCE EXPLAINED

Main Meal	Quality	Light Meal/ Side Dish	Staple	Convenience
Regular meal	Quality ingredients	Side dish	Value for money	Don't have time to cook
Meal with adults	Quality pasta	Treat for family	Special meals	Quick to prepare
Informal meals	Nutritious pasta	Light meal	Instead of takeout	
	Recipe taste		Would doctor up	
	No artificial ingredients		On hand	
	Doesn't stick			
	Appetizing appearance			
	Light taste			
	Manufacturer you can trust			
(41%)	(39%)	(20%)	(0%)	(0%)

Exhibit 11A Positioning Map–Quality vs. Light Meal/Side Dish (General Population Female)

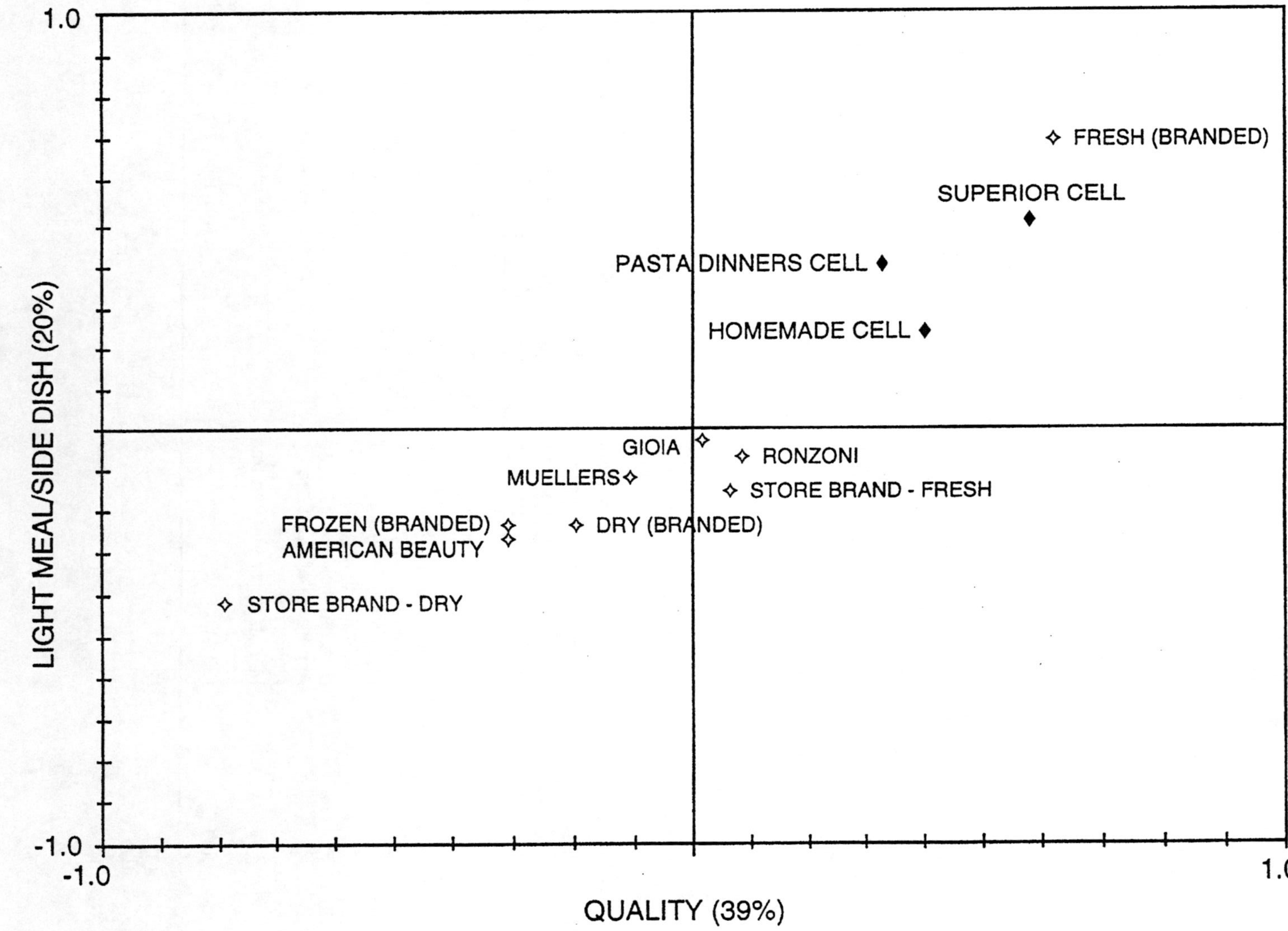

Exhibit 11B Positioning Map–Quality vs. Ordinary Main Meal (General Population Female)

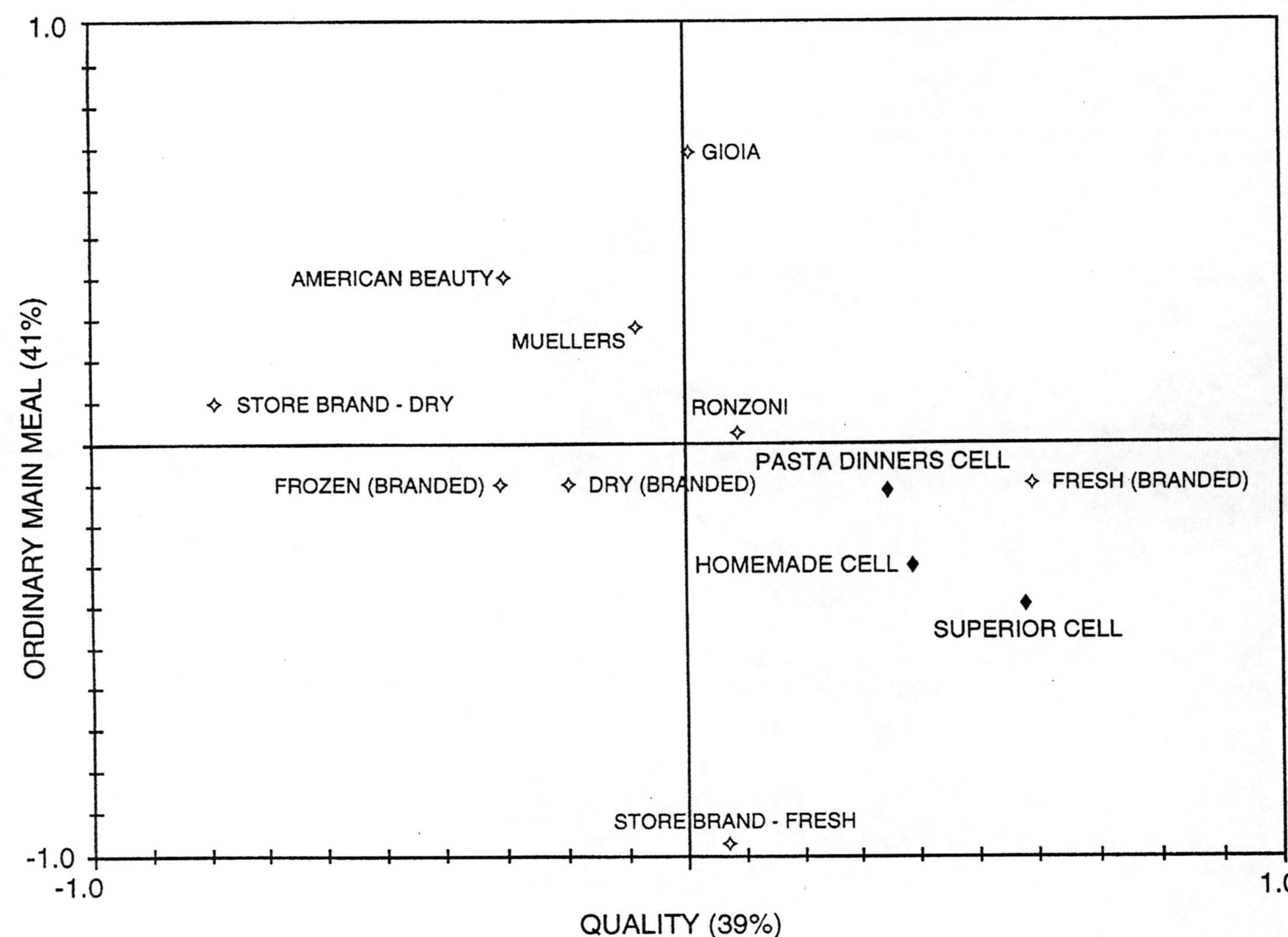

Exhibit 12 Contadina Pasta and Sauce, Products and Prices

Introducing Contadina® Superiore

A complete line of fresh pastas and sauces that are superior to any pasta or sauce you've tried before.

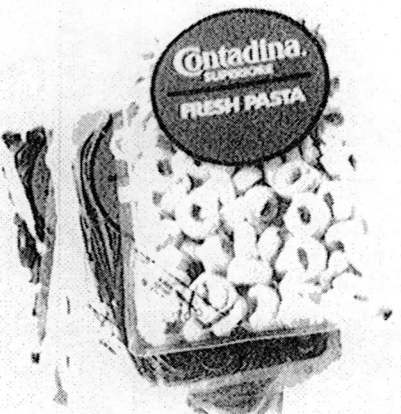

Fresh pastas so light in texture and rich in flavor they even taste good before you add our sauce.

Contadina Superiore fresh pasta is different from the pasta you're used to. Your first mouthful will reveal its lighter texture and richer taste.

Why are our fresh pastas so light in texture and taste?

First, our ingredients: we use only the finest durum wheat flour and whole eggs. Our filled pastas contain select meats, Italian cheeses, fine herbs and spices. Naturally, no preservatives, artificial colors or flavors come near our pastas.

Most importantly, we package our pastas immediately after we make them, and rush them in chilled trucks to the refrigerated case in your local supermarket. This special care retains the soft, moist texture of the noodles and keeps the flavor fresh and light.

Look for the date on each package (just like milk). It guarantees you the freshest, lightest pasta you can eat.

And because we keep Contadina Superiore refrigerator fresh, it cooks in a fraction of the time that dry or frozen pasta takes. Our fresh pastas are never gummy or starchy after cooking, either, so they don't need rinsing.

Contadina Superiore Fresh Pastas: You'll taste pasta in a whole new light.

VARIETIES: (Each 9 oz. package makes 2 main courses or 4 side dishes)	PRICES
Strand pastas (Linguine, Fettucine, Angel's Hair)	$1.99
Filled Pastas (Ravioli, Tortellini, Tortelloni, Agnolotti)	$2.99

Look for our pastas in the refrigerated section of your grocery store.

Pasta sauce that's freshly made—and refrigerated—to capture the savory balance of our select ingredients.

One taste of Contadina Superiore Fresh Pasta Sauces and you'll know how pasta sauce was meant to taste.

We start by using the finest possible ingredients: Our red sauces are made from plump, sun-ripened tomatoes, selected fresh vegetables, fine herbs and spices. The delicate white sauces are made from fresh cream, real butter, Italian cheeses and carefully chosen seasonings. Our savory herb sauce is made with fresh basil, virgin olive oil, Parmesan cheese and pine nuts.

And, of course, we never use preservatives, artificial flavorings or colorings in our sauces.

After blending and cooking, each sauce is carefully packaged and then refrigerated to maintain its fresh taste. We even "freshness-date" each portion to make sure you always get consistently fresh tasting sauces.

So look for Contadina Superiore Fresh Pasta Sauces in the refrigerated section of your grocery store—and get all the flavor out of a sauce that we put into it.

VARIETIES: (Each container of sauce makes 3 [illegible] main courses or [illegible] 8 side dishes)	PRICES
Plum Tomato: with a touch of parmesan (15 oz)	$1.99
Bolognese: tomato with meat (15 oz)	$2.49
Alfredo: cream, butter, parmesan, romano (11 oz)	$2.49
White Clam: cream, white wine, clams, garlic (11 oz)	$2.79
Pesto: fresh basil, cheese, olive oil, herbs, nuts and spices (7 oz)	$2.79

Exhibit 13 Mean Concept Attribute Ratings Before Trial (based on a 10-point scale where 10 = Agree Strongly)

	Takeout Pizza Heavy Users' Evaluation of Takeout Pizza[a] n=128	Kit Favorable Users' Evaluation of Contadina Kit[b] n=115	Frozen Pizza Users' Evaluation of Frozen Pizza[c] n=129
Is a product kids would like	9.4	9.0	7.5
Is a product for the whole family	8.9	8.8	6.7
Is convenient	9.1	8.8	7.6
Appropriate for informal meals any day of the week	8.9	8.4	6.5
Would taste fresh	9.3	8.7	4.7
Comes in varieties I like	9.4	8.8	5.9
Is easy to prepare	--	8.6	7.9
Is easy to serve	9.1	8.5	7.2
Is made from high quality ingredients	8.4	8.1	4.9
Has the type of crust I like	9.0	8.2	5.1
Has no artificial ingredients or preservatives	8.0	7.8	4.5
Would taste good	9.0	7.9	5.2
Would not have a soggy crust	7.8	7.6	4.9
Is appropriate for special meals	7.2	6.1	3.2

[a] In the Pizza Kit sample of 200 people, there were 128 heavy takeout pizza users. Heavy usage is defined as once every 2-3 weeks or more often.

[b] In the Pizza Kit sample of 200 people, there were 115 people favorable to the concept (Top Two Box).

[c] In the Pizza Kit sample of 200 people, there were 129 people who had purchased frozen pizza in the past 12 months.

Exhibit 14 Mean Concept Attribute Ratings Before Trial (based on a 10-point scale where 10 = Agree Strongly)

	Takeout Pizza Heavy Users' Evaluation of Takeout Pizza[a] n=135	Assembled Favorable Users' Evaluation of Assembled Pizza[b] n=102	Frozen Pizza Users' Evaluation of Frozen Pizza[c] n=144
Is a product kids would like	9.3	8.7	7.7
Is a product for the whole family	9.2	8.9	7.5
Is convenient	9.0	8.7	7.8
Appropriate for informal meals any day of the week	8.8	8.6	7.5
Would taste fresh	9.2	8.2	4.9
Comes in varieties I like	9.3	8.3	6.8
Is easy to prepare	N/A	9.0	7.8
Is easy to serve	8.9	8.4	7.0
Is made from high quality ingredients	8.5	8.1	5.3
Has the type of crust I like	9.1	8.1	5.1
Has no artificial ingredients or preservatives	8.0	8.1	4.6
Would taste good	9.1	7.9	5.5
Would not have a soggy crust	8.6	7.6	5.0
Is appropriate for special meals	7.6	6.0	3.3

[a]In the Assembled Pizza sample of 200 people, there were 135 heavy takeout pizza users. Heavy usage is defined as once every 2-3 weeks or more often.

[b]In the Assembled Pizza sample of 200 people, there were 104 people favorable to the concept (Top Two Box).

[c]In the Assembled Pizza sample of 200 people, there were 144 people who had purchased frozen pizza in the past 12 months.

Exhibit 15 Substitution of Contadina Pizza for Another Pizza Product

	% of Last Pizza Eating Occasions (n=60)[a]	% of Next 10 Pizza Eating Occasions (n=60)
Contadina pizza		28%
Takeout/delivered pizza[b]	75%	58%
Frozen pizza from supermarket	16%	9%
Fresh pizza from supermarket	5%	1%
Homemade pizza	4%	4%

Note:

[a]Of the 115 respondents favorable to the kit concept, 60 said they would buy Contadina pizza instead of another product.

[b]To be read: 75% of the last 10 pizza-eating occasions were takeout/delivered pizza for those respondents favorable to Contadina pizza and who would buy it instead of another product. If Contadina was available, these respondents indicated that takeout/delivered pizza would account for 58% of their next 10 pizza-eating occasions.

Exhibit 16 BASES II Study–Concept Board Pizza and Toppings

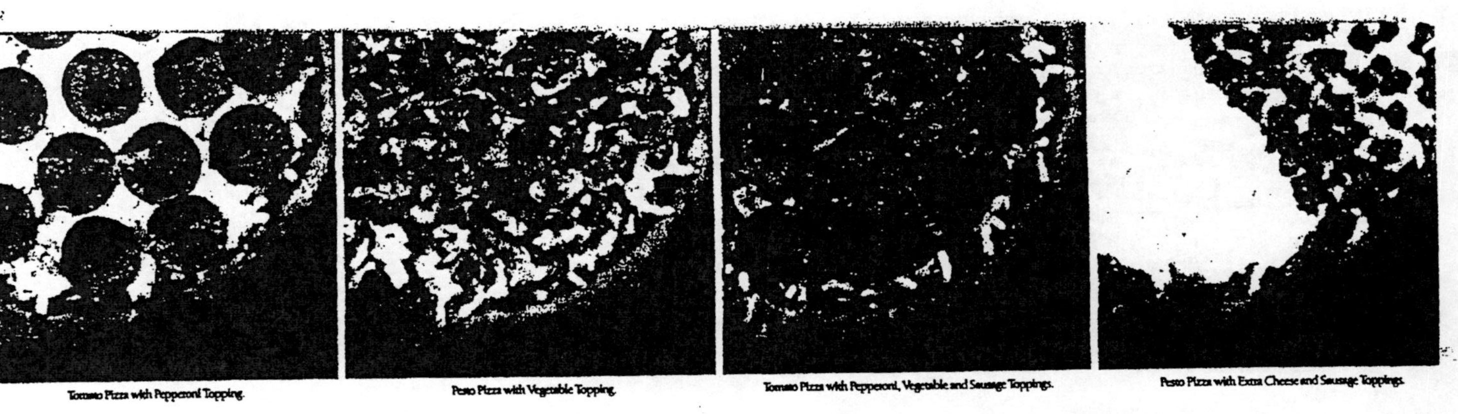
Tomato Pizza with Pepperoni Topping. Pesto Pizza with Vegetable Topping. Tomato Pizza with Pepperoni, Vegetable and Sausage Toppings. Pesto Pizza with Extra Cheese and Sausage Toppings.

New Contadina Fresh Pizza.

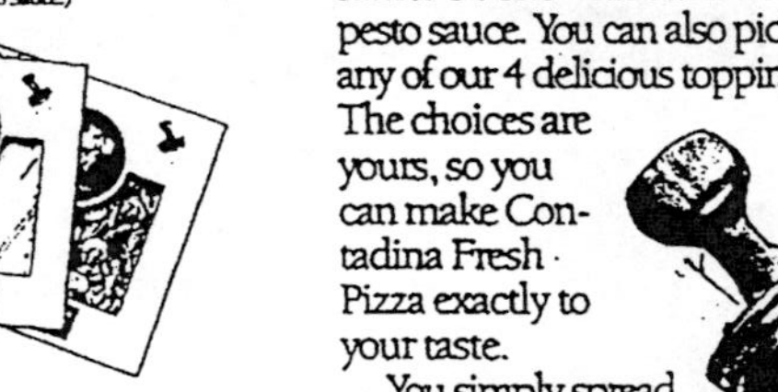
Contadina Fresh Pizza: Crust, Sauce and Cheese. (Available with Tomato or Pesto Sauce.)

Contadina Fresh Pizza Toppings: Pepperoni, Italian Sausage, Extra Cheese, and Vegetable (Mushrooms and Bell Peppers). Each topping sold separately.

Now you can make fresh-baked pizza just the way you like, in minutes.

Contadina Fresh™ has created a delicious new way to enjoy pizza: We've made it easy for you to combine the highest-quality ingredients into a pizza that comes out just the way you like.

To start, just choose a Contadina Fresh package with crust, cheese, and our thick, rich tomato sauce. Or one with our flavorful pesto sauce. You can also pick up any of our 4 delicious toppings. The choices are yours, so you can make Contadina Fresh Pizza exactly to your taste.

You simply spread on the sauce, sprinkle on the cheese, and add any combination of our toppings, or your own favorites. You even choose how crisp the crust is, because you set the baking time.

And it's so easy, you can do it all in less than 15 minutes, from start to piping-hot pizza, fresh from your oven.

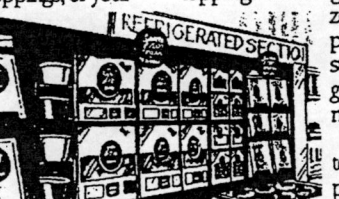

Look for Contadina Fresh Pizza in your grocer's refrigerated section.

Of course your first bite of Contadina Fresh Pizza will tell you we've used only the finest ingredients. Like the choicest pepperoni and Italian sausage. Select mushrooms and peppers. Distinctive cheeses. And sauces that only Contadina Fresh could create.

What's more, to keep the flavors fresh, our pizzas and toppings are refrigerated, not frozen. And each package is date-stamped, to *guarantee* freshness.

It all adds up to a great-tasting pizza, made just the way you like. Piping hot and fresh from your oven, in a matter of minutes.

Contadina Fresh Pizza	
Crust, Tomato Sauce, and Cheese (Serves 2-3)	$6.39
Crust, Pesto Sauce, and Cheese (Serves 2-3)	$6.39
Contadina Fresh Pizza Toppings (Each sold separately)	
Pepperoni	$1.29
Italian Sausage	$1.29
Extra Cheese	$1.29
Vegetable (Mushrooms and Bell Peppers)	$1.29

Exhibit 17 BASES II Study–Concept Board Pizza Only

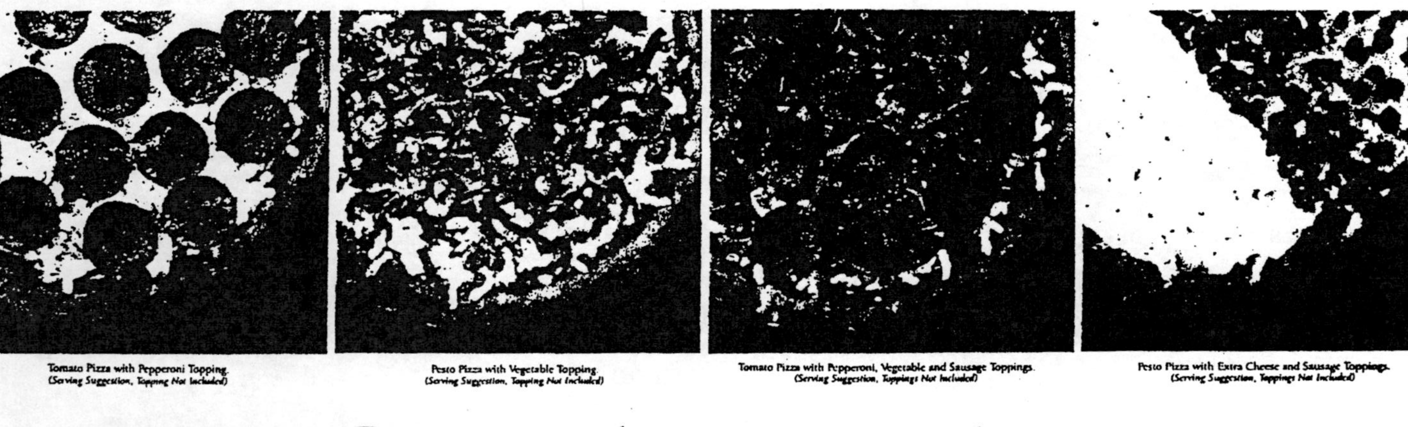

Tomato Pizza with Pepperoni Topping. (Serving Suggestion, Topping Not Included)

Pesto Pizza with Vegetable Topping. (Serving Suggestion, Topping Not Included)

Tomato Pizza with Pepperoni, Vegetable and Sausage Toppings. (Serving Suggestion, Toppings Not Included)

Pesto Pizza with Extra Cheese and Sausage Toppings. (Serving Suggestion, Toppings Not Included)

New Contadina Fresh Pizza.

Now you can make fresh-baked pizza just the way you like, in minutes.

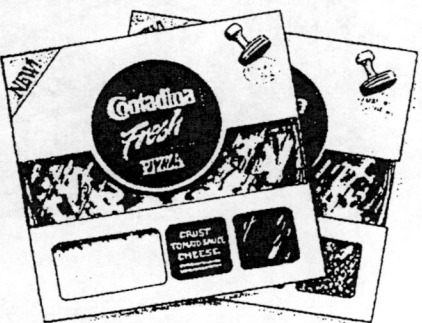

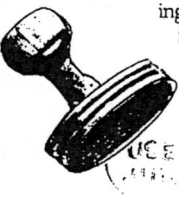

Contadina Fresh Pizza: Crust, Sauce and Cheese. (Available with Tomato or Pesto Sauce.)

Contadina Fresh™ has created a delicious new way to enjoy pizza: We've made it easy for you to combine the highest quality ingredients into a pizza that comes out just the way you like.

To start, just choose a Contadina Fresh package with crust, cheese, and our thick, rich tomato sauce. Or one with our flavorful pesto sauce. Just add your own delicious toppings to make Contadina Fresh Pizza exactly to your taste.

You simply spread on the sauce, sprinkle on the cheese, and add your own favorite toppings. You even choose how crisp the crust is, because you set the baking time.

And it's so easy, you can do it all in less than 15 minutes, from start to piping-hot pizza, fresh from your oven.

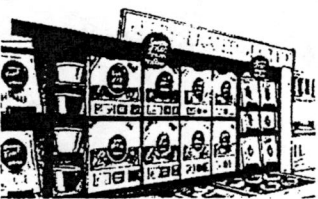

Look for Contadina Fresh Pizza in your grocer's refrigerated section

Of course, your first bite of Contadina Fresh Pizza will tell you we've used only the finest ingredients. Like the finest flour for our crust. Distinctive cheeses. And sauces that only Contadina Fresh could create. What's more, to keep the flavors fresh, our pizzas are refrigerated, not frozen. And each package is date stamped to *guarantee* freshness.

It all adds up to a great-tasting pizza, made just the way you like. Piping-hot and fresh from your oven, in a matter of minutes.

Contadina Fresh Pizza	
Crust, Tomato Sauce, and Cheese (Serves 2-3)	$6.39
Crust, Pesto Sauce, and Cheese (Serves 2-3)	$6.39

Exhibit 18 BASES II Study—Claimed Source of Volume

	Trial	Repeat Purchase
Frozen Pizza	32%	38%
Home Delivered	13	19
Fresh/Deli Pizza	6	2
Refrigerated Pizza	2	5
Restaurant Pizza	2	4
Pizza Kits	2	2
Other Products	11	12
None	32	14

Respondents were asked the following question at concept and after use: At your first purchase, what product would you replace in order to buy this new product? (IF PIZZA, PROBE TYPE:) Is that frozen, home-delivered, fresh from a supermarket deli or refrigerated case, eaten at a restaurant, take-out, homemade, or from a pizza kit?

Exhibit 19 Concept Likes and Dislikes—BASES II Study—Pizza & Toppings, Pizza Only

	Pizza and Toppings			Pizza Only[a,b]	
	Total (n=399) %	Favorable (n=304) %	Unfavorable (n=95) %	Favorable (n=76) %	Unfavorable (n=52) %
Concept Likes					
Can add amount oftoppings desired	34	37	23	53	
Quick/easy to prepare	21	23	16	18	
Bakes in 15 minutes	11	12	7	12	
Already prepared/made	8	8	5	12	
Can purchase all items in one place	3	4	--	6	
Fresh	21	21	19	17	
Fresh pizza tastes better	18	19	15	26	
Dated for freshness	11	13	6	17	
Fresh ingredients	8	9	6	16	
General taste/flavor	28	30	24	44	
Variety of toppings	23	25	15	--	
Texture/Consistency	16	17	11	21	
Good price	9	10	5	17	
Can buy toppings separately	7	8	4	--	
Natural no preservatives	4	3	4	2	
Like Contadina Fresh	14	15	11	9	
Dislikes					
Too expensive/more than take out/delivery/ restaurant	26	21	44		39
General taste/flavor	12	8	26		13
Too small	2	2	4		5
Prefer pizza already made	4	2	11		17
Nothing Disliked	49	59	15		13

[a]Of the 198 Pizza Only respondents, 116 were favorable to the concept. At the end of the Pizza Only interview respondents were asked if they thought the pizza came with toppings or just the sauce and cheese. Of those, 65% (76 people) understood that the pizza came with just sauce and cheese. Of the 82 unfavorable to the concept, 63% (52 people) understood that the pizza came with just sauce and cheese.

[b]The concept interview for the Pizza Only option was brief. Therefore there are limited diagnostics. For example, those favorable were asked why they were favorable, those unfavorable why they disliked the concept.

Exhibit 20 Mean Concept Attribute Ratings—Pizza and Toppings

	Pizza and Toppings		
	Total (n=399)	Favorable (n=304)	Unfavorable (n=95)
Mean Concept Attribute Ratings			
Would taste better than frozen pizza	9.0	9.3	8.1
Has toppings in varieties you like	8.5	8.8	7.3
Would be better tasting because you make it the way you like it	8.4	9.0	6.5
Would taste fresh baked	8.4	8.8	7.1
Would taste good	8.1	8.5	7.0
Would taste as good as take-out or home delivered pizza	7.3	7.9	5.6
Would be quick to prepare	8.8	9.1	8.1
Would be easy to prepare	8.8	9.0	8.1
Is a convenient way to have pizza at home	8.4	8.9	7.0
Is made by a manufacturer you trust	8.7	8.9	7.9
Is made with fresh ingredients	8.5	8.8	7.7
Is a high quality product	8.3	8.7	7.1
Is appropriate for the whole family	8.7	9.1	7.6
Is appropriate for kids	8.7	9.0	7.8
Would make a good snack	8.4	8.7	7.3
Would make a complete meal	7.8	8.3	6.5
Is a good value for the money	6.8	7.4	4.8

Ten-point scale where 10=Agree Strongly, 1=Disagree Strongly

Exhibit 21 Key Measures—BASES II Study—Contadina Users and Nonusers
(This exhibit is to be read in conjunction with **Table C**)

Sample	Pizza & Topping	Pizza Only	Pizza & Topping (Includes 100 Contadina Pasta Users)		Pizza Only (Includes 35 Contadina Pasta Users)	
			Users	Nonusers	Users	Nonusers
	n=399	n=198	n=181	n=318	n=78	n=155
Definitely would buy	17%	15%	30%	15%	22%	12%
Probably would buy	59%	43%	57%	59%	48%	42%
Top two box	76%	58%	87%	74%	70%	54%
Mean likability[a]	4.3	4.1	4.5	4.3	4.4	4.0
Price/value mean[b]	3.2	3.2	3.3	3.2	3.4	3.2
Price/value mean for toppings[c]	3.4	n/a	3.5	3.6	n/a	n/a

[a]Six-point scale with 6 being like extremely
[b]Five-point scale with 5 being very good value
[c]Five-point scale with 5 being very good value

Exhibit 22 Product Uniqueness—BASES II Study—Pizza and Toppings Before and After Use, Before Use Pizza Only

	Pizza and Toppings		Pizza Only
	Before Use n=399 (%)	After Use n=186[a] (%)	Before Use n=198 (%)
Extremely new and different	16	16	15
Very new and different	43	33	38
Somewhat new and different	32	38	36
Slightly new and different	7	10	8
Not at all new and different	3	3	3
Mean Concept Uniqueness (5 pt. scale)	3.6	3.5	3.5

[a]From the original random sample of 399 respondents, 186 participated in the in-home use test.

Exhibit 23 Reasons for Favorable/Unfavorable After Use Purchase Intent, Suggested Product Improvements: Pizza and Toppings

	Favorable (n=130)[a] %	Unfavorable (n=56) %
Favorable		
Fresh pizza tastes better	33	
Like crust	13	
Right amount of spiciness/seasoning	11	
Like taste	10	
Like extra cheese toppings	9	
Like tomato sauce	5	
Variety of toppings	8	
Quick/easy to prepare	34	
Already prepared/made	11	
Can add amount toppings/ingredients desired	9	
Convenient to have on hand	7	
Good reasonable price	10	
Like serving size	9	
Crispy crust not soggy	16	
Husband/children family like	9	
Suggested Improvements		
Improve overall taste/flavor	7	22
Add more sauce	10	5
Improve the sauces	2	8
Add more cheese	3	0
Lower Price	23	33
Make crust less tough	5	9
No improvement needed	33	7
Unfavorable		
Too expensive		33
More expensive than restaurant/take-out		13
Dislike sauce		11
Not enough sauce		6
Crust too chewy		7
Prefer pizza already made		4
Husband/children/family don't like		7

[a]From the original random sample of 399 respondents, 186 participated in the in-home use test, 130 of them were "favorable."

Exhibit 24 Typical Price Consumers Would Pay for 12″ Pizza Serving Two-Three People (In Home Use Test Respondents)

	Total n=186 %	Favorable n=130 %	Unfavorable n=56 %	Frozen/Fresh n=34 %	Delivered/ Takeout n=143 %
$3.00 or Less	9.7	9.4	9.9	14.3	8.4
$3.01 - 4.00	10.5	8.5	15.0	16.7	8.3
$4.01 - 5.00	17.1	15.4	20.8	27.9	15.3
$5.01 - 6.00	11.5	10.7	13.4	7.3	13.2
$6.01 - 7.00	14.2	12.6	18.1	20.1	12.5
$7.01 - 8.00	12.8	14.1	9.7	5.2	14.4
$8.01 - 9.00	7.0	9.4	1.3	2.3	8.6
$9.01 - 10.00	10.4	12.6	5.2	4.7	12.4
Over $10.00	5.8	6.9	3.6	8.0	5.8
Mean Price	$6.49	$6.32	$5.72	$5.73	$6.75

Note: The average retail price for Contadina pizza and toppings is about $8.00 (assuming 1.25 toppings per pizza).

HARVARD | BUSINESS | SCHOOL

9-504-016
REV: JULY 10, 2006

YOUNGME MOON
JOHN QUELCH

Starbucks: Delivering Customer Service

In late 2002, Christine Day, Starbucks' senior vice president of administration in North America, sat in the seventh-floor conference room of Starbucks' Seattle headquarters and reached for her second cup of toffee-nut latte. The handcrafted beverage—a buttery, toffee-nut flavored espresso concoction topped with whipped cream and toffee sprinkles—had become a regular afternoon indulgence for Day ever since its introduction earlier that year.

As she waited for her colleagues to join her, Day reflected on the company's recent performance. While other retailers were still reeling from the post-9/11 recession, Starbucks was enjoying its 11th consecutive year of 5% or higher comparable store sales growth, prompting its founder and chairman, Howard Schultz, to declare: "I think we've demonstrated that we are close to a recession-proof product."[1]

Day, however, was not feeling nearly as sanguine, in part because Starbucks' most recent market research had revealed some unexpected findings. "We've always taken great pride in our retail service," said Day, "but according to the data, we're not always meeting our customers' expectations in the area of customer satisfaction."

As a result of these concerns, Day and her associates had come up with a plan to invest an additional $40 million annually in the company's 4,500 stores, which would allow each store to add the equivalent of 20 hours of labor a week. "The idea is to improve speed-of-service and thereby increase customer satisfaction," said Day.

In two days, Day was due to make a final recommendation to both Schultz and Orin Smith, Starbucks' CEO, about whether the company should move forward with the plan. "The investment is the EPS [earnings per share] equivalent of almost seven cents a share," said Day. In preparation for her meeting with Schultz and Smith, Day had asked one of her associates to help her think through the implications of the plan. Day noted, "The real question is, do we believe what our customers are telling us about what constitutes 'excellent' customer service? And if we deliver it, what will the impact be on our sales and profitability?"

---

[1] Jake Batsell, "A Grande Decade for Starbucks," *The Seattle Times*, June 26, 2002.

Company Background

The story of how Howard Schultz managed to transform a commodity into an upscale cultural phenomenon has become the stuff of legends. In 1971, three coffee fanatics—Gerald Baldwin, Gordon Bowker, and Ziev Siegl—opened a small coffee shop in Seattle's Pike Place Market. The shop specialized in selling whole arabica beans to a niche market of coffee purists.

In 1982, Schultz joined the Starbucks marketing team; shortly thereafter, he traveled to Italy, where he became fascinated with Milan's coffee culture, in particular, the role the neighborhood espresso bars played in Italians' everyday social lives. Upon his return, the inspired Schultz convinced the company to set up an espresso bar in the corner of its only downtown Seattle shop. As Schultz explained, the bar became the prototype for his long-term vision:

> The idea was to create a chain of coffeehouses that would become America's "third place." At the time, most Americans had two places in their lives—home and work. But I believed that people needed another place, a place where they could go to relax and enjoy others, or just be by themselves. I envisioned a place that would be separate from home or work, a place that would mean different things to different people.

A few years later, Schultz got his chance when Starbucks' founders agreed to sell him the company. As soon as Schultz took over, he immediately began opening new stores. The stores sold whole beans and premium-priced coffee beverages by the cup and catered primarily to affluent, well-educated, white-collar patrons (skewed female) between the ages of 25 and 44. By 1992, the company had 140 such stores in the Northwest and Chicago and was successfully competing against other small-scale coffee chains such as Gloria Jean's Coffee Bean and Barnie's Coffee & Tea.

That same year, Schultz decided to take the company public. As he recalled, many Wall Street types were dubious about the idea: "They'd say, 'You mean, you're going to sell coffee for a dollar in a paper cup, with Italian names that no one in America can say? At a time in America when no one's drinking coffee? And I can get coffee at the local coffee shop or doughnut shop for 50 cents? Are you kidding me?'"[2]

Ignoring the skeptics, Schultz forged ahead with the public offering, raising $25 million in the process. The proceeds allowed Starbucks to open more stores across the nation.

By 2002, Schultz had unequivocally established Starbucks as the dominant specialty-coffee brand in North America. Sales had climbed at a compound annual growth rate (CAGR) of 40% since the company had gone public, and net earnings had risen at a CAGR of 50%. The company was now serving 20 million unique customers in well over 5,000 stores around the globe and was opening on average three new stores a day. (See **Exhibits 1–3** for company financials and store growth over time.)

What made Starbucks' success even more impressive was that the company had spent almost nothing on advertising to achieve it. North American marketing primarily consisted of point-of-sale materials and local-store marketing and was far less than the industry average. (Most fast-food chains had marketing budgets in the 3%–6% range.)

For his part, Schultz remained as chairman and chief global strategist in control of the company, handing over day-to-day operations in 2002 to CEO Orin Smith, a Harvard MBA (1967) who had joined the company in 1990.

---

[2] Batsell.

The Starbucks Value Proposition

Starbucks' brand strategy was best captured by its "live coffee" mantra, a phrase that reflected the importance the company attached to keeping the national coffee culture alive. From a retail perspective, this meant creating an "experience" around the consumption of coffee, an experience that people could weave into the fabric of their everyday lives.

There were three components to this experiential branding strategy. The first component was the coffee itself. Starbucks prided itself on offering what it believed to be the highest-quality coffee in the world, sourced from the Africa, Central and South America, and Asia-Pacific regions. To enforce its exacting coffee standards, Starbucks controlled as much of the supply chain as possible—it worked directly with growers in various countries of origin to purchase green coffee beans, it oversaw the custom-roasting process for the company's various blends and single-origin coffees, and it controlled distribution to retail stores around the world.

The second brand component was service, or what the company sometimes referred to as "customer intimacy." "Our goal is to create an uplifting experience every time you walk through our door," explained Jim Alling, Starbucks' senior vice president of North American retail. "Our most loyal customers visit us as often as 18 times a month, so it could be something as simple as recognizing you and knowing your drink or customizing your drink just the way you like it."

The third brand component was atmosphere. "People come for the coffee," explained Day, "but the ambience is what makes them want to stay." For that reason, most Starbucks had seating areas to encourage lounging and layouts that were designed to provide an upscale yet inviting environment for those who wanted to linger. "What we have built has universal appeal," remarked Schultz. "It's based on the human spirit, it's based on a sense of community, the need for people to come together."[3]

Channels of Distribution

Almost all of Starbucks' locations in North America were company-operated stores located in high-traffic, high-visibility settings such as retail centers, office buildings, and university campuses.[4] In addition to selling whole-bean coffees, these stores sold rich-brewed coffees, Italian-style espresso drinks, cold-blended beverages, and premium teas. Product mixes tended to vary depending on a store's size and location, but most stores offered a variety of pastries, sodas, and juices, along with coffee-related accessories and equipment, music CDs, games, and seasonal novelty items. (About 500 stores even carried a selection of sandwiches and salads.)

Beverages accounted for the largest percentage of sales in these stores (77%); this represented a change from 10 years earlier, when about half of store revenues had come from sales of whole-bean coffees. (See **Exhibit 4** for retail sales mix by product type; see **Exhibit 5** for a typical menu board and price list.)

Starbucks also sold coffee products through non-company-operated retail channels; these so-called "Specialty Operations" accounted for 15% of net revenues. About 27% of these revenues came from North American food-service accounts, that is, sales of whole-bean and ground coffees to hotels, airlines, restaurants, and the like. Another 18% came from domestic retail store licenses that, in

---

[3] Batsell.

[4] Starbucks had recently begun experimenting with drive-throughs. Less than 10% of its stores had drive-throughs, but in these stores, the drive-throughs accounted for 50% of all business.

North America, were only granted when there was no other way to achieve access to desirable retail space (e.g., in airports).

The remaining 55% of specialty revenues came from a variety of sources, including international licensed stores, grocery stores and warehouse clubs (Kraft Foods handled marketing and distribution for Starbucks in this channel), and online and mail-order sales. Starbucks also had a joint venture with Pepsi-Cola to distribute bottled Frappuccino beverages in North America, as well as a partnership with Dreyer's Grand Ice Cream to develop and distribute a line of premium ice creams.

Day explained the company's broad distribution strategy:

> Our philosophy is pretty straightforward—we want to reach customers where they work, travel, shop, and dine. In order to do this, we sometimes have to establish relationships with third parties that share our values and commitment to quality. This is a particularly effective way to reach newcomers with our brand. It's a lot less intimidating to buy Starbucks at a grocery store than it is to walk into one of our coffeehouses for the first time. In fact, about 40% of our new coffeehouse customers have already tried the Starbucks brand before they walk through our doors. Even something like ice cream has become an important trial vehicle for us.

Starbucks Partners

All Starbucks employees were called "partners." The company employed 60,000 partners worldwide, about 50,000 in North America. Most were hourly-wage employees (called *baristas*) who worked in Starbucks retail stores. Alling remarked, "From day one, Howard has made clear his belief that partner satisfaction leads to customer satisfaction. This belief is part of Howard's DNA, and because it's been pounded into each and every one of us, it's become part of our DNA too."

The company had a generous policy of giving health insurance and stock options to even the most entry-level partners, most of whom were between the ages of 17 and 23. Partly as a result of this, Starbucks' partner satisfaction rate consistently hovered in the 80% to 90% range, well above the industry norm,[5] and the company had recently been ranked 47th in the *Fortune* magazine list of best places to work, quite an accomplishment for a company with so many hourly-wage workers.

In addition, Starbucks had one of the lowest employee turnover rates in the industry—just 70%, compared with fast-food industry averages as high as 300%. The rate was even lower for managers, and as Alling noted, the company was always looking for ways to bring turnover down further: "Whenever we have a problem store, we almost always find either an inexperienced store manager or inexperienced baristas. Manager stability is key—it not only decreases partner turnover, but it also enables the store to do a much better job of recognizing regular customers and providing personalized service. So our goal is to make the position a lifetime job."

To this end, the company encouraged promotion from within its own ranks. About 70% of the company's store managers were ex-baristas, and about 60% of its district managers were ex-store managers. In fact, upon being hired, all senior executives had to train and succeed as baristas before being allowed to assume their positions in corporate headquarters.

[5] Industrywide, employee satisfaction rates tended to be in the 50% to 60% range. Source: Starbucks, 2000.

Delivering on Service

When a partner was hired to work in one of Starbucks' North American retail stores, he or she had to undergo two types of training. The first type focused on "hard skills" such as learning how to use the cash register and learning how to mix drinks. Most Starbucks beverages were handcrafted, and to ensure product quality, there was a prespecified process associated with each drink. Making an espresso beverage, for example, required seven specific steps.

The other type of training focused on "soft skills." Alling explained:

> In our training manual, we explicitly teach partners to connect with customers—to enthusiastically welcome them to the store, to establish eye contact, to smile, and to try to remember their names and orders if they're regulars. We also encourage partners to create conversations with customers using questions that require more than a yes or no answer. So for example, "I noticed you were looking at the menu board—what types of beverages do you typically enjoy?" is a good question for a partner to ask.

Starbucks' "Just Say Yes" policy empowered partners to provide the best service possible, even if it required going beyond company rules. "This means that if a customer spills a drink and asks for a refill, we'll give it to him," said Day. "Or if a customer doesn't have cash and wants to pay with a check (which we aren't supposed to accept), then we'll give her a sample drink for free. The last thing we want to do is win the argument and lose the customer."

Most barista turnover occurred within the first 90 days of employment; if a barista lasted beyond that, there was a high probability that he or she would stay for three years or more. "Our training ends up being a self-selection process," Alling said. Indeed, the ability to balance hard and soft skills required a particular type of person, and Alling believed the challenges had only grown over time:

> Back in the days when we sold mostly beans, every customer who walked in the door was a coffee connoisseur, and it was easy for baristas to engage in chitchat while ringing up a bag. Those days are long gone. Today, almost every customer orders a handcrafted beverage. If the line is stretching out the door and everyone's clamoring for their coffee fix, it's not that easy to strike up a conversation with a customer.

The complexity of the barista's job had also increased over time; making a *venti tazoberry and crème,* for instance, required 10 different steps. "It used to be that a barista could make every variation of drink we offered in half a day," Day observed. "Nowadays, given our product proliferation, it would take 16 days of eight-hour shifts. There are literally hundreds of combinations of drinks in our portfolio."

This job complexity was compounded by the fact that almost half of Starbucks' customers customized their drinks. According to Day, this created a tension between product quality and customer focus for Starbucks:

> On the one hand, we train baristas to make beverages to our preestablished quality standards—this means enforcing a consistent process that baristas can master. On the other hand, if a customer comes in and wants it their way—extra vanilla, for instance—what should we do? Our heaviest users are always the most demanding. Of course, every time we customize, we slow down the service for everyone else. We also put a lot of strain on our baristas, who are already dealing with an extraordinary number of sophisticated drinks.

One obvious solution to the problem was to hire more baristas to share the workload; however, the company had been extremely reluctant to do this in recent years, particularly given the economic downturn. Labor was already the company's largest expense item in North America (see **Exhibit 3**), and Starbucks stores tended to be located in urban areas with high wage rates. Instead, the company had focused on increasing barista efficiency by removing all non-value-added tasks, simplifying the beverage production process, and tinkering with the facility design to eliminate bottlenecks.

In addition, the company had recently begun installing automated espresso machines in its North American cafés. The *verismo* machines, which decreased the number of steps required to make an espresso beverage, reduced waste, improved consistency, and had generated an overwhelmingly positive customer and barista response.

Measuring Service Performance

Starbucks tracked service performance using a variety of metrics, including monthly status reports and self-reported checklists. The company's most prominent measurement tool was a mystery shopper program called the "Customer Snapshot." Under this program, every store was visited by an anonymous mystery shopper three times a quarter. Upon completing the visit, the shopper would rate the store on four "Basic Service" criteria:

- **Service**—Did the register partner verbally greet the customer? Did the barista and register partner make eye contact with the customer? Say thank you?
- **Cleanliness**—Was the store clean? The counters? The tables? The restrooms?
- **Product quality**—Was the order filled accurately? Was the temperature of the drink within range? Was the beverage properly presented?
- **Speed of service**—How long did the customer have to wait? The company's goal was to serve a customer within three minutes, from back-of-the-line to drink-in-hand. This benchmark was based on market research which indicated that the three-minute standard was a key component in how current Starbucks customers defined "excellent service."

In addition to Basic Service, stores were also rated on "Legendary Service," which was defined as "behavior that created a memorable experience for a customer, that inspired a customer to return often and tell a friend." Legendary Service scores were based on secret shopper observations of service attributes such as partners initiating conversations with customers, partners recognizing customers by name or drink order, and partners being responsive to service problems.

During 2002, the company's Customer Snapshot scores had increased across all stores (see **Exhibit 7**), leading Day to comment, "The Snapshot is not a perfect measurement tool, but we believe it does a good job of measuring trends over the course of a quarter. In order for a store to do well on the Snapshot, it needs to have sustainable processes in place that create a well-established pattern of doing things right so that it gets 'caught' doing things right."

Competition

In the United States, Starbucks competed against a variety of small-scale specialty coffee chains, most of which were regionally concentrated. Each tried to differentiate itself from Starbucks in a different way. For example, Minneapolis-based Caribou Coffee, which operated more than 200 stores in nine states, differentiated itself on store environment. Rather than offer an upscale, pseudo-European atmosphere, its strategy was to simulate the look and feel of an Alaskan lodge, with knotty-pine cabinetry, fireplaces, and soft seating. Another example was California-based Peet's Coffee & Tea, which operated about 70 stores in five states. More than 60% of Peet's revenues came from the sale of whole beans. Peet's strategy was to build a super-premium brand by offering the freshest coffee on the market. One of the ways it delivered on this promise was by "roasting to order," that is, by hand roasting small batches of coffee at its California plant and making sure that all of its coffee shipped within 24 hours of roasting.

Starbucks also competed against thousands of independent specialty coffee shops. Some of these independent coffee shops offered a wide range of food and beverages, including beer, wine, and liquor; others offered satellite televisions or Internet-connected computers. Still others differentiated themselves by delivering highly personalized service to an eclectic clientele.

Finally, Starbucks competed against donut and bagel chains such as Dunkin Donuts, which operated over 3,700 stores in 38 states. Dunkin Donuts attributed half of its sales to coffee and in recent years had begun offering flavored coffee and noncoffee alternatives, such as Dunkaccino (a coffee and chocolate combination available with various toppings) and Vanilla Chai (a combination of tea, vanilla, honey, and spices).

Caffeinating the World

The company's overall objective was to establish Starbucks as the "most recognized and respected brand in the world."[6] This ambitious goal required an aggressive growth strategy, and in 2002, the two biggest drivers of company growth were retail expansion and product innovation.

Retail Expansion

Starbucks already owned close to one-third of America's coffee bars, more than its next five biggest competitors combined. (By comparison, the U.S.'s second-largest player, Diedrich Coffee, operated fewer than 400 stores.) However, the company had plans to open 525 company-operated and 225 licensed North American stores in 2003, and Schultz believed that there was no reason North America could not eventually expand to at least 10,000 stores. As he put it, "These are still the early days of the company's growth."[7]

The company's optimistic growth plans were based on a number of considerations:

- First, coffee consumption was on the rise in the United States, following years of decline. More than 109 million people (about half of the U.S. population) now drank coffee every day, and an additional 52 million drank it on occasion. The market's biggest growth appeared to be among drinkers of specialty coffee,[8] and it was estimated that about one-third of all U.S. coffee consumption took place outside of the home, in places such as offices, restaurants, and coffee shops. (See **Exhibit 6**.)

---

[6] Starbucks 2002 Annual Report.

[7] Dina ElBoghdady, "Pouring It On: The Starbucks Strategy? Locations, Locations, Locations," *The Washington Post*, August 25, 2002.

[8] National Coffee Association.

- Second, there were still eight states in the United States without a single company-operated Starbucks; in fact, the company was only in 150 of the roughly 300 metropolitan statistical areas in the nation.

- Third, the company believed it was far from reaching saturation levels in many existing markets. In the Southeast, for example, there was only one store for every 110,000 people (compared with one store for every 20,000 people in the Pacific Northwest). More generally, only seven states had more than 100 Starbucks locations.

Starbucks' strategy for expanding its retail business was to open stores in new markets while geographically clustering stores in existing markets. Although the latter often resulted in significant cannibalization, the company believed that this was more than offset by the total incremental sales associated with the increased store concentration. As Schultz readily conceded, "We self-cannibalize at least a third of our stores every day."[9]

When it came to selecting new retail sites, the company considered a number of criteria, including the extent to which the demographics of the area matched the profile of the typical Starbucks drinker, the level of coffee consumption in the area, the nature and intensity of competition in the local market, and the availability of attractive real estate. Once a decision was made to move forward with a site, the company was capable of designing, permitting, constructing, and opening a new store within 16 weeks. A new store typically averaged about $610,000 in sales during its first year; same-store sales (comps) were strongest in the first three years and then continued to comp positively, consistent with the company average.

Starbucks' international expansion plans were equally ambitious. Starbucks already operated over 300 company-owned stores in the United Kingdom, Australia, and Thailand, in addition to about 900 licensed stores in various countries in Asia, Europe, the Middle East, Africa, and Latin America. (Its largest international market was Japan, with close to 400 stores.) The company's goal was to ultimately have 15,000 international stores.

Product Innovation

The second big driver of company growth was product innovation. Internally, this was considered one of the most significant factors in comparable store sales growth, particularly since Starbucks' prices had remained relatively stable in recent years. New products were launched on a regular basis; for example, Starbucks introduced at least one new hot beverage every holiday season.

The new product development process generally operated on a 12- to 18-month cycle, during which the internal research and development (R&D) team tinkered with product formulations, ran focus groups, and conducted in-store experiments and market tests. Aside from consumer acceptance, whether a product made it to market depended on a number of factors, including the extent to which the drink fit into the "ergonomic flow" of operations and the speed with which the beverage could be handcrafted. Most importantly, the success of a new beverage depended on partner acceptance. "We've learned that no matter how great a drink it is, if our partners aren't excited about it, it won't sell," said Alling.

In recent years, the company's most successful innovation had been the 1995 introduction of a coffee and non-coffee-based line of Frappuccino beverages, which had driven same-store sales primarily by boosting traffic during nonpeak hours. The bottled version of the beverage (distributed

[9] ElBoghdady.

by PepsiCo) had become a $400 million[10] franchise; it had managed to capture 90% of the ready-to-drink coffee category, in large part due to its appeal to non-coffee-drinking 20-somethings.

Service Innovation

In terms of nonproduct innovation, Starbucks' stored-value card (SVC) had been launched in November 2001. This prepaid, swipeable smart card—which Schultz referred to as "the most significant product introduction since Frappuccino"[11]—could be used to pay for transactions in any company-operated store in North America. Early indications of the SVC's appeal were very positive: After less than one year on the market, about 6 million cards had been issued, and initial activations and reloads had already reached $160 million in sales. In surveys, the company had learned that cardholders tended to visit Starbucks twice as often as cash customers and tended to experience reduced transaction times.

Day remarked, "We've found that a lot of the cards are being given away as gifts, and many of those gift recipients are being introduced to our brand for the first time. Not to mention the fact that the cards allow us to collect all kinds of customer-transaction data, data that we haven't even begun to do anything with yet."

The company's latest service innovation was its T-Mobile HotSpot wireless Internet service, introduced in August 2002. The service offered high-speed access to the Internet in selected Starbucks stores in the United States and Europe, starting at $49.99 a month.

Starbucks' Market Research: Trouble Brewing?

Interestingly, although Starbucks was considered one of the world's most effective marketing organizations, it lacked a strategic marketing group. In fact, the company had no chief marketing officer, and its marketing department functioned as three separate groups—a market research group that gathered and analyzed market data requested by the various business units, a category group that developed new products and managed the menu and margins, and a marketing group that developed the quarterly promotional plans.

This organizational structure forced all of Starbucks' senior executives to assume marketing-related responsibilities. As Day pointed out, "Marketing is everywhere at Starbucks—it just doesn't necessarily show up in a line item called 'marketing.' Everyone has to get involved in a collaborative marketing effort." However, the organizational structure also meant that market- and customer-related trends could sometimes be overlooked. "We tend to be great at measuring things, at collecting market data," Day noted, "but we are not very disciplined when it comes to using this data to drive decision making." She continued:

> This is exactly what started to happen a few years ago. We had evidence coming in from market research that contradicted some of the fundamental assumptions we had about our brand and our customers. The problem was that this evidence was all over the place—no one was really looking at the "big picture." As a result, it took awhile before we started to take notice.

---

10 Refers to sales at retail. Actual revenue contribution was much lower due to the joint-venture structure.

11 Stanley Holmes, "Starbucks' Card Smarts," *BusinessWeek*, March 18, 2002.

Starbucks' Brand Meaning

Once the team did take notice, it discovered several things. First, despite Starbucks' overwhelming presence and convenience, there was very little image or product differentiation between Starbucks and the smaller coffee chains (other than Starbucks' ubiquity) in the minds of specialty coffeehouse customers. There *was* significant differentiation, however, between Starbucks and the independent specialty coffeehouses (see **Table A** below).

Table A Qualitative Brand Meaning: Independents vs. Starbucks

Independents:
- Social and inclusive
- Diverse and intellectual
- Artsy and funky
- Liberal and free-spirited
- Lingering encouraged
- Particularly appealing to younger coffeehouse customers
- Somewhat intimidating to older, more mainstream coffeehouse customers

Starbucks:
- Everywhere—the trend
- Good coffee on the run
- Place to meet and move on
- Convenience oriented; on the way to work
- Accessible and consistent

Source: Starbucks, based on qualitative interviews with specialty-coffeehouse customers.

More generally, the market research team discovered that Starbucks' brand image had some rough edges. The number of respondents who strongly agreed with the statement "Starbucks cares primarily about making money" was up from 53% in 2000 to 61% in 2001, while the number of respondents who strongly agreed with the statement "Starbucks cares primarily about building more stores" was up from 48% to 55%. Day noted, "It's become apparent that we need to ask ourselves, 'Are we focusing on the right things? Are we clearly communicating our value and values to our customers, instead of just our growth plans?'" (see **Table B** below).

Table B The Top Five Attributes Consumers Associate with the Starbucks Brand

- Known for specialty/gourmet coffee (54% strongly agree)
- Widely available (43% strongly agree)
- Corporate (42% strongly agree)
- Trendy (41% strongly agree)
- Always feel welcome at Starbucks (39% strongly agree)

Source: Starbucks, based on 2002 survey.

The Changing Customer

The market research team also discovered that Starbucks' customer base was evolving. Starbucks' newer customers tended to be younger, less well-educated, and in a lower income bracket than Starbucks' more established customers. In addition, they visited the stores less frequently and had very different perceptions of the Starbucks brand compared to more established customers (see **Exhibit 8**).

Furthermore, the team learned that Starbucks' historical customer profile—the affluent, well-educated, white-collar female between the ages of 24 and 44—had expanded. For example, about half of the stores in southern California had large numbers of Hispanic customers. In Florida, the company had stores that catered primarily to Cuban-Americans.

Customer Behavior

With respect to customer behavior, the market research team discovered that, regardless of the market—urban versus rural, new versus established—customers tended to use the stores the same way. The team also learned that, although the company's most frequent customers averaged 18 visits a month, the typical customer visited just five times a month (see **Figure A** below).

Figure A Customer Visit Frequency

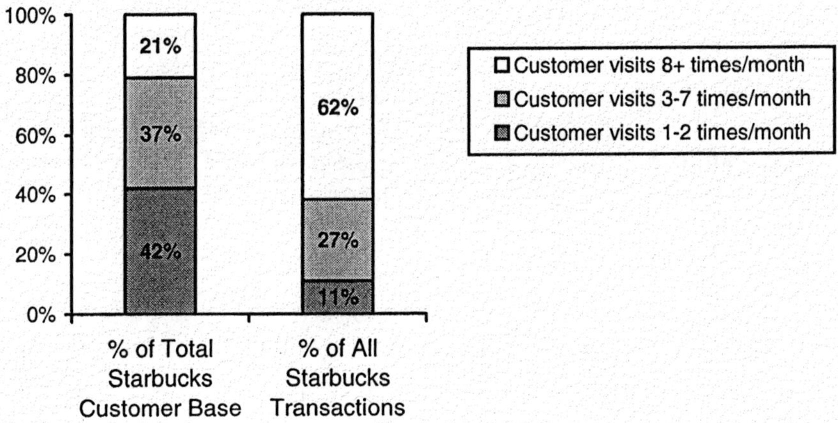

Source: Starbucks, 2002.

Measuring and Driving Customer Satisfaction

Finally, the team discovered that, despite its high Customer Snapshot scores, Starbucks was not meeting expectations in terms of customer satisfaction. The satisfaction scores were considered critical because the team also had evidence of a direct link between satisfaction level and customer loyalty (see **Exhibit 9** for customer satisfaction data).

While customer satisfaction was driven by a number of different factors (see **Exhibit 10**), Day believed that the customer satisfaction gap could primarily be attributed to a *service gap* between Starbucks scores on key attributes and customer expectations. When Starbucks had polled its customers to determine what it could do to make them feel more like valued customers, "improvements to service"—in particular, speed-of-service—had been mentioned most frequently (see **Exhibit 11** for more information).

Rediscovering the Starbucks Customer

Responding to the market research findings posed a difficult management challenge. The most controversial proposal was the one on the table before Day—it involved relaxing the labor-hour controls in the stores to add an additional 20 hours of labor, per week, per store, at a cost of an extra $40 million per year. Not surprisingly, the plan was being met with significant internal resistance. "Our CFO is understandably concerned about the potential impact on our bottom line," said Day. "Each $6 million in profit contribution translates into a penny a share. But my argument is that if we move away from seeing labor as an expense to seeing it as a customer-oriented investment, we'll see a positive return." She continued:

> We need to bring service time down to the three-minute level in all of our stores, regardless of the time of day. If we do this, we'll not only increase customer satisfaction and build stronger long-term relationships with our customers, we'll also improve our customer throughput. The goal is to move each store closer to the $20,000 level in terms of weekly sales, and I think that this plan will help us get there.

In two days, Day was scheduled to make a final recommendation to Howard Schultz and Orin Smith about whether the company should roll out the $40 million plan. In preparation for this meeting, Day had asked Alling to help her think through the implications of the plan one final time. She mused:

> We've been operating with the assumption that we do customer service well. But the reality is, we've started to lose sight of the consumer. It's amazing that this could happen to a company like us—after all, we've become one of the most prominent consumer brands in the world. For all of our focus on building the brand and introducing new products, we've simply stopped talking about the customer. We've lost the connection between satisfying our customers and growing the business.

Alling's response was simple: "We know that both Howard and Orin are totally committed to satisfying our retail customers. Our challenge is to tie customer satisfaction to the bottom line. What evidence do we have?"

Exhibit 1 Starbucks' Financials, FY 1998 to FY 2002 ($ in millions)

	FY 1998	FY 1999	FY 2000	FY 2001	FY 2002
Revenue					
Co-Owned North American	1,076.8	1,375.0	1,734.9	2,086.4	2,583.8
Co-Owned Int'l (UK, Thailand, Australia)	25.8	48.4	88.7	143.2	209.1
Total Company-Operated Retail	1,102.6	1,423.4	1,823.6	2,229.6	2,792.9
Specialty Operations	206.1	263.4	354.0	419.4	496.0
Net Revenues	**1,308.7**	**1,686.8**	**2,177.6**	**2,649.0**	**3,288.9**
Cost of Goods Sold	578.5	747.6	961.9	1,112.8	1,350.0
Gross Profit	**730.2**	**939.2**	**1,215.7**	**1,536.2**	**1,938.9**
Joint-Venture Income[a]	1.0	3.2	20.3	28.6	35.8
Expenses:					
Store Operating Expense	418.5	543.6	704.9	875.5	1,121.1
Other Operating Expense	44.5	54.6	78.4	93.3	127.2
Depreciation & Amortization Expense	72.5	97.8	130.2	163.5	205.6
General & Admin Expense	77.6	89.7	110.2	151.4	202.1
Operating Expenses	**613.1**	**785.7**	**1,023.8**	**1,283.7**	**1,656.0**
Operating Profit	**109.2**	**156.7**	**212.3**	**281.1**	**310.0**
Net Income	**68.4**	**101.7**	**94.5**	**181.2**	**215.1**
% Change in Monthly Comparable Store Sales[b]					
North America	5%	6%	9%	5%	7%
Consolidated	5%	6%	9%	5%	6%

Source: Adapted from company reports and Lehman Brothers, November 5, 2002.

[a]Includes income from various joint ventures, including Starbucks' partnership with the Pepsi-Cola Company to develop and distribute Frappuccino and with Dreyer's Grand Ice Cream to develop and distribute premium ice creams.

[b]Includes only company-operated stores open 13 months or longer.

Exhibit 2 Starbucks' Store Growth

	FY 1998	FY 1999	FY 2000	FY 2001	FY 2002
Total North America	**1,755**	**2,217**	**2,976**	**3,780**	**4,574**
Company-Operated	1,622	2,038	2,446	2,971	3,496
Licensed Stores[a]	133	179	530	809	1,078
Total International	**131**	**281**	**525**	**929**	**1,312**
Company-Operated	66	97	173	295	384
Licensed Stores	65	184	352	634	928
Total Stores	**1,886**	**2,498**	**3,501**	**4,709**	**5,886**

Source: Company reports.

[a]Includes kiosks located in grocery stores, bookstores, hotels, airports, and so on.

Exhibit 3 Additional Data, North American Company-Operated Stores (FY2002)

	Average
Average hourly rate with shift supervisors and hourly partners	$ 9.00
Total labor hours per week, average store	360
Average weekly store volume	$15,400
Average ticket	$ 3.85
Average daily customer count, per store	570

Source: Company reports.

Exhibit 4 Product Mix, North American Company-Operated Stores (FY2002)

	Percent of Sales
Retail Product Mix	
Coffee Beverages	77%
Food Items	13%
Whole-Bean Coffees	6%
Equipment & Accessories	4%

Source: Company reports.

Exhibit 5 Typical Menu Board and Price List for North American Company-Owned Store

Espresso Traditions Classic Favorites	Tall	Grande	Venti
Toffee Nut Latte	2.95	3.50	3.80
Vanilla Latte	2.85	3.40	3.70
Caffe Latte	2.55	3.10	3.40
Cappuccino	2.55	3.10	3.40
Caramel Macchiato	2.80	3.40	3.65
White Chocolate Mocha	3.20	3.75	4.00
Caffe Mocha	2.75	3.30	3.55
Caffe Americano	1.75	2.05	2.40

Espresso	Solo	Doppio
Espresso	1.45	1.75

Extras	
Additional Espresso Shot	.55
Add flavored syrup	.30
Organic milk & soy available upon request	

Frappuccino Ice Blended Beverages	Tall	Grande	Venti
Coffee	2.65	3.15	3.65
Mocha	2.90	3.40	3.90
Caramel Frappuccino	3.15	3.65	4.15
Mocha Coconut (limited offering)	3.15	3.65	4.15

Crème Frappuccino Ice Blended Crème	Tall	Grande	Venti
Toffee Nut Crème	3.15	3.65	4.15
Vanilla Crème	2.65	3.15	3.65
Coconut Crème	3.15	3.65	4.15

Tazo Tea Frappuccino Ice Blended Teas	Tall	Grande	Venti
Tazo Citrus	2.90	3.40	3.90
Tazoberry	2.90	3.40	3.90
Tazo Chai Crème	3.15	3.65	4.15

Brewed Coffee	Tall	Grande	Venti
Coffee of the Day	1.40	1.60	1.70
Decaf of the Day	1.40	1.60	1.70

Cold Beverages	Tall	Grande	Venti
Iced Caffe Latte	2.55	3.10	3.50
Iced Caramel Macchiato	2.80	3.40	3.80
Iced Caffe Americano	1.75	2.05	3.40

Coffee Alternatives	Tall	Grande	Venti
Toffee Nut Crème	2.45	2.70	2.95
Vanilla Crème	2.20	2.45	2.70
Caramel Apple Cider	2.45	2.70	2.95
Hot Chocolate	2.20	2.45	2.70
Tazo Hot Tea	1.15	1.65	1.65
Tazo Chai	2.70	3.10	3.35

Whole Beans: Bold Our most intriguing and exotic coffees	½ lb	1 lb
Gold Coast Blend	5.70	10.95
French Roast	5.20	9.95
Sumatra	5.30	10.15
Decaf Sumatra	5.60	10.65
Ethiopia Sidame	5.20	9.95
Arabian Mocha Sanani	8.30	15.95
Kenya	5.30	10.15
Italian Roast	5.20	9.95
Sulawesi	6.10	11.65

Whole Beans: Smooth Richer, more flavorful coffees	½ lb	1 lb
Espresso Roast	5.20	9.95
Decaf Espresso Roast	5.60	10.65
Yukon Blend	5.20	9.95
Café Verona	5.20	9.95
Guatemala Antigua	5.30	10.15
Arabian Mocha Java	6.30	11.95
Decaf Mocha Java/SWP	6.50	12.45

Whole Beans: Mild The perfect introduction to Starbucks coffees	½ lb	1 lb
Breakfast Blend	5.20	9.95
Lightnote Blend	5.20	9.95
Decaf Lightnote Blend	5.60	10.65
Colombia Narino	5.50	10.45
House Blend	5.20	9.95
Decaf House Blend	5.60	10.65
Fair Trade Coffee	5.95	11.45

Source: Starbucks location: Harvard Square, Cambridge, Massachusetts, February 2003.

Exhibit 6 Total U.S. Retail Coffee Market (includes both in-home and out-of-home consumption)

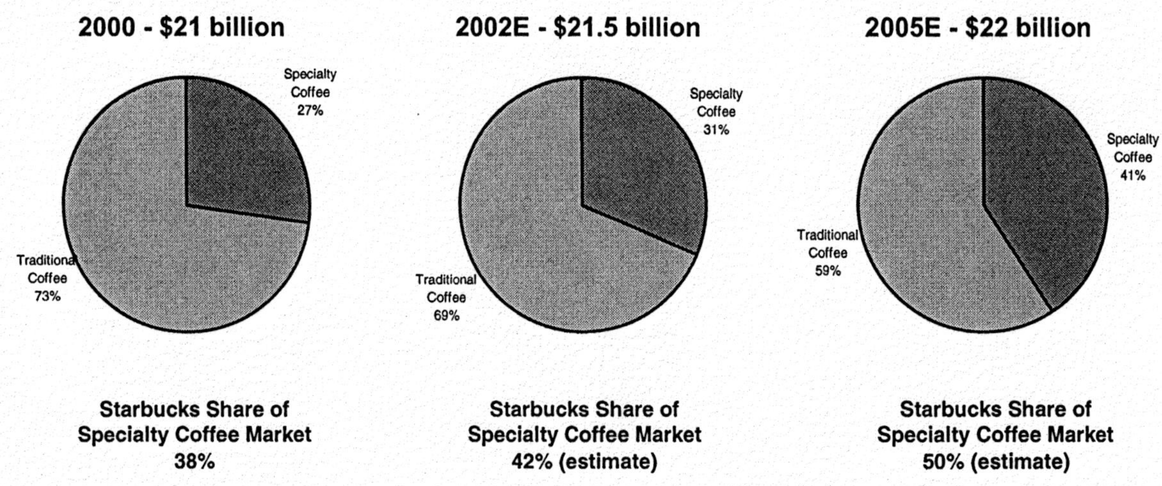

Starbucks Share of Specialty Coffee Market 38%

Starbucks Share of Specialty Coffee Market 42% (estimate)

Starbucks Share of Specialty Coffee Market 50% (estimate)

Other estimates[a] for the U.S. retail coffee market in 2002:

- In the home, specialty coffee[b] was estimated to be a $3.2 billion business, of which Starbucks was estimated to have a 4% share.
- In the food-service channel, specialty coffee was estimated to be a $5 billion business, of which Starbucks was estimated to have a 5% share.
- In grocery stores, Starbucks was estimated to have a 7.3% share in the ground-coffee category and a 21.7% share in the whole-beans category.
- It was estimated that over the next several years, the overall retail market would grow less than 1% per annum, but growth in the specialty-coffee category would be strong, with compound annual growth rate (CAGR) of 9% to 10%.
- Starbucks' U.S. business was projected to grow at a CAGR of approximately 20% top-line revenue growth.

Source: Adapted from company reports and Lehman Brothers, November 5, 2002.

[a]The value of the retail coffee market was difficult to estimate given the highly fragmented and loosely monitored nature of the market (i.e., specialty coffeehouses, restaurants, delis, kiosks, street carts, grocery and convenience stores, vending machines, etc.).

[b]Specialty coffee includes espresso, cappuccino, latte, café mocha, iced/ice-blended coffee, gourmet coffee (premium whole bean or ground), and blended coffee.

Exhibit 7 Customer Snapshot Scores (North American stores)

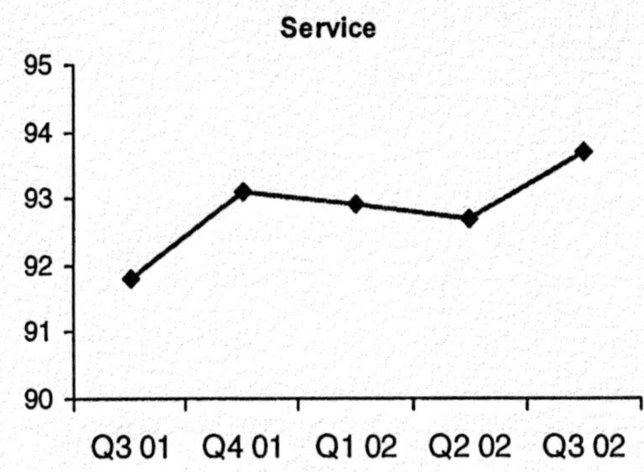

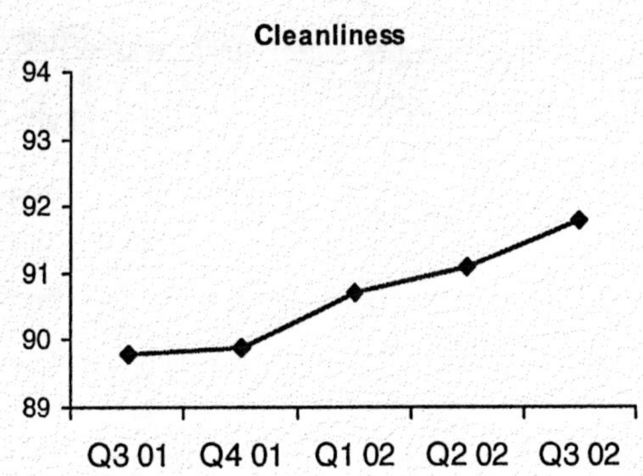

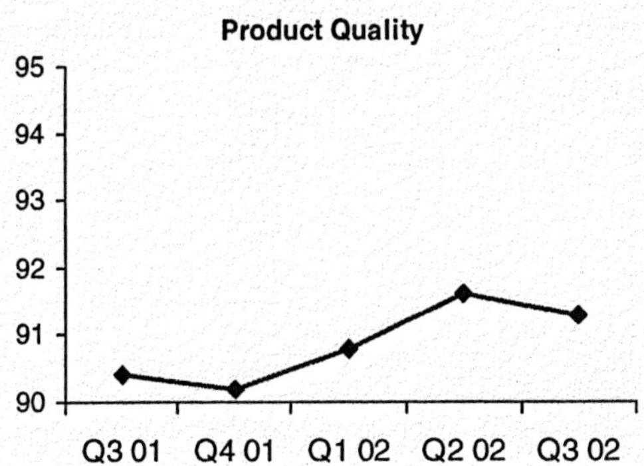

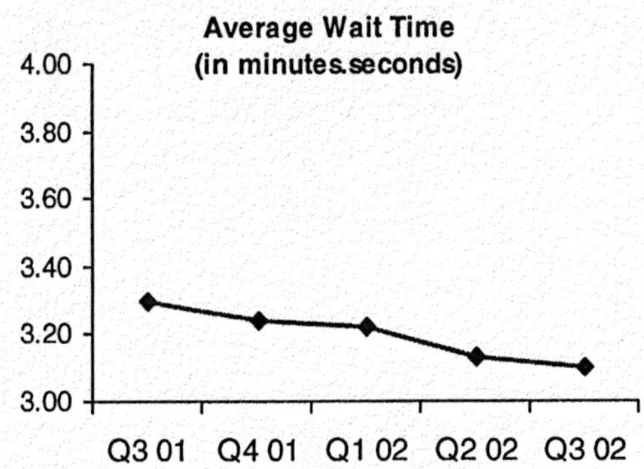

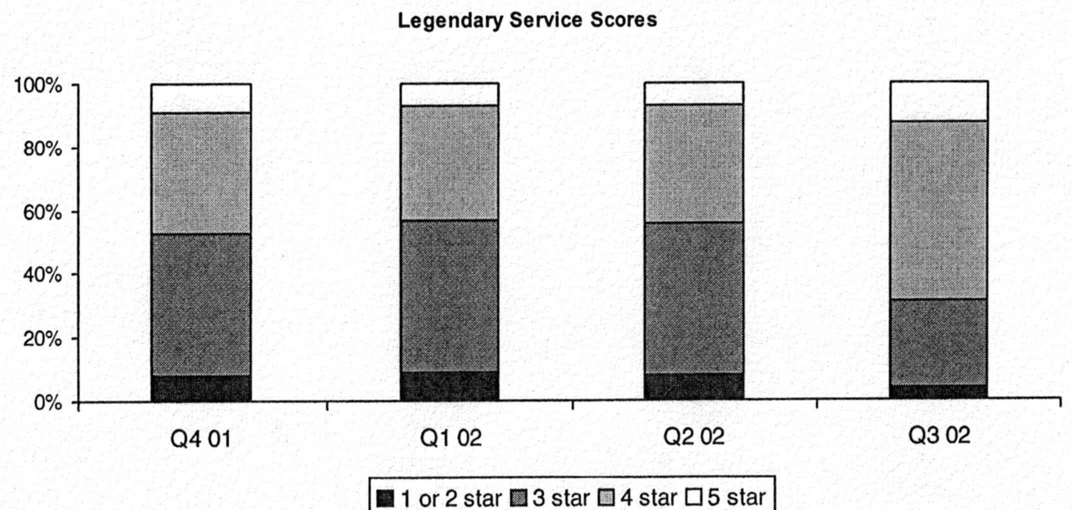

Source: Company information.

Exhibit 8 Starbucks' Customer Retention Information

% of Starbucks' customers who first started visiting Starbucks . . .	
In the past year	27%
1–2 years ago	20%
2–5 years ago	30%
5 or more years ago	23%

Source: Starbucks, 2002. Based on a sample of Starbucks' 2002 customer base.

	New Customers (first visited in past year)	Established Customers (first visited 5+ years ago)
Percent female	45%	49%
Average Age	36	40
Percent with College Degree +	37%	63%
Average income	$65,000	$81,000
Average # cups of coffee/week (includes at home and away from home)	15	19
Attitudes toward Starbucks:		
High-quality brand	34%	51%
Brand I trust	30%	50%
For someone like me	15%	40%
Worth paying more for	8%	32%
Known for specialty coffee	44%	60%
Known as the coffee expert	31%	45%
Best-tasting coffee	20%	31%
Highest-quality coffee	26%	41%
Overall opinion of Starbucks	**25%**	**44%**

Source: Starbucks, 2002. "Attitudes toward Starbucks" measured according to the percent of customers who agreed with the above statements.

Exhibit 9 Starbucks' Customer Behavior, by Satisfaction Level

	Unsatisfied Customer	Satisfied Customer	Highly Satisfied Customer
Number of Starbucks Visits/Month	3.9	4.3	7.2
Average Ticket Size/Visit	$3.88	$4.06	$4.42
Average Customer Life (Years)	1.1	4.4	8.3

Source: Self-reported customer activity from Starbucks survey, 2002.

Exhibit 10 Importance Rankings of Key Attributes in Creating Customer Satisfaction

To be read: *83% of Starbucks' customers rate a clean store as being highly important (90+ on a 100-point scale) in creating customer satisfaction.*

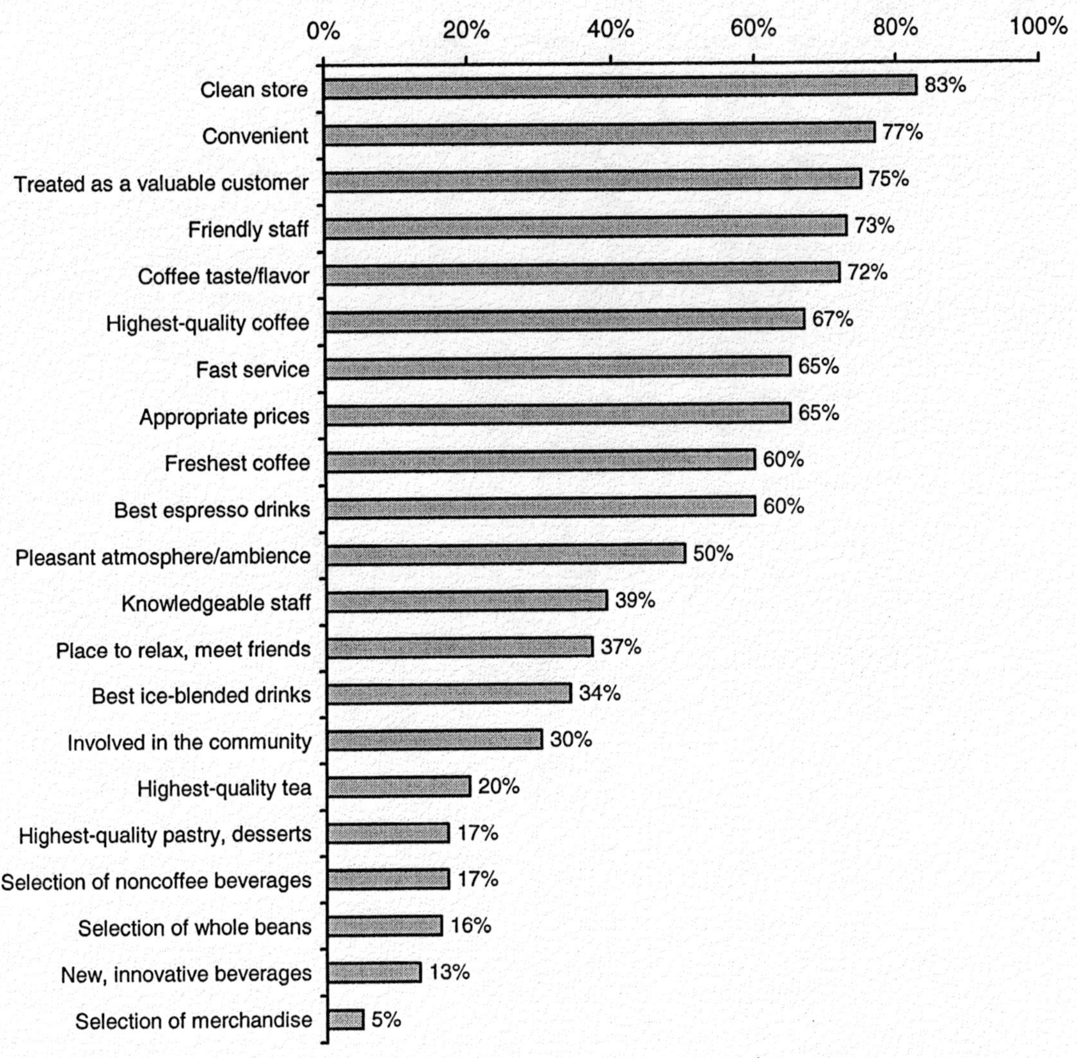

Source: Self-reported customer activity from Starbucks survey, 2002.

Exhibit 11 Factors Driving "Valued Customer" Perceptions

How could Starbucks make you feel more like a valued customer?	% Responses
Improvements to Service (total)	**34%**
Friendlier, more attentive staff	19%
Faster, more efficient service	10%
Personal treatment (remember my name, remember my order)	4%
More knowledgeable staff	4%
Better service	2%
Offer Better Prices/Incentive Programs (total)	**31%**
Free cup after x number of visits	19%
Reduce prices	11%
Offer promotions, specials	3%
Other (total)	**21%**
Better quality/Variety of products	9%
Improve atmosphere	8%
Community outreach/Charity	2%
More stores/More convenient locations	2%
Don't Know/Already Satisfied	**28%**

Source: Starbucks, 2002. Based on a survey of Starbucks' 2002 customer base, including highly satisfied, satisfied, and unsatisfied customers.

9-504-028
REV: FEBRUARY 17, 2005

GAIL MCGOVERN

Virgin Mobile USA: Pricing for the Very First Time

When Richard Branson called me to discuss the CEO position at Virgin Mobile USA, I quickly considered the opportunity: a chance to be the chief executive of a newly formed start-up in an overcrowded, increasingly mature, capital-intensive, highly competitive industry. Oh yeah, I should also mention that this is not an industry known for its customer service and we'd be entering with a brand that had little U.S. name recognition except for possibly as an airline. But then I thought, "It's these kinds of opportunities where a team can define itself, and if this could be pulled off, it would be unbelievable."

—Dan Schulman, CEO, Virgin Mobile USA

Schulman accepted the challenge in the summer of 2001 and began to assemble a team to develop the new Virgin-branded service with a launch date of July 2002. Schulman had 18 years of telecommunications experience with AT&T and had most recently been CEO of Priceline.com. He would need to draw on his experiences from both firms to create an appealing offer that would take off in a saturated market. His goal was to achieve a run rate in which Virgin Mobil would have 1 million total subscribers by the end of the first year, and 3 million by year four.[1]

One of the key decisions for Virgin Mobile USA was the selection of a pricing strategy that would attract and retain subscribers.

Company Background

Virgin, a U.K.-based company led by Sir Richard Branson, was one of the top three most recognized brands in Britain. The company had a history of brand extensions—more than any other major firm in the past 20 years—resulting in a vast portfolio consisting of more than 200 different corporate entities involved in everything from planes and trains to beverages and cosmetics. What tied all of these businesses together were the values of the Virgin brand:

> We believe in making a difference. In our customers' eyes, Virgin stands for value for money, quality, innovation, fun and a sense of competitive challenge. ... We look for opportunities where we can offer something better, fresher and more valuable, and we seize them. We often move into areas where the customer has traditionally received a poor deal,

[1] Numbers in this case are disguised for competitive reasons and utilize primary data from industry analysts.

Professor Gail McGovern prepared this case. HBS cases are developed solely as the basis for class discussion. Certain details have been disguised. Cases are not intended to serve as endorsements, sources of primary data, or illustrations of effective or ineffective management.

and where the competition is complacent. . . . We are pro-active and quick to act, often leaving bigger and more cumbersome organizations in our wake.[2]

Many of the company's ventures, such as Virgin Music Group, had proven to be phenomenally successful; others, such as Virgin Cola, had resulted in failure. Virgin's cellular operations in the U.K. had been among the company's success stories—Virgin had signed up approximately 2.5 million customers in just three years. The venture had broken new ground by being the country's first mobile virtual network operator (MVNO), which meant that rather than investing in and running a network in-house, the company leased network space from another firm, Deutsche Telekom.

In Singapore, however, the story had been different. There, the company's cellular service—a joint venture with Singapore Telecommunications—had run into difficulties, attracting fewer than 30,000 subscribers after its launch in October 2001. The Singapore MVNO had recently shut its doors, and although both partners had agreed that the market had been too saturated to sustain a new entrant, some analysts had offered another explanation for the failure: Virgin's hip and trendy positioning had failed to strike a chord in the Singapore market.

Despite this setback, Virgin had forged ahead with its plans to launch a wireless phone service in the U.S. Utilizing the MVNO model once again, the company had entered into a 50-50 joint venture with Sprint in which Virgin Mobile USA's services would be hosted on Sprint's PCS network. (Sprint was in the process of updating its network and increasing its capacity, so that it had ample capacity to allow for additional users.) Under the agreement, Virgin Mobile would purchase minutes from Sprint on an as-used basis.

"The nice thing about this model is that we don't have to worry about huge fixed costs or the physical infrastructure," said Schulman. "We can focus on what we do best—understanding and meeting customer needs."

The Crowded Cellular Market: Identifying a Niche

The team leading Virgin Mobile USA was acutely aware of the overcrowded nature of the mobile communications industry in the United States. At the end of 2001, the U.S. had six national carriers and a number of regional and affiliate providers. Industry penetration was close to 50% with about 130 million subscribers, and the market was considered to have reached maturity. (Please see **Exhibit 1** for subscribers by carrier.)

Among consumers aged 15 to 29, however, penetration was significantly lower, and the growth rate among this demographic was projected to be robust for the next five years.[3] (Please see **Exhibit 2** for growth rates.)

Still, as Schulman observed, "The big players haven't targeted this segment." One reason was that young consumers often had poor credit quality. "These are people who don't necessarily have credit cards and often don't pass the credit checks that the cellular contracts require," Schulman noted.

In addition, in an industry in which the average cost to acquire a customer was roughly $370, many carriers did not believe it was worth acquiring consumers who might not use their cell phones on a frequent basis. "The assumption is that if you're not using the phone for business or if you don't

---

[2] Source: Company Web site.

[3] Source: Strategis Group.

already subscribe to a cell phone service, then you're probably not going to be someone who uses their cell phone a lot," explained Schulman. In fact, the average monthly cell phone bill for the national carriers was $52, representing about 417 minutes of use. Because the cost to serve a customer was roughly $30 a month, the carriers tended to be wary of acquiring low-value subscribers.

Despite these challenges, the Virgin Mobile team decided that this segment represented the greatest opportunity. "This is a market that has been underserved by the existing carriers," explained Schulman. "They have specific needs that haven't been met." He continued:

> A lot of the consumers in this age group are in flux in their lives. They're either in college, they're just leaving their home, or they may be getting their first cell phone. Their usage is probably inconsistent. One month, they may not use the phone at all, and another month, they may use it quite a bit, depending on whether they're on vacation or in school.
>
> Their calling patterns are different from the typical businessperson. They're more open to new things, like text messaging and downloading information using their phones. And they're more likely to use ring tones, faceplates, and graphics. In fact, some of them need to go to "ring tone anonymous," that's how addicted they are. Phones are more than a tool for these young people; they're a fashion accessory and a personal statement.

VirginXtras

The rock in our slingshot in this battle of David versus many Goliaths is focus. By focusing exclusively on the youth market from the ground up, we're putting ourselves in a position to serve these customers in a way that they've never been served before.

—Dan Schulman

The Virgin Mobile USA team quickly began to seek ways to develop a value proposition that would appeal to the youth market. Because revenue for mobile entertainment was projected to increase steadily over the next few years (see **Exhibit 3**), the team decided that a key part of the Virgin Mobile service would involve the delivery of content, features, and entertainment, which they called "VirginXtras." To this end, the company signed an exclusive, multiyear content and marketing agreement with MTV networks to deliver music, games, and other MTV-, VH1-, and Nickelodeon-based content to Virgin Mobile subscribers. (See **Exhibit 4** for screenshots.) The deal ensured that subscribers would have access to MTV-branded accessories and phones, as well as branded content such as graphics, ring tones, text alerts, and voice mail. The company would also receive promotional airtime on MTV's channels and Web site. And under the agreement, Virgin Mobile subscribers would be able to use their phones to vote for their favorite videos on shows like MTV's "Total Request Live." As Schulman put it:

> We're taking cell phone content to a whole new level. It's a great match: MTV Networks is home to some of the most recognized youth brands in the country; it has unparalleled reach for the under-30 market. The Virgin brand is all about fun, honesty, and great value for money, which is what our target market wants. You put the two together, and you've got some of the most exciting cell phone features in the market. It's a powerful relationship for us.

In addition to the MTV-branded content, the Virgin Mobile service would also include the following VirginXtras:

- **Text Messaging**. Schulman believed text messaging was a key selling point for youth: "The number of text messages tends to skyrocket during school hours. Kids discreetly text message while they're in class. Part of the reason why they communicate like this is so their parents don't see who they call. It's a very private form of communication for them."

- **Online Real-Time Billing.** For additional privacy from their parents, kids would not have call detail on monthly bills. Virgin Mobile would provide a Web site with a record of individual calls on a real-time basis.

- **Rescue Ring**. Virgin Mobile subscribers would be able to schedule a "rescue ring," which would call them at a prearranged time to provide them with an "escape" in case a date was not going well. If the date was going well, they could always tell the "caller" that they would get back to them tomorrow.

- **Wake-Up Call**. For those who needed a little help getting out of bed in the morning, Virgin Mobile USA would offer its customers the chance to wake up to original messages from a variety of cheeky celebrity personalities.

- **Ring Tones.** A large selection of tunes would be available for subscribers to download if they wanted to customize their ring tones, ranging from hip hop to rock to the Sponge Bob Square Pants anthem.

- **Fun Clips.** These audio clips would consist of news tidbits, jokes, gossip, sports information, and more.

- **The Hit List.** Subscribers would be able to use their handsets to listen to and vote on a top 10 list of hit songs. After voting, customers would be able to hear the percentage of other subscribers who either "loved it" or "hated it."

- **Music Messenger.** This service would let subscribers tap into a top 10 song list and then would shoot a message to a friend allowing them to check out a hot new track.

- **Movies.** This service would provide movie descriptions, show times, and allow subscribers to buy tickets in advance using their phones.

The Virgin team believed that these features would appeal to the youth market, generate additional usage, and create loyalty. Schulman elaborated: "Our market research indicates that VirginXtras will attract and retain the youth segment. Not only will these features be appealing, but we also believe they will be addictive and will bond our customers to their cell phones."

Purchasing the Service

Most cellular providers sold their services in their own proprietary retail outlets, kiosks in malls, high-end electronic stores (e.g., Radio Shack), specialty stores, and so on. Because these retail outlets typically employed high-touch salespeople, most providers paid high sales commissions to ensure hands-on service.

In contrast, the Virgin Mobile team had already decided to adopt a different channel strategy that was more closely aligned to its target-market selection. Schulman explained:

> We've decided to distribute in channels where youth shop. This means places like Target, Sam Goody music stores, and Best Buy. In these stores, kids are used to buying consumer electronics products. They're used to buying a CD player or an MP3 player. So we've decided to package our products in consumer electronics packaging. Instead of being in a box locked behind some counter, we've created a clamshell, clear, see-through package where consumers can pick up the phone without a salesperson helping them and purchase it like they would any other consumer electronics product.

Cellular carriers historically purchased handsets from cell phone manufacturers such as Nokia, Motorola, Samsung, and Lucky Goldstar. Although the cost per handset generally ranged from $150 to $300, carriers typically charged end users between $60 and $90.[4] This handset subsidy was an accepted part of the carrier's acquisition costs.

Virgin had a contract with handset manufacturer Kyocera by which it would buy phones for anywhere from $60 to $100 depending on the features and functions of the phones.[5] The first two basic models would be named the "Party Animal" (a Kyocera 2119) and the "Super Model" (a Kyocera 2255). Both would come bundled with interchangeable faceplates that would be decorated with eye-catching colors and patterns (see **Exhibit 5** for sample phones) and would be nestled inside one of Virgin Mobile's bright red clamshell-style Starter Packs (see **Exhibit 6** for pictures of packaging).

The Starter Packs would be easily visible on large point-of-sale displays (see **Exhibit 7**) that the company would make available to its retailers. The company had entered into distribution agreements with Target and Best Buy, both of which charged lower commissions than traditional industry channels—$30 per phone, versus an industry average of $100.[6] The Starter Packs would also be available at retailers such as Sam Goody, Circuit City, Media Play, and Virgin Megastores. In total, the company expected its phones to be available at more than 3,000 U.S. retail outlets by the time the service launched in July.

Advertising

> *Unless you're between 14 and 24, you're probably never going to see our ads. If you ever see us on "60 Minutes," then you know we've gone astray. Think WB, MTV, and Comedy Central [three youth-oriented networks].*
>
> —Dan Schulman

The U.S. cellular industry was projected to spend about $1.8 billion in advertising in 2002. Most national carriers had huge ad budgets; for example, Verizon Wireless alone was expected to spend more than $650 million advertising in major media in 2002.[7] Virgin Mobile USA's advertising budget was miniscule by comparison: approximately $60 million.

Still, Schulman was determined to make the most of the limited budget. "By definition, the big players need to be all things to all people. They are throwing huge amounts of money into messages

4 Source: Morgan Stanley research.

5 Numbers are disguised for competitive reasons.

6 Numbers are disguised for competitive reasons.

7 Source: TNS Media Intelligence/CMR. For the national carriers, advertising spending typically ranged from $75 to $105 per customer acquired.

that are largely undifferentiated," he said. "Our goal is different; we want to break through the clutter. Our advantage is that we've got a much tighter focus on a much narrower target market; this means we have to be able to get our message out more efficiently than our competitors."

The team had already decided on an advertising campaign that it believed was quirky, offbeat, and completely different from competitive ad treatments. The ads would feature teens and would make use of strange, often-indecipherable metaphors. As Howard Handler, Virgin Mobile's Chief Marketing Officer, put it, "We need to stand out from the rest of the crowd, which means that we need to deliver ads that are not run-of-the-mill. They need to be more entertaining and more unique in their creative execution." In addition, the company was working with youth magazine editors of publications such as *The Complex*, *Vibe*, and *XXL* to publish "advertorials," pieces extolling Virgin Mobile to their readers. "These are the opinion-leading magazines," Handler said. "Getting their buy-in is important for us."

Virgin Mobile was also planning a number of high-profile street marketing events. These events would feature paid performers—dancers and gymnasts dressed in red from head to toe—who would engage in various stunts.

Finally, the team was in the process of planning a highly unusual event to kick off the launch of the Virgin Mobile USA service. The plan called for the cast of *The Full Monty*, a Broadway show, to appear with Sir Richard Branson, dangling from a building in New York City's Time Square, wearing nothing but a large, strategically placed cell phone. (See **Exhibit 8** for pictures from the launch.)

The Pricing Decision

We knew that we couldn't afford to get pricing wrong when we designed our offer. It can make or break your success. Consequently, we did a tremendous amount of market research among our target segment, and one thing became clear: Our audience did not trust the industry pricing plans. They all advertise "free this" and "free that," but young people know that there are a lot of hidden charges, and they resent this. These are savvy consumers, and they hate feeling like they're being conned. So we've got an opportunity to use pricing as a way to differentiate ourselves from the competition.

—Dan Schulman

Over 90% of all subscribers in the U.S. had contractual agreements with their cellular providers. The contracts were generally for a period of one to two years, and they required a rigorous credit check. Many plans had established "buckets" of minutes. Customers could sign up for a bucket of 300 minutes, for example. However, if they actually used more than 300 minutes, they were penalized with extremely high rates (e.g., 40 cents/minute) for the overage. If they used fewer than 300 minutes, they were still charged the fixed monthly fee, which then drove up their price per minute.

The carriers typically charged less for off-peak than on-peak minutes, but the off-peak period had shrunk over time. Originally, off-peak had begun at 6:00 p.m.; the starting time had since shifted to 7:00 p.m., then 8:00 p.m., and finally 9:00 p.m. Some carriers such as Cingular charged a monthly fee (about $7) to move the peak time back one hour. Schulman noted:

> The industry is making money from customer confusion. As a customer, you need to use minutes within the tight range that you signed up for in order to get a good rate. Your on-peak and off-peak minutes have to be in the right mix too. If all customers actually signed up for the optimal plan for their usage, the carriers would be making far less money than they are today.

In fact, the industry's pricing plans were quite rational if customers would always select the right plan for their usage patterns. (Please refer to **Exhibit 9a**.) However, customers usually could not predict their usage. Virgin Mobile studied hundreds of customers and found that the prices they actually paid varied widely. (Please refer to **Exhibit 9b**.) Schulman continued:

> Often customers *think* that they use more minutes than they *actually* use. For example, in our target segment, the majority of young people actually use from 100 to 300 minutes per month. However, if you ask them to predict their usage, they'll often come up with a much higher number. Other people will try to pick lower bucket plans to avoid high monthly fees. Then they'll get a $100 bill because they didn't realize that it would cost them 40 cents for every minute above the bucket.

Adding to consumer resentment was the fact that most carriers slapped on additional fees to add to the monthly bill. Schulman explained: "The carriers will only tell you about the monthly bucket fee; they won't mention the taxes you'll have to pay or the universal services charge that you'll have to pay. There are a bunch of one-time costs that are loaded on top of the bill that they don't advertise. So even if you end up being exactly right in your bucket, a $29 plan ends up being a $35 plan."

Schulman and his team carefully considered various pricing strategies. Although the pricing possibilities were endless, the team believed that there were realistically three viable options. Schulman said: "We're trying to be as open-minded as possible. We have the luxury of starting from scratch, so this is an opportunity to fix some of the problems that are endemic in this industry. Our only constraints are that (1) we want to make sure our prices are competitive, (2) we want to make sure we can make money, and (3) we don't want to trigger off competitive reactions."

Option 1—"Clone the Industry Prices"

The first option was to merely "clone" the existing industry price structure. (See **Exhibit 10a** for Option 1 pricing.) All of the major carriers paid high commissions to salespeople to explain their complicated pricing structures and to perform credit checks. (In fact, 30% of prospective customers failed to pass these credit checks.) Given Virgin Mobile's nontraditional channel strategy, its pricing message would have to be relatively simple. Schulman said, "With this first option, we would simply be telling consumers that we're priced competitively with everyone else, but with a few key advantages like differentiated applications [MTV] and superior customer service."

In addition, Virgin Mobile could attempt to differentiate from the competition by offering better off-peak hours and fewer hidden fees. "We know that consumers are sick of hidden fees and they hate off-peak deals that start at 9 p.m., so we'd be addressing a real sore spot among young people," said Schulman.

He added, "The nice thing about this idea is that it's easy to promote. People may not like the pricing plans, but given all the money the industry spends to promote them, the customers are used to 'buckets' and peak/off-peak distinctions. Given our limited advertising budget, it may be a stretch for us to break through with anything different. We could also put it on our packaging so that even without the help of a salesperson, consumers would get the message."

Option 2—"Price Below the Competition"

The second option was to adopt a similar pricing *structure* as that of the rest of the industry, with *actual* prices slightly below those of the competition. That is, Virgin Mobile would maintain the buckets and volume discounts, but its price per minute would be set below the industry average for certain key buckets (see **Exhibit 10b**).

"This option would allow us to tell consumers that we're cheaper, plain and simple. Because our target market generally uses between 100 and 300 minutes per month, that's where consumers would get the best price," said Schulman. "Under this option, we could also offer better off-peak hours and fewer hidden fees, but I don't know if that would be necessary if our price per minute was clearly below the competition. We wouldn't want to leave too much money on the table."

Option 3—"A Whole New Plan"

The third option was the most radical. The idea was to start from scratch and come up with an entirely different pricing structure, one that was significantly different from anything offered by the competition. The pricing variables that Schulman was toying with included:

- **The role of contracts.** Did it make sense to shorten the term of the subscription contracts, or perhaps even eliminate the contracts altogether? Contracts provided carriers with a hedge against churn and a guaranteed annuity stream; yet even with the contracts, cellular providers struggled with an industry churn rate that averaged 2% per month. If Virgin Mobile were to shorten or eliminate such contracts, the risk would be that its churn rate would skyrocket. In fact it was estimated that churn would climb to 6% each month.[8]

  Schulman added:

  > From a marketing perspective, there's no question that it would be great if we could announce to the world that we've eliminated contracts. Keep in mind that, if you're under 18, you can't even enter into a contract with a cellular provider. Your parents need to do it for you. So eliminating contracts would be a big advantage for us from a customer-acquisition standpoint. Of course, in terms of retention, contracts are a safety net. So the question is, does it make sense for us to try to fly without a safety net?

- **Prepaid versus post-paid.** The vast majority (92%) of current cell phone subscribers in the U.S. had post-paid plans, which meant that they were billed monthly on the basis of their contract. Prepaid arrangements, in which consumers purchased a number of minutes in advance, were unusual because of prohibitive pricing (generally, between 35 and 50 cents per minute, and as high as 75 cents per minute). Most prepaid customers used their phones on an occasional basis as a safety device: "They just keep them in their glove compartment," as Schulman put it. Many of these customers had poor credit; in fact, the reason prepaid plans appealed to them was that such plans required no credit checks. Customers therefore thought that prepaid arrangements were a stigma, and the prepaid offers tended to attract low-usage customers. Still, in countries such as Finland and the U.K., prepaid arrangements were commonplace, accounting for the majority of new gross adds.

  Schulman knew that the risks of adopting a prepaid pricing structure were significant. U.S. carriers were extremely wary of prepaying consumers because of their high churn rates; prepaying consumers tended to exhibit no loyalty to a provider once they had used up all of their prepaid minutes. If Virgin Mobile were to adopt a prepaid pricing structure, the danger was that the company would never be able to recoup its customer acquisition costs. In fact,

[8] Source: Morgan Stanley research.

industry analysts estimate that total acquisition costs would have to be at or below $100 per new gross add for prepaid to be viable.[9]

In addition, there were a number of related issues to consider. A prepaid pricing structure would require some mechanism—perhaps via the Web or through physical phone cards—whereby consumers could easily add minutes to their phone.

- **Handset subsidies**. Most carriers purchased handsets from cell phone manufacturers such as Nokia, Motorola, and Samsung at a cost per handset ranging from $150 to $300 for the industry. The carriers then subsidized the cost of the handset to end users. This subsidy—which was typically about $100 to $200—was part of the customer acquisition cost.

  "We're debating all of our options here," said Schulman, "everything from increasing the subsidy so that our phones are cheaper than the competition, to lowering the subsidy as a way of getting consumers to feel more invested and loyal towards our service."

- **Hidden fees and off-peak hours.** "One of our goals is to offer a service that is priced so simply that consumers don't need a math degree to figure it out," noted Schulman. "One way to do this would be to eliminate *all* hidden fees, including taxes, universal service charges, *everything*. It would literally be 'what you see is what you get.' However, this would mean rolling all of those hidden costs into our pricing structure in such a way that our pricing feels competitive to our target market, and yet we still make money."

  As for off-peak hours, "We need to think about what makes sense for our target customer," said Schulman. "These kids don't lead the same kind of lifestyle as the typical business-person, so our service should define off-peak with that in mind."

As Schulman reviewed the various options for pricing, he realized the importance of laying the foundation for future profitability. "There's this assumption that you can't target young people and make money," he said. "Our goal is to prove otherwise. Ideally, every customer we acquire will have positive lifetime value (LTV) for us." (See **Exhibit 11** for LTV details.)

"That's why this pricing decision is so critical," he continued. "If we can figure out a way to create value so that we can successfully enter a very competitive and saturated market, and also create profitability with this target segment, then we will have truly accomplished something big."

---

[9] Source: Morgan Stanley research.

Exhibit 1 Wireless Subscribers in the United States, by Carrier (Q4 2001, in millions)

Carrier	Subscribers
AT&T (affiliates)	20.5
Cingular	21.7
Verizon	29.5
VoiceStream	6.5
Alltel	6.7
Sprint	14.5
U.S. Cellular	3.5
Leap	1.1
Other Carriers	26.1
Total	130.0

Source: Adapted from The Yankee Group.

Exhibit 2 Mobile Penetration by Age Group

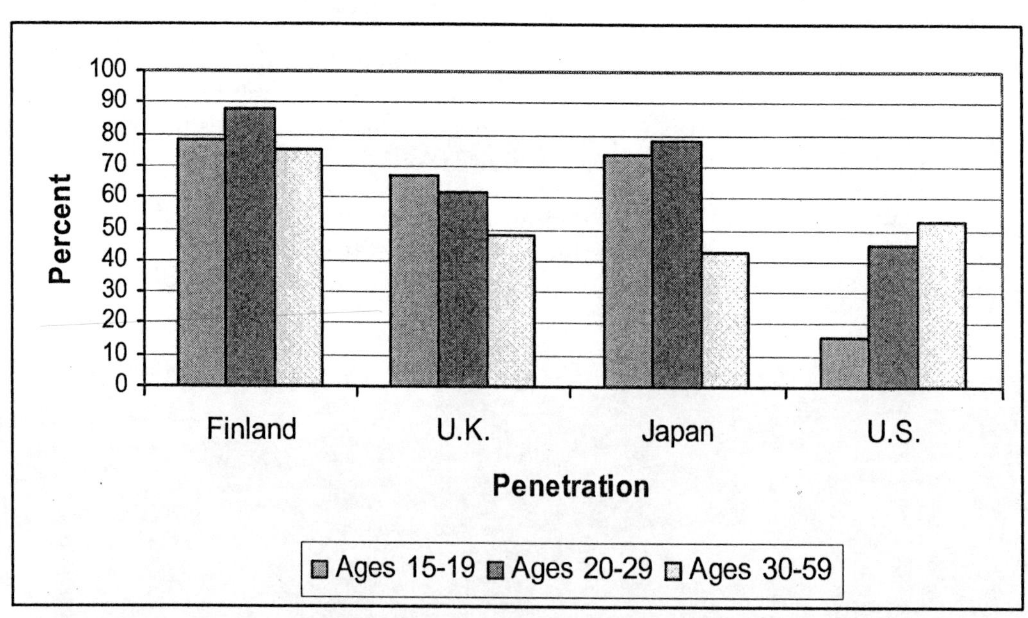

Source: Adapted from IDC, Salomon Smith Barney.

Exhibit 3 Revenue from Mobile Entertainment Services

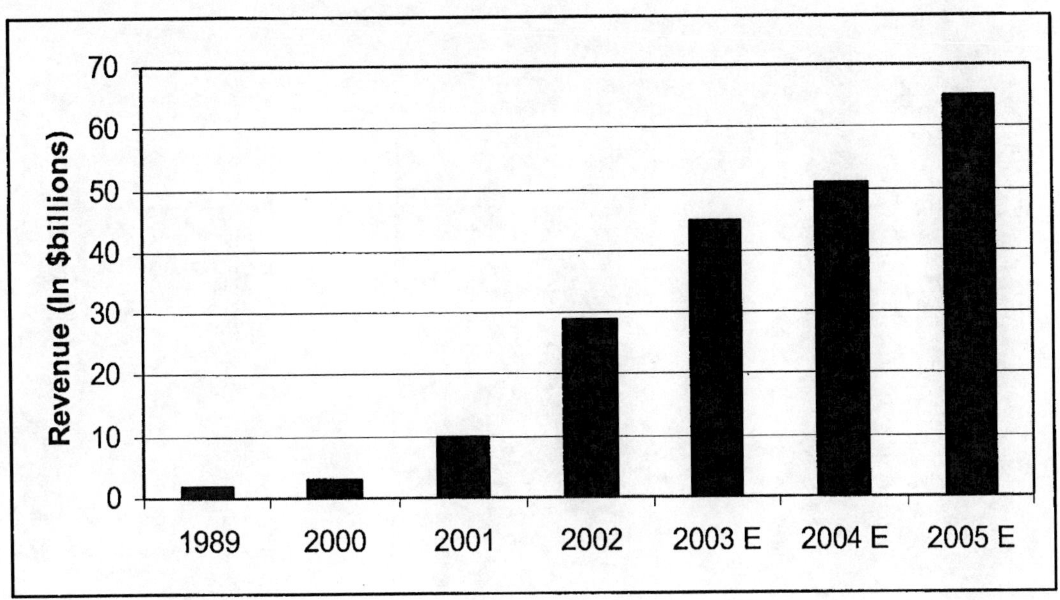

Source: Adapted from The Yankee Group.

Note: Revenues include video, audio, graphics, and games.

Exhibit 4 Screenshots of Virgin Mobile USA Content

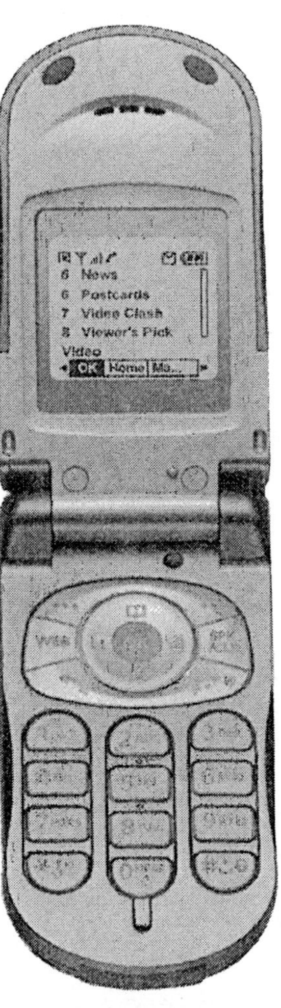

Source: Company Web site.

Exhibit 5 Virgin Mobile USA Handset Models

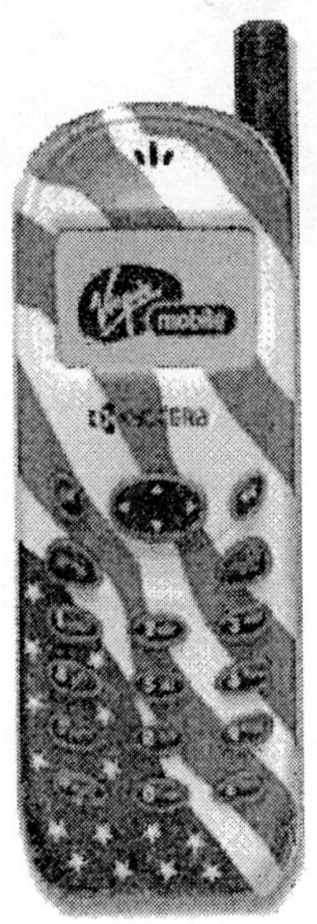

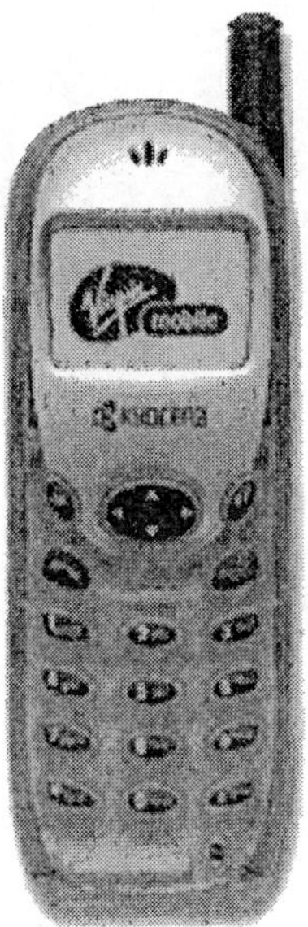

Source: Company Web site.

Note: Phones in second row show various faceplates for a single model.

Exhibit 6 Virgin Mobile USA: The Super Model Starter Pack (clamshell packaging)

Source: Company Web site.

Exhibit 7 Virgin Mobile USA Point-of-Sale Displays

Source: Company Web site.

Exhibit 8 Picture of Branson at Launch

Source: *Forbes* Magazine, October 7, 2002.

Exhibit 9a Calling Plans—Industry Prices

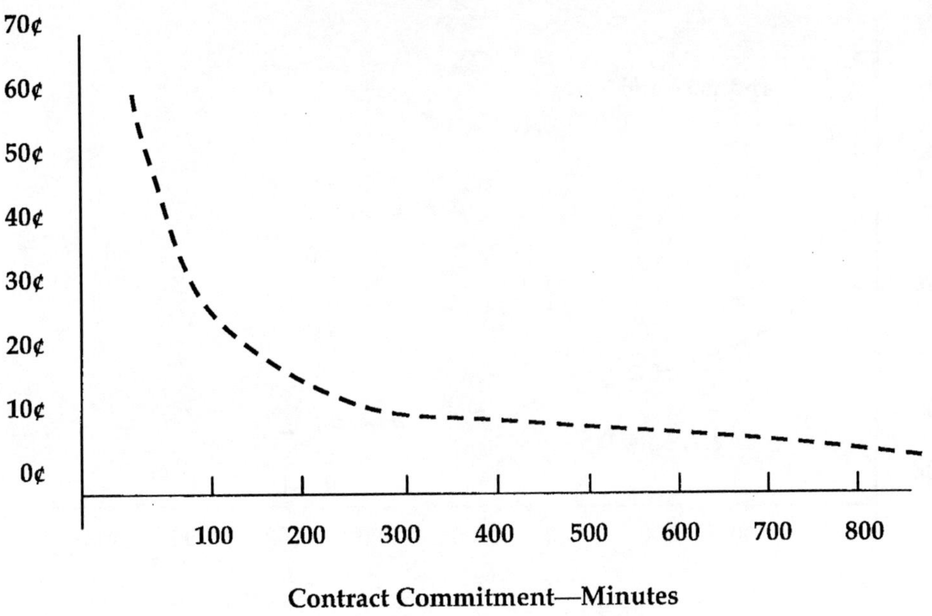

Source: Adapted from company data, Morgan Stanley research.

Exhibit 9b Actual Prices Paid by Customers

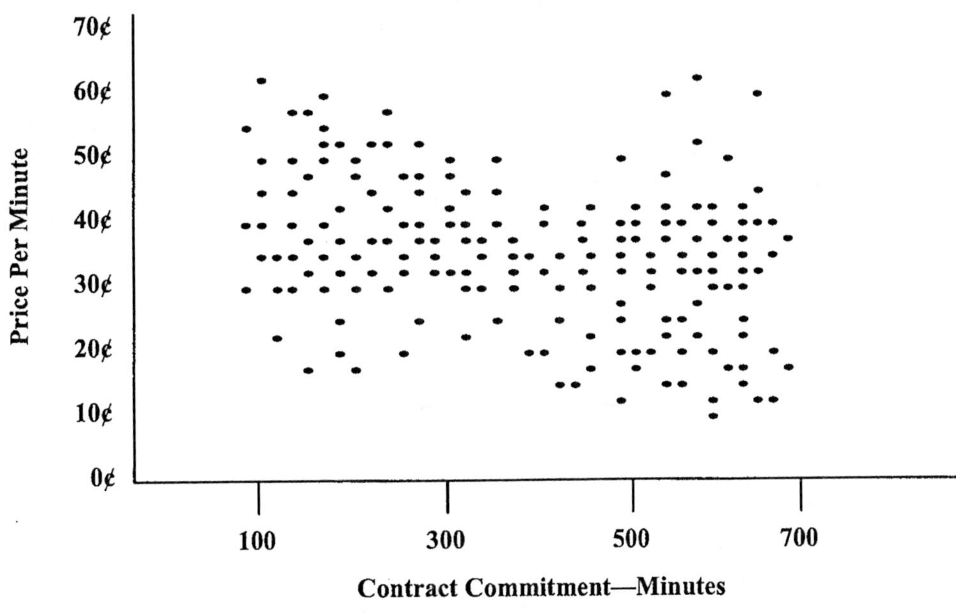

Source: Adapted from company data, Morgan Stanley research.

Exhibit 10a Option 1 Pricing Structure

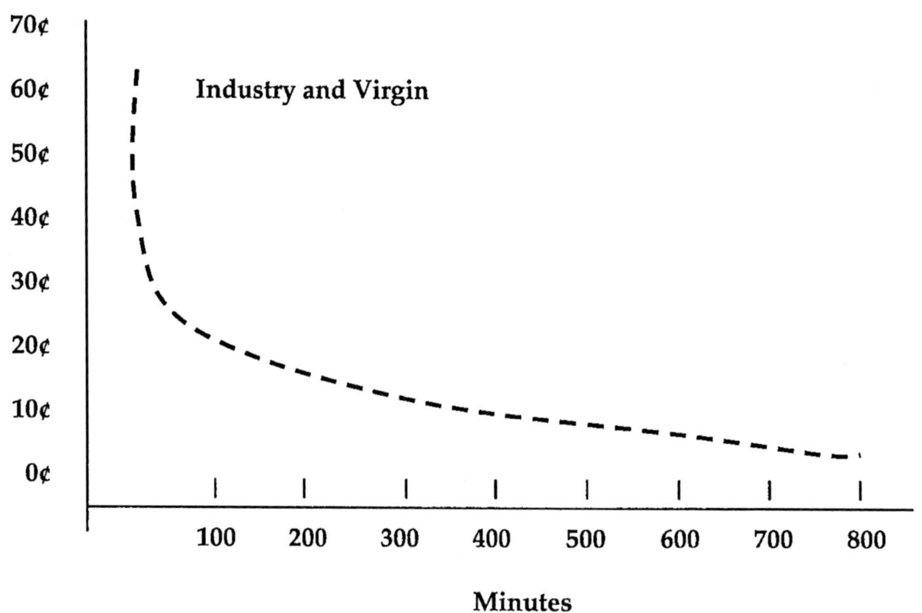

Source: Adapted from company data, Morgan Stanley research.

Exhibit 10b Option 2 Pricing Structure

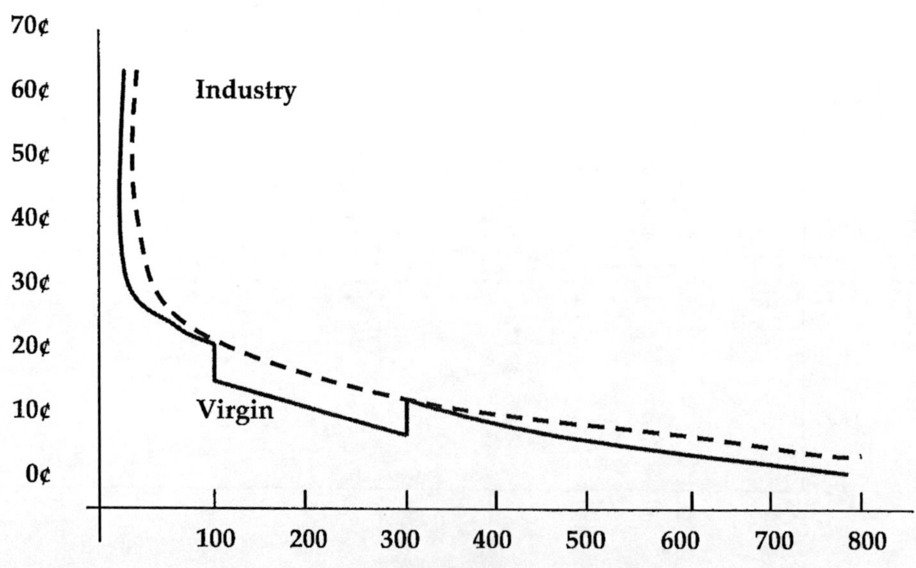

Source: Adapted from company data, Morgan Stanley research.

Note: Prices are for a blend of on- and off-peak minutes, with off-peak beginning at 9:00 p.m. Each additional off-peak hour reduces average price per minute by approximately 1.5 cents.

Exhibit 11 Calculating Lifetime Value (LTV) for Cellular Subscribers

In general, lifetime value (LTV) for a customer is calculated as follows:

$$LTV = \sum_{a=1}^{N} \frac{(M_a) r^{(a-1)}}{(1+i)^a} - AC$$

where

N = the number of years over which the relationship is calculated

M_a= the margin the customer generates in year a

r = the retention rate ($r^{(a-1)}$is the survival rate for year a)

i = the interest rate

AC = the acquisition cost

Source: Adapted from "Customer Profitability and Lifetime Value," HBS Note 503-019.

In the cellular industry, margin is relatively fixed across periods. Therefore, one can simplify the above expression by assuming an infinite economic life (i.e., letting $N \rightarrow \infty$), which leads to:

$$LTV = \frac{M}{1-r+i} - AC$$

Monthly Margin = average revenue per unit per month (ARPU) – monthly cost to serve (CCPU, or cash cost per user)

The components of AC were advertising per gross add, the sales commission paid per subscriber, and the handset subsidy provided to the subscriber.

CCPU consisted of customer-care costs, network costs (the cost of using Sprint's network), IT costs, and overhead. Industry analysts estimated that Virgin Mobile's CCPU would be constant at 45% of revenues during its first year of operations, since most of Virgin's costs were variable. Monthly churn was estimated to be 2% for customers under contract and 6% for prepaid customers.[a]

Interest rates were 5%.

[a]Numbers disguised for competitive reasons.

HARVARD | BUSINESS | SCHOOL

9-506-009

REV: SEPTEMBER 5, 2006

ANITA ELBERSE
JEHOSHUA ELIASHBERG
JULIAN VILLANEUVA

Polyphonic HMI: Mixing Music and Math

So few songs actually become hits—Las Vegas gives you better odds than the music industry! You might as well just put a million dollars on red and spin the wheel . . .

—Ric Wake, Independent Music Producer

In late 2003, the management team of Barcelona-based Polyphonic HMI was preparing to launch an artificial intelligence tool that they believed had the potential to create tremendous value for the music industry. The technology, referred to as Hit Song Science (HSS), analyzed the mathematical characteristics of music (by isolating aspects such as melody, tempo, pitch, rhythm, and chord progression) and compared them with characteristics of past music hits, making it possible to determine a song's hit potential. Mike McCready, the CEO of Polyphonic, explained:

> The music industry has always used two criteria to determine if a song will be a success. One is that it sounds like a hit. They have professionals at the music labels who are paid to determine if a song sounds like a hit. And two is that they have an idea how they can bring the artist and the song to the market. The problem is that the industry has about a 10% success rate: only one in 10 songs that get promoted ever charts. We add a third criterion—that it has to have optimal mathematical patterns—and significantly increase success rates.

"This piece of technology is truly special," he raved. "In one of our early tests, HSS generated unusually high scores for Norah Jones, a jazz singer who most industry insiders expected to have limited commercial impact but whose album later rose to the top of the charts. We also correctly predicted each of the hits of rock band Maroon 5."

Nevertheless, Polyphonic was having its share of problems. Initial sales pitches had met with resistance. "When we tell music executives about the concept, they typically look at us with glazed eyes, check their watch, and think of an excuse why they need to leave as soon as possible. Many people simply cannot imagine that science might play a role," said Tracie Reed, Polyphonic's vice president. In addition, the company had to abandon efforts to market a music recommendation system based on the same technology to retailers when hardware partners could not be found. Funds were running very low as a result—McCready himself had agreed to forgo his monthly paychecks in exchange for company stock.

Professors Anita Elberse, Jehoshua Eliashberg (The Wharton School, Philadelphia), and Julian Villaneuva (IESE Business School, Barcelona) prepared this case. HBS cases are developed solely as the basis for class discussion. Some nonpublic data have been disguised and some business details have been simplified to aid classroom discussion. Cases are not intended to serve as endorsements, sources of primary data, or illustrations of effective or ineffective management.

At this point, Antonio Trias, the creator of much of the HSS technology, provided Polyphonic with a personal investment of $150,000. Armed with what McCready called a "shoestring budget," the Polyphonic team was faced with several pressing questions. What was the best target market for this piece of technology—record companies, producers, or unsigned artists? And what was a suitable marketing plan? Specifically, how should the product be positioned, priced, and marketed?

Company Background

Polyphonic HMI was a subsidiary of Grupo AIA, a company that used its expertise in the area of artificial intelligence and the natural sciences (such as mathematics and physics) to solve complex business problems. Founded in 1988, AIA was headquartered in Barcelona but also had operations in Mexico and the U.S. It generated just over $5 million in revenues in 2002. Many of the approximately 50 employees, including four of the five top managers, had Ph.Ds in fields such as mathematics, physics, and engineering. "AIA is known for approaching business problems from different scientific perspectives," said Regina Llopis, AIA's CEO. "Our Ph.Ds are often working on one specific business problem, each from a different point of view. Together, they come up with a solution."

AIA operated in a wide range of industry settings, ranging from energy and finance to telecom and e-business. For example, its product portfolio covered a planning and monitoring tool for electric grid network operators, a money-laundering detection system for financial institutions, and a network interconnections management system for telecommunications providers. All products were artificial-intelligence and natural-science applications. Its list of clients was dominated by several of the main Spanish companies in banking (such as Caja Madrid, Grupo Santander, and La Caixa), utilities (such as Red Eléctrica de España, Endesa, and Gas Natural), and telecommunications (like Auna) but also included major players in those sectors in Europe, Latin America, and the U.S.

Polyphonic HMI, founded in 2002, was AIA's first foray into the entertainment sector. As the name implies,[1] Polyphonic was established specifically to market Grupo AIA's artificial-intelligence tools to the music industry. Its top managers, consisting of Jimena Llopis (executive chairman), McCready (chief executive officer), and Reed (vice president for North America) each had a background in music. They had assembled an experienced advisory board, which included Thomas Mottola, one of the music world's most prominent artist managers who previously had served as chairman and CEO of Sony Music Entertainment, and Ric Wake, a leading producer who scored numerous hits with artists such as Taylor Dane, Mariah Carey, and Celine Dion. Brief biographies for the management team and advisory board are provided in **Exhibit 1**.

Polyphonic's management team worked with a small group of dedicated scientists and other staff members and had access to experts in the Grupo AIA parent organization. The annual fixed costs of operating Polyphonic were estimated to be around $500,000.

Basic Technology

The technology underlying HSS found its origins in an extensive analysis of millions of songs. This covered nearly all music released by music labels since the 1950s, and the database was updated weekly with new releases. Polyphonic devised a way to "listen to" a piece of music and isolate

---

[1] The term "polyphony" refers to "music with two or more independent melodic parts sounded together" (Source: *The American Heritage Dictionary of the English Language*, Fourth Edition, Houghton Mifflin Company). HMI stands for "human media interface."

particular patterns. The process, referred to as "spectral deconvolution," considered over 25 characteristics in total, including melody, harmony, tempo, pitch, octave, beat, rhythm, fullness of sound, noise, brilliance, and chord progression. Based on its mathematical characteristics, each song was then mapped onto a multidimensional grid called the "music universe." **Exhibit 2** provides some details.

Songs with mathematical similarities are positioned very close to one another in this universe. According to McCready, the technology organized music in ways that sometimes seemed counter-intuitive:

> Our technology reflects the mathematical patterns in the music—not necessarily the sound of music. For example, as far as the melody pattern is concerned, one composition by Beethoven could fall on one end, and another composition by Beethoven on the opposite end of the universe. Similarly, one Beethoven composition could fall very close to a song by rock band U2 or pop singer Mariah Carey.

Music Recommendation System

Polyphonic had initially used the technology to develop a music recommendation system. The idea was to develop a device placed in music stores that provided recommendations to shoppers, thereby helping retailers to increase sales. McCready explained:

> Many people walk into music stores looking for something new, but they just don't know how to look for it. We believe people don't just like a certain genre of music but that they like specific mathematical patterns that transverse music genres—genres are just marketing terms. Our recommendation system locked onto that idea: we asked what music a consumer liked, matched that to our universe of music, and used that information to recommend other music.

Polyphonic planned to license the technology to retailers such as Best Buy, HMV, and Virgin Megastores for up to a quarter of a million dollars a year. It had developed the software needed for the system and counted on partners to develop the accompanying hardware. Unfortunately, the difficult economic situation—annual music sales were sharply decreasing—caused reluctance among retailers and hardware providers. "The sales cycles with the hardware providers proved to be extremely long. We are a small, tenuously financed company, and we could not afford to ride this out," said McCready, "so we went back to the drawing board. We knew we had to come up with another application of the technology."

Hit Song Science

That new application became HSS. McCready explained how the idea emerged:

> Antonio Trias, the vice president for innovation at AIA, figured out that hit songs had common mathematical properties. He had gone back to the music universe and had initially focused on songs that had made it to the Singles Top 40 of the leading music chart, the Billboard Hot 100,[2] in the past five years. When he found that there were only about 50 to 60 hit clusters—not an infinitely large number—we realized the potential of the idea.

[2] Each week, the Billboard Hot 100 ranked singles based on sales and radio airplay. The chart was compiled by Nielsen Broadcast Data Systems and Nielsen Soundscan and published in the music trade publication *Billboard Magazine*.

McCready and his team felt the existence of clusters was evidence for the view that hit songs share certain mathematical patterns. Consequently, the extent to which new releases "fit" those clusters should indicate their hit potential (see **Figure A**). McCready said:

> We can take an unreleased album and examine how the songs on that album map onto the clusters. If a song falls *within* one of these clusters, we can't necessarily say that it will be a hit. We just know it has the potential. The song has to conform to a couple of other criteria in order to become a hit: it has to sound like a hit, be promoted like a hit, and be marketable. But if a song falls *outside* of the clusters, we know it will probably not become a hit.

Figure A Hit Song Science: A New Album Mapped onto Hit Clusters

Source: Polyphonic HMI.

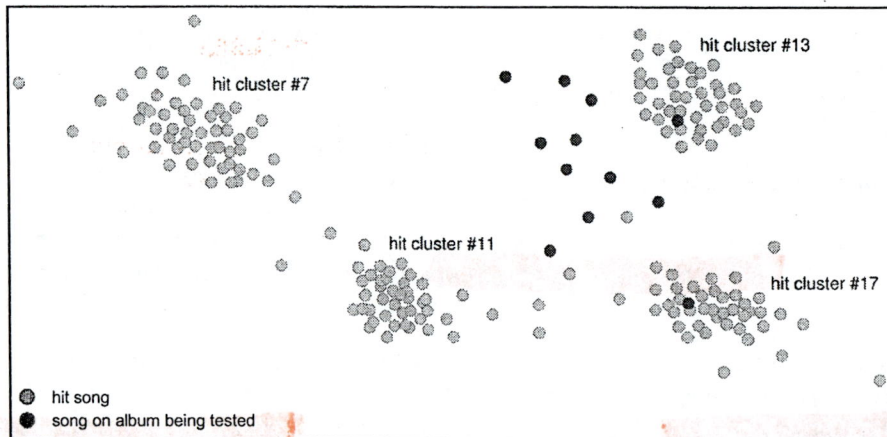

The closeness to a cluster was indicated with a "Hit Song Science score" on a scale of 1–10, with higher scores indicating a great hit potential. The clustering technique also allowed Polyphonic to provide insights into the coherence of an album, that is, the extent to which songs fall into the same or nearby clusters, and a list of songs with similar mathematical properties.

Figure B Hit Song Science: A New Album Mapped onto Hit Clusters (with weights)

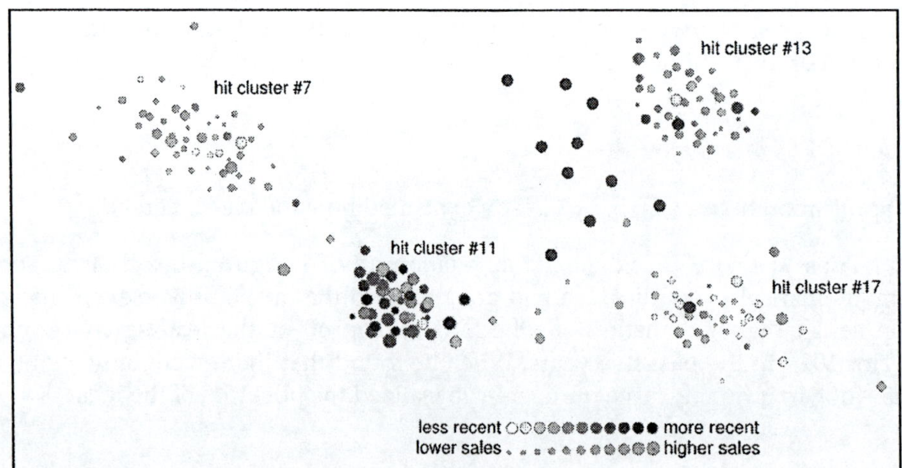

Source: Polyphonic HMI.

Additional testing led to further refinements. For example, by giving higher weights to songs in the universe with higher sales levels, Polyphonic scientists could better pinpoint the significance of a cluster. Similarly, by focusing on more recent successes among the songs in the universe, they could incorporate the extent to which tastes might change over time (see **Figure B**).

As of late 2003, AIA and Polyphonic had spent about $600,000 developing HSS. Now that the technology was in place, generating reports for clients was relatively inexpensive. McCready estimated it took about two hours, at a total cost of $300, to analyze an album with 10 songs.

The Music Industry[3]

The worldwide market for recorded music was worth over $32 billion at the retail level in 2002 (see **Exhibits 3a** and **3b** for a breakdown of sales by region and country). The number one market, the U.S., was a strong force in the world's music business, both as a place of origination of new music and as a consumer of music products. In 2002, about 30% of all the recorded music was produced there, and the size of the retail market was well over $12 billion, or 39% of worldwide sales (see **Exhibit 4** for manufacturers' shipments). European countries accounted for 34% of worldwide sales in 2002, with the U.K., Germany, France, Italy, and Spain being the largest markets.

Most major regions of the world had endured several consecutive years of falling music sales, which many industry insiders attributed to online and offline piracy. Although legal online downloads were still a small fraction of total sales, the rise of music distribution via the internet was beginning to affect music consumption. **Exhibit 5** provides insights into consumption patterns.

Recording Music

Artists The music recording process typically started with the artists who wrote song lyrics, composed music, and performed music. Recognized talent and some new artists typically had contracts with a "label" within a record company that stipulated the terms under which they were to deliver one or more albums. They were supported by legal advisors, managers, and agents who helped them negotiate contracts, book concerts, and schedule recording sessions, among other things.

McCready estimated that there were about 10,000 artists with a record contract in the U.S. and Europe, but only several hundred with some name recognition and commercial success. Tens of thousands—if not hundreds of thousands—of artists were hoping to secure such a contract. "Every high school has a band who think they will be the next big thing," said McCready. Unsigned artists often used "demo" (demonstration) recordings to attract a music publisher's interest. "Record companies are always on the lookout for good, new material, and labels may receive three to four hundred demos a week," mentioned McCready, "but only a small fraction of those demos lead to record contracts." When labels signed artists, they usually required an artist to deliver several albums over a certain period and work exclusively for that label during that time.

Record companies There were five big companies, "the majors," that dominated the recorded music business: BMG Entertainment, EMI, Sony Music, Universal Music Group, and Warner Music Group (see **Exhibit 6** for their 2002 market shares). Each of those companies had various labels and music publishing companies under their umbrellas. For example, Universal Music Group incorporated at least a dozen labels aimed at the U.S. market, including Motown, Interscope, Geffen,

[3] This section draws on Harold L. Vogel, *Entertainment Industry Economics* (Cambridge, UK: Cambridge University Press, 2001).

MCA, Universal Classics, Universal Records, Universal South, and Universal/Island, and three times as many labels aimed at international markets. Some labels covered all music types, whereas others specialized in certain music genres. In the U.S. alone, there were also tens of thousands of small and midsized record companies. **Figure C** depicts how labels are commonly organized.

Figure C Typical Organization of a Record Label

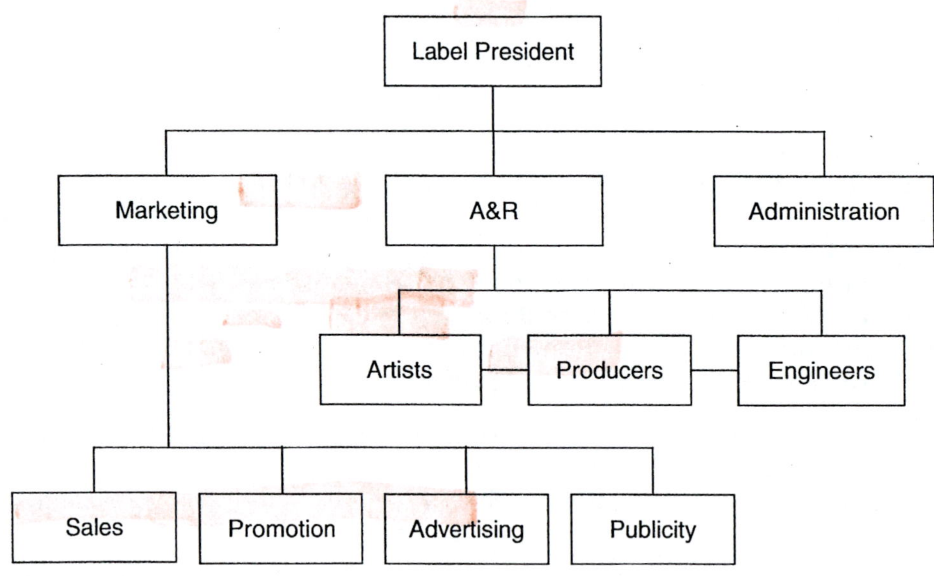

Source: Casewriters.

When labels signed an artist, they typically had an in-house producer, known as an artist-and repertoire (A&R) person, guide the project. "A&R executives are usually young people who really like music and who have convinced somebody that they have 'good ears,'" said McCready. Quique Tejada, an A&R director at Spanish record company Vale Music, explained his role: "I prepare the launch of new artists. I look for talent, find songs that they can record, select the best producer for each project, participate in the recording process, and check the master recordings. I am responsible for 20 artists." "An A&R executive is shepherding a band he has discovered through their early career development," added McCready. "He wants to make sure that their music is successful, because his career rides on that success. Most A&R people have a career span of three to four years. Those with a longer career span really become somebody in the music industry—people know who they are."

Nurturing talent was a critical activity for record companies. The lion's share of a record company's revenues was generated through its established artists—not new artists. For Warner Music Group, for example, established artists accounted for almost 90% of the $1.7 billion in revenues from newly released titles in 2003.

Producers In addition, artists often worked with independent producers who, much like the A&R people, helped the artist select music and develop a music style, oversaw recording schedules, recruited engineers, and watched over recording budgets. "A producer can be responsible for a lot of things—writing the song, recording the song, mixing and editing it, making sure it has the right vibe. The producer is the pivot between the label, the publisher, the manager, and the artist," explained independent producer Wake. "A good producer can see what an artist is supposed to sound like and come up with the right sound, or take an artist who has a vision and help him or her realize it." He added: "I once saw a performance by a girl named Leslie Wonderman and just had a strong feeling, a special sensation, that she could be a star. I turned her into Taylor Dane, found a sound that worked for her, and helped her score several huge hits."

According to Wake, there were only about 20 to 30 top producers who were responsible for the majority of successes, a larger group of a few hundred producers who had a hit once in a while, and thousands of people trying to establish themselves as producers.

Deals among Artists, Producers, and Record Labels

The deals among artists, producers, and labels could be structured in a number of ways. In some cases, the label signed the artist and hired an in-house producer, compensated through salary plus perhaps some royalties, to handle the project. In other cases, the label retained an independent producer or company to deliver a master recording for an artist under contract. In a third variation, independent artists and producers made a master recording and then tried to sell the master to a label.

Income from music came from three different royalty streams. Mechanical royalties were mostly derived from the sale of music recordings. Performance royalties were earned each time music was performed (by radio stations, orchestras, nightclub singers, and so on). Synchronization royalties were paid for music played to visual images and soundtracks.

A record company typically paid an artist recording a new album an up-front fee and, once sales had passed a level that allowed the company to fully recover its costs, also a sales-based payment. The latter depended on the artist's track record and stature but usually varied between 5% and 15% of the record's suggested retail price.

Industry contracts generally dictated that most of the costs of making a record were to be repaid out of the artist's up-front fee and royalties. "A record contract is essentially a loan from the record company to the artist," clarified McCready. Managers and talent agents alone extracted between 25% and 40% of a performer's income. Outside producers usually received a production fee and often also negotiated a royalty of 1% to 5% of the suggested retail price. Production fees varied dramatically, according to Wake: "A Mariah Carey record may be close to a million dollars in production fees, but a first record by a new artist might have only cost $100,000."

Marketing and Distributing Music

The recording process ends with the delivery of a completed master. At this point, record companies start planning a marketing campaign for the album (or individual singles) and establish a timetable for the physical production and distribution of records.

Although practices differed across labels, the record label president and marketing director generally made final decisions about marketing strategies, but the A&R person also often played a role. "Our marketing department develops and executes a marketing plan for each of our artists, but I participate in that process as well," remarked Tejada about the procedure at Vale Music. "In my role as the A&R director, I am most frequently in contact with the artists and know what strategies will work for them. At our weekly marketing meetings, which are led by our president and attended by all 12 of our executives, I often speak out on marketing issues."

One of the most important decisions for a label usually was which single of an album (with on average of 10 songs) to release first. "Virtually all mainstream albums released nowadays are accompanied by a single," said McCready. "Radio airplay is the primary advertising vehicle for popular albums—and you need a single to get on the radio. The same is true for music television, which is also an important advertising channel—you need a strong single to get on MTV."

Particularly for new artists, the first single was often a make-or-break situation. "I have heard of many situations where albums were left to 'die' when the first single underperformed," said McCready. "When that happens, labels commonly decide not to release any more singles by that artist and essentially give up on the advertising campaign. It could be the end of the artist's career."

Marketing music was expensive. "The release of a single usually involves at least $300,000 in marketing expenditures—and that is just what they will spend on the first single for an unknown artist," said McCready. "Labels may spend in excess of $1 million to promote the single of an established star like Mariah Carey." Often, labels did not expect to make that money back on single sales, according to McCready: "The album, not the single, will often deliver the lion's share of revenues." In the U.S., the first single and the album were typically released at the same time.

Marketing campaigns involved anything from the production of music videos to concert tours, cooperative advertising with retailers, in-store merchandising materials, radio and television commercials, and press kits. To promote the song and get it played on the radio, free records were often sent to hundreds of radio stations. Because radio was a significant factor in introducing new artists and songs to consumers and because popular music stations were able to add at most three or four new cuts per week to their lists, competition for airplay was intense. After bribery (so-called payola) of radio stations had been outlawed in the 1960s, record labels had turned to hiring independent promoters to ensure airplay for new songs or paying "advertising" fees for a song's first spins on the radio. Generating significant airplay for a song could easily cost $100,000 in promotion fees alone.

The lion's share of recorded music was distributed in a physical form, on a compact disc. Each year, approximately 30,000 new full (album) CDs were brought to the market. Not all of those albums were aimed at a broad, mainstream audience—McCready estimated that about 2,500 of the albums released each year were accompanied by one or more CD singles. The distribution arms of the five majors accounted for the large majority of shipments of all discs.

The suggested retail price to consumers of a full (album) CD was just under $17 in the U.S.; music retailers paid about $10.50 for a CD. As contractual terms among labels, artists, and other parties often differed substantially, the breakdown of costs for labels could vary widely. Record labels typically sought a margin of at least 30% of the price to retailers, after paying royalties to artists, fees to the publisher (about 5% of the price to retailers), manufacturing and distribution costs (about 10% of the price to retailers), administrative expenses (also about 10% of the price to retailers), A&R expenses (often as much as 15% of the price to retailers), and marketing and promotion costs.

CD singles were typically priced between $3 and $5. Although the large majority of consumers continued to buy music offline and in the form of albums, the rise of online distribution channels also stimulated downloads of individual songs, which were typically priced around a dollar each.

A Hit-and-Miss Business

The vast majority of music released never became a hit. Ken Bunt, an executive at Disney's Hollywood Records, commented on the uncertainty surrounding new releases: "Releases in the music business traditionally are a big gamble. We can spend millions of dollars to put a product on the market and not be sure whether there will be any demand for it or whether it will get any airplay." For each label, the few successes covered the losses made on the many failed titles. For example, in late 2003, Norah Jones seemed well on her way to single-handedly preventing a market share decline for her label, Blue Note, which was part of EMI.

Exhibit 7a and **Exhibit 7b** list the top-selling albums and singles in the U.S. in 2002. As **Exhibit 7a** shows, the year's 25 highest-ranked albums sold just below 3 million units on average. A total of 65 albums sold over 1 million units in 2002. In that same year, just over 120 albums achieved "Platinum" status, indicating sales of at least 1 million units over their lifetime. In contrast, in that same year, only two singles reached the 1 million sales mark.

It was a well-known industry fact that less than 15% of music titles released were profitable. According to McCready, having a single on the weekly Billboard Singles Top 40 chart was the best, albeit not a perfect, indicator of a label's ability to recover its production and marketing costs. He estimated that fewer than 300, or about 10%, of the approximately 3,000 singles released each year made it to the Billboard Singles Top 40. Similarly, he estimated, only 10% of all 2,500 albums had at least one single that made it to the Singles Top 40. (The difference was caused by albums that had more than one successful single.)

Based on information obtained from an industry expert, McCready had compiled key statistics (see **Table A)** to "guesstimate" the likely revenues in each case:

Table A Estimated Revenues for Singles and Albums with and without a Top 40 Chart Position

Expected Revenues for . . .	Low Estimate	Medium Estimate	High Estimate
A single that does not reach the Singles Top 40	$0	$10,000	$100,000
A single that reaches the Singles Top 40	$100,000	$200,000	$2,000,000
An album with a single that does not reach the Singles Top 40	$0	$90,000	$300,000
An album with a single that reaches the Singles Top 40	$300,000	$2,000,000	$40,000,000

Source: Polyphonic HMI.

"Averages are not very meaningful in the music business," remarked McCready. "You either lose a lot of money with a dud, or you win a lot of money with a hit." He added: "And of course a runaway smash hit can generate significantly more than $40 million in album sales, especially if the song makes it into a movie or advertising campaign. Some albums bring in $90 million in revenues! Unfortunately, such hits don't come around very often."

Most record companies engaged in research activities to help them forecast sales levels for the titles in their portfolios. "Everyone has their own technique," remarked McCready. "One top record-label executive, Antonio 'LA' Reid, likes to round up kids out on the streets in New York and let them listen to new artists and new songs. Clive Davis, another famous executive, prides himself on his 'ears'—unless it sounds like a hit to him, it is not, and he does not want to know what anybody else thinks." "Some labels still work completely on gut instinct," agreed Hollywood Records' Bunt. "But we do not stick our head in the sand. We almost always do some focus group or online testing beforehand and play it for people ahead of the release, asking them if they would want to hear it on their favorite radio station."

So-called call-out research was the most popular research method. Record companies would enlist the help of market research companies, which called respondents at home, walked them through a prescripted screening process and, if the respondents qualified based on demographics, music listening behavior, or other characteristics, submit them to a music test. They played specific "hooks" (15- to 30-second fragments) of songs respondents were asked to rate, for example by using the push buttons on their phone or by directly giving their score to the interviewer. Depending on the number of people surveyed and the method used, "Call-out studies usually cost the record labels between $5,000 and $7,000 per song," according to McCready. "Internet polling starts at around $3,000," he added, "and focus group research can cost record labels as much as $10,000 per song."

"Despite these traditional research techniques and executives' gut instincts," said McCready, "only one out of every 10 songs that gets promoted as a single actually charts. I have spoken with A&R people who pride themselves on a success rate that is 2% or 3% higher than average."

Hit Song Science: Improved Odds?

HSS, McCready argued based on the results of initial tests, could give the industry much better odds. "The analyses we have performed for music released in the U.S. in the past six months suggest that Hit Song Science can achieve a success rate of 80%—we correctly predicted whether a single would reach the Singles Top 40 eight out of 10 times," he said. **Table B** reflects the results of a representative sample.

Table B Hit Song Science's Success Rates: A Sample

Artist	Song Title	HSS Rating > 7.00	Weeks in the Singles Top 40	Highest Chart Position
Outkast	Hey Ya!	Yes	29	1
Clay Aiken	This Is The Night	Yes	6	1
Santana Feat. Alex Band	Why Don't You & I	Yes	28	6
R. Kelly	Step In The Name Of Love	Yes	22	9
Monica	So Gone	No	13	9
t.A.t.U.	All The Things She Said	Yes	26	12
Daniel Bedingfield	If You're Not The One	Yes	15	12
Uncle Kracker Feat. Dobie Gray	Drift Away	Yes	17	13
Brad Paisley	I Wish You'd Stay	No	0	--
Jennifer Hanson	Beautiful Goodbye	No	0	--

Source: Polyphonic HMI.

"If a song scores an HSS rating of 7.00 or higher, we believe it has the potential to become a hit," McCready explained. "It turns out we were correct in nine of these 10 examples. Only 'So Gone,' a song by Monica, just missed our cutoff point. It was released anyway and actually performed quite well." He added: "However, on two other songs with low HSS ratings, 'I Wish You'd Stay,' by Brad Paisley, and 'Beautiful Goodbye,' by Jennifer Hanson, we were right—they were released but never made it to the charts."

As of late 2003, despite an extensive search, the Polyphonic management team was not aware of any comparable products. "It is up to us to show that science—Hit Song Science—can radically improve the odds of success in the music industry," McCready said, "and if we succeed, we will dramatically alter the business."

Developing a Marketing Strategy for Hit Song Science

Armed with a budget of only $150,000, the management team faced the task of developing a marketing strategy for Polyphonic's breakthrough product. They had to resolve two particularly pressing questions.

Two Questions

What was the best target market? The team felt Hit Song Science could be valuable for three target markets: record labels, producers, and unsigned artists.

- For **record labels,** HSS could be helpful in at least three ways: in deciding whether to market an album, in selecting which song to release first, and even in testing new artists looking for a record deal.
- For **producers,** HSS offered a chance to test songs or albums at some stage during the production process and "tweak" them to maximize their hit potential.
- For **unsigned artists,** HSS could add value in that it helped them check the hit potential of their songs and thus find out whether they had a shot at making it in the industry.

In light of the budgetary and time constraints, McCready thought Polyphonic should initially limit itself to one target market. Several questions ran through his mind. Which market would represent the largest opportunity for Polyphonic? Where would the company achieve the highest return on its efforts? And where could it generate sales relatively quickly? In addition, within each market, should Polyphonic aim for a specific type of customer?

What was a suitable marketing plan? Once a decision on the target market had been made, the management team had to develop a marketing plan for that target market. They had decided to sell reports based on the HSS technology—and not the exclusive rights to the technology itself, for example—but several other questions remained.

- **How should HSS be positioned?** Specifically, what benefit of HSS should be emphasized for the chosen target market?
- **What price should be charged?** What price would allow Polyphonic to break even on HSS? Was the price for call-out research a good guideline for pricing decisions? Or was a higher price justified?
- **How should Polyphonic approach the selling process?** The management team realized its budget did not allow for much advertising and favored a proactive selling approach.

Related to the pricing decision, the Polyphonic team also debated whether it was worthwhile to offer potential customers a free trial. "We have received some requests for free trials from people who have heard about us, and we expect more calls when we generate more publicity," said Executive Chairman Jimena Llopis. "We are keen to prove our concept," she continued, "but we are unsure whether handing out free trials left and right is a good strategy."

"We need people to really understand what our product does and reach the right people with our message," said McCready. He pointed to the report on the Norah Jones album that Polyphonic had prepared for Blue Note Records (see **Exhibit 8**). "It may be a bit overwhelming at first to read these reports, but eventually people will recognize what we bring to the table."

When it came to designing a sales procedure, the management team recognized the need to act decisively. They had acquired three relevant industry directories: the "A&R Registry," which provided contact details for A&R people at major and independent labels (see **Exhibit 9** for a sample page); the "Producer Registry," which listed over 1,600 producers and engineers along with their selected credits and contact details; and Billboard's "International Talent and Touring Guide" with contacts for about 10,000 artists. Where and how should the team start?

Music and Math: A Challenging Mix

Polyphonic's managers knew that marketing HSS would not be easy, but they were encouraged by initial responses from potential customers who had been asked to test the product. For instance, Hollywood Records executive Bunt had been enthusiastic: "This business has always been run by instinct and gut, and even my own colleagues might have a hard time believing this, but my experiences with Hit Song Science have been fantastic. HSS has been extremely accurate on the tracks that we have taken to commercial radio."

Producer Wake agreed: "When this product came along I was very skeptical. So I put together a crazy album with some really bad songs and some really good ones, just to see what would happen. When Mike sent a report back, it clearly showed the duds and the hits. Now that I have tested it, I realize that this is an amazing tool for producers."

However, not all music industry insiders were impressed, initial sales pitches had met with considerable resistance, and early news reports on HSS voiced some concerns. "What creates a hit is that people have an emotional reaction to a song, in particular the lyrics. It is difficult to believe that a machine could gauge that," said one artist manager quoted in *The New York Times*.[4] Another musician added, "I doubt pop music could get any worse" and called it "a meaningless tool." "There are always musicians who will do something different," argued a third expert. "They could possibly be missed out if the industry pensions off A&R people and relies too much on this data-crunching machine."

"Hit Song Science is to the music industry what the X-ray machine was to medicine. The first time someone told a doctor he could look inside a patient's body without cutting it open, it probably sounded like science fiction too," said McCready about the challenge in front of him. "But in the end, the X-ray machine is a tool that helps the doctor see something that he could not see before, and he can use that information to make better decisions. That is exactly what Hit Song Science does, and that is what matters. I know that we are just a millimeter away from this thing taking off."

---

[4] "Antiwar Song, With Whimsey," *The New York Times*, March 12, 2003.

Exhibit 1 Biographies for Polyphonic's Management Team and Advisory Board

Management Team

Jimena Llopis (Executive Chairman) joined Grupo AIA in July 1998. She started in the Banking and Finance Unit, where she later held the position of Assistant Manager. In 2000 she created the Internet and Telecommunications Business Unit, and was the Director of this Unit until 2002. She is currently Group AIA's Vice President of New Business Development. Llopis holds Bachelor and Master's degrees (with honors) in Mathematics from the Universidad Simon Bolivar, and a Ph.D. degree in Sciences at the Universidad Central, both in Venezuela. She has held various research positions, including a tenured professorship at Universidad Simon Bolivar, and visiting positions at the Massachusetts Institute of Technology and the Mathematical Science Research Institute at Berkeley. Since 2002, she is also a researcher at Barcelona's Pompeu Fabra University. Llopis studied Music, including piano, harmony, counterpoint and composition, for twelve years at the Music School Juan Jose Landaeta in Venezuela.

Mike McCready (Chief Executive Officer) is an experienced entrepreneur and marketing executive at companies like ConsumerDesk and IconMedialab. He has spent several years within the music industry, five of which as a marketing manager at Barcelona Promoció, a firm that manages the Olympic venues in Barcelona including the Palau Sant Jordi and the Olympic Stadium. At Barcelona Promoció, he worked on the contracting of many of the city's major concerts and was responsible for bringing large events to Barcelona, including the 2002 MTV European Music Awards. McCready also consulted for Swedish music portal deo.com. Mike is a hobbyist musician. In 2000, he became the first American to publish a CD in Catalan, which was released by the second largest independent music label in Catalonia, DiscMedi.

Tracie Reed (Vice President, North America) is an experienced music retail executive in both the U.K. and the U.S. She worked as a senior executive for The Music Land Group for eight years, four of which she spent in London opening new stores for the company. She held a variety of marketing and merchandising positions at the company's Minneapolis headquarters and was the Director of Merchandising for the Superstore Division before leaving the company to work in the senior merchandising position at CDNOW, one of the largest online music retailers. At CDNOW she was responsible for brokering partnerships and large strategic relationships, among other things. She helped sell CDNOW to BMG before leaving the company. Reed also has consulted for independent music labels, artists, and retailers.

Advisory Board (Selected Members)

Lorin Hollander made his Carnegie Hall debut at the age of eleven. A child prodigy who composed music at age three and performed the Well-Tempered Clavier of Bach at five, he has since performed with every major symphony orchestra in the world and is a veteran of nearly 2,500 performances: with orchestra, in recital, lecture/recital, chamber ensemble as pianist, symphony and choral conductor. He has collaborated with Bernstein, Mehta, Ozawa, Monteux, and Szell, among many others. He performed in the soundtrack of the movie "Sophie's Choice," and has recorded for RCA Victor, Columbia, Angel and Delos and PianoDisc.

Thomas D. Mottola is one of the most highly regarded and influential executives in the music business. He most recently served as Chairman and CEO Sony Music Entertainment. During his tenure, he transformed Sony into a highly successful global music company. Along the way, he developed and nurtured many of popular music's top icons, from Celine Dion, Barbra Streisand, Bruce Springsteen, and Gloria Estefan, to Destiny's Child, Jennifer Lopez, Mariah Carey, and Nas, among others. Mottola joined Sony (then CBS Records) in 1988 as the youngest President in CBS history. Prior to joining CBS, Mottola was a prominent artist manager, and successfully launched the careers of artists such as Hall & Oates, Carly Simon and John Mellencamp.

Vic Sarjoo is a money manager, investment banker and business consultant. He has worked for Merrill Lynch, Chase and Citicorp, and founded VSAM Global Asset Management, a private investment management and investment banking boutique, in 1998.

Antoni Trias is the creator of much of the core technology that drives Polyphonic HMI's music analysis tool. He holds a Ph.D. degree (Cum Laude) in Physics from the Universidad Autónoma de Barcelona. He was a visiting postdoctoral research fellow from 1974 to 1976 at the Lawrence Berkeley Laboratory of the University of California. Later, he was a tenured professor in Theoretical Physics at the Universidad Simón Bolívar in Venezuela, and a visiting professor at the State University of New York in Stony Brook (where he worked with Nobel Prize Laureate C.N. Yang, among others). In 1985 he returned to Spain, where he taught at the Universitat Autónoma de Barcelona, and the Universitat Politècnica de Catalunya. Trias is a founding partner, Vice Chairman, and R&D Director of AIA.

Ric Wake presides over a musical empire that encompasses The W&R Group, a thriving production company, Notation Music, a publishing division which oversees the work of 30 songwriters and whose success include covers by Jennifer Lopez, Marc Anthony, and Celine Dion, and two state of the art recording studios. Since the late 1980s, when he masterminded a string of hits for newcomer Taylor Dayne, Wake has been a highly successful producer and remixer. Among the projects he has been involved in are Mariah Carey's hit "Someday" and Jennifer Lopez's "Love Don't Cost A Thing." He produced and remixed four multi-platinum Celine Dion albums, and scored a Grammy Award for producing the multi-platinum soundtrack to the film "Chicago: The Musical."

Source: Polyphonic HMI.

Exhibit 2 Polyphonic's Technology: The Basics

- Polyphonic considered 25 characteristics of music, including beat, chord progression, duration, fullness of sound, harmony, melody, octave, pitch, rhythm, sonic brilliance, and tempo.
- In a process known as "spectral deconvolution," it isolated each of the patterns in a song, compared them on an appropriate scale, and scored each song accordingly. For example, for tempo, the process could be depicted as follows:

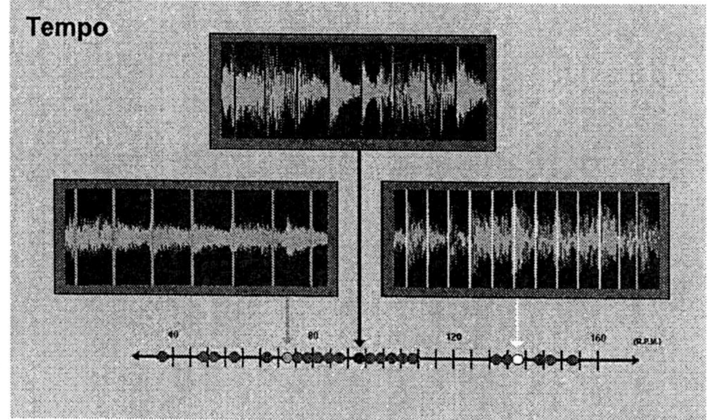

The figure shows three fragments of songs, each with a distinct temporal pattern and each scored accordingly. As indicated on the scale (where each dot represents one song), the one on the left has the slowest, and the one on the right the fastest pace.

- Based on its scores on the characteristics, each song was mapped onto a multidimensional grid called the "music universe." The below figure illustrates the process for two characteristics (i.e., two dimensions), namely tempo and duration:

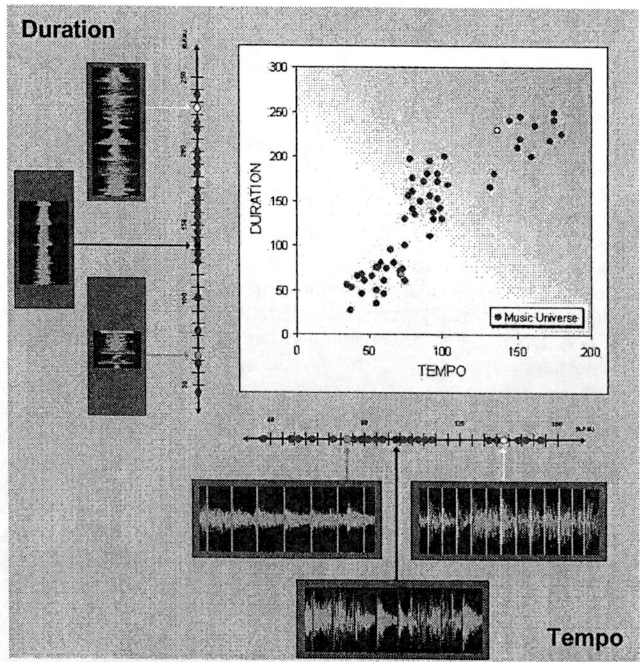

Source: Polyphonic HMI.

Exhibit 3a Regions' Share of Music Sales, 2002

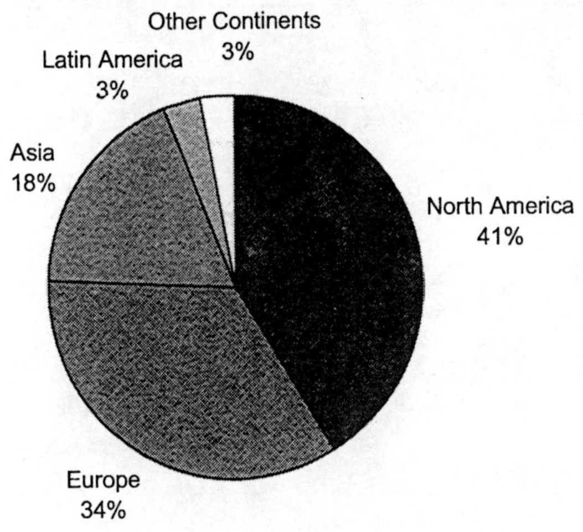

Source: Adapted from International Federation of the Phonographic Industry (IFPI).

Exhibit 3b Top 10 Music Markets, by Retail Value, 2002

	Units (in millions)						Retail Value ($ millions)	Annual Growth in Unit Sales
	Singles	LPs[a]	MCs[b]	CDs	DVD	VHS		
U.S.	8.4	1.7	32.4	803.3	10.7	3.5	12,609	-10.4%
Japan	77.1	2.2	4.6	228.9	11.0	2.1	5,001	-9.9%
U.K.	52.5	2.2	1.9	221.6	3.6	1.5	2,936	-0.9%
Germany	39.0	1.1	14.3	179.4	3.8	3.3	2,091	-4.7%
France	40.5	0.5	5.0	130.4	3.1	0.8	2,070	3.1%
Canada	0.6	-	1.1	57.0	1.6	1.2	621	-5.4%
Italy	3.5	0.0	3.4	36.8	0.4	0.2	565	9.3%
Spain	2.2	0.0	2.4	61.7	0.5	0.0	551	-17.9%
Australia	11.9	0.0	0.6	49.2	2.4	0.2	532	-3.0%
Mexico	0.6	0.0	2.9	51.1	-	0.9	462	-3.3%
Top 10 Markets	**236.3**	**7.7**	**68.6**	**1819.4**	**37.1**	**13.7**	**22,442**	
All Markets	**265.0**	**8.6**	**478.9**	**2,247.1**	**63.6**	**16.1**	**32,281**	

Source: Adapted from International Federation of the Phonographic Industry (IFPI).

[a] LP denotes "long-playing phonograph record."

[b] MC denotes "microcassette."

Exhibit 4 U.S. Music Manufacturers' Unit Shipments and Dollar Value (in millions)

	1994	1995	1996	1997	1998	1999	2000	2001	2002
CD Album									
Units Shipped	662	723	779	753	847	939	943	882	803
Dollar Value[a]	8,465	9,377	9,935	9,915	11,416	12,816	13,215	12,909	12,044
CD Single									
Units Shipped	9	22	43	67	56	56	34	17	5
Dollar Value	56	111	184	273	213	222	143	79	20
Cassette									
Units Shipped	345	273	225	173	159	124	76	45	31
Dollar Value	2,976	2,304	1,905	1,523	1,420	1,062	626	363	210
Music Video									
Units Shipped	11	13	17	19	26	17	15	10	4
Dollar Value	231	220	236	324	496	311	202	138	52
DVD Audio									
Units Shipped	-	-	-	-	-	-	-	0	0
Dollar Value	-	-	-	-	-	-	-	6	9
DVD Video									
Units Shipped	-	-	-	-	1	3	3	8	11
Dollar Value	-	-	-	-	12	66	80	191	236
Other[b]									
Units Shipped	106	96	90	72	60	39	23	16	9
Dollar Value	571	528	510	527	650	419	261	191	96
Total Units[c]	**1,123**	**1,113**	**1,137**	**1,063**	**1,124**	**1,161**	**1,079**	**969**	**860**
Total Value	**12,068**	**12,320**	**12,534**	**12,237**	**13,711**	**14,585**	**14,324**	**13,741**	**12,614**

Source: Adapted from Recording Industry Association of America (RIAA).

[a]Dollar value reflects the total suggested retail list prices of shipments.

[b]Includes cassette single, LP/EP, and vinyl single.

[c]Total units and total value include shipments to retail and direct and special markets.

Exhibit 5 Profile of Music Consumers[a]

	1994	1995	1996	1997	1998	1999	2000	2001	2002
What genre was purchased?									
Rock	35.1	33.5	32.6	32.5	25.7	25.2	24.8	24.4	24.7
Rap/Hip-Hop[b]	7.9	6.7	8.9	10.1	9.7	10.8	12.9	11.4	13.8
R&B/Urban[c]	9.6	11.3	12.1	11.2	12.8	10.5	9.7	10.6	11.2
Country	16.3	16.7	14.7	14.4	14.1	10.8	10.7	10.5	10.7
Pop	10.3	10.1	9.3	9.4	10.0	10.3	11.0	12.1	9.0
Religious[d]	3.3	3.1	4.3	4.5	6.3	5.1	4.8	6.7	6.7
Classical	3.7	2.9	3.4	2.8	3.3	3.5	2.7	3.2	3.1
Jazz	3.0	3.0	3.3	2.8	1.9	3.0	2.9	3.4	3.2
Soundtracks	1.0	0.9	0.8	1.2	1.7	0.8	0.7	1.4	1.1
Oldies	0.8	1.0	0.8	0.8	0.7	0.7	0.9	0.8	0.9
New Age	1.0	0.7	0.7	0.8	0.6	0.5	0.5	1.0	0.5
Children's	0.4	0.5	0.7	0.9	0.4	0.4	0.6	0.5	0.4
Other[e]	5.3	7.0	5.2	5.7	7.9	9.1	8.3	7.9	8.1
In which format?									
Full-length CDs	58.4	65.0	68.4	70.2	74.8	83.2	89.3	89.2	90.5
Full-length cassettes	32.1	25.1	19.3	18.2	14.8	8.0	4.9	3.4	2.4
Singles (all types)	7.4	7.5	9.3	9.3	6.8	5.4	2.5	2.4	1.9
Music videos/video DVDs	0.8	0.9	1.0	0.6	1.0	0.9	0.8	1.1	0.7
DVD audio	NA	NA	NA	NA	NA	NA	NA	1.1	1.3
Digital download	NA	NA	NA	NA	NA	NA	NA	0.2	0.5
Vinyl LPs	0.8	0.5	0.6	0.7	0.7	0.5	0.5	0.6	0.7
Through which channel?									
Record store	53.3	52.0	49.9	51.8	50.8	44.5	42.4	42.5	36.8
Other store	26.7	28.2	31.5	31.9	34.4	38.3	40.8	42.4	50.7
Tape/record club	15.1	14.3	14.3	11.6	9.0	7.9	7.6	6.1	4.0
TV, newspaper, magazine ad or 800 number	3.4	4.0	2.9	2.7	2.9	2.5	2.4	3.0	2.0
Internet[f]	NA	NA	NA	0.3	1.1	2.4	3.2	2.9	3.4

Source: Adapted from Recording Industry Association of America (RIAA).

[a] Peter Hart Research conducts a national telephone survey of past-month music buyers (over 2,900 per year). Data from the survey is weighted by age and sex and then projected to reflect the U.S. population age 10 and over. The reliability of the data is +/– 1.8% at a 95% confidence level. With respect to genre, consumers were asked to classify their music purchases; they are not assigned a particular category by Hart Research.

[b] "Rap": Includes rap and hip-hop.

[c] "R&B": Includes R&B, blues, dance, disco, funk, fusion, Motown, reggae, soul.

[d] "Religious": Includes Christian, gospel, inspirational, religious, and spiritual.

[e] "Other": Includes ethnic, standards, big band, swing, Latin, electronic, instrumental, comedy, humor, spoken word, exercise, language, folk, and holiday music.

[f] "Internet": Does not include record club purchases made over the Internet.

Exhibit 6 Major Record Companies' Share of Music Sales (2002)

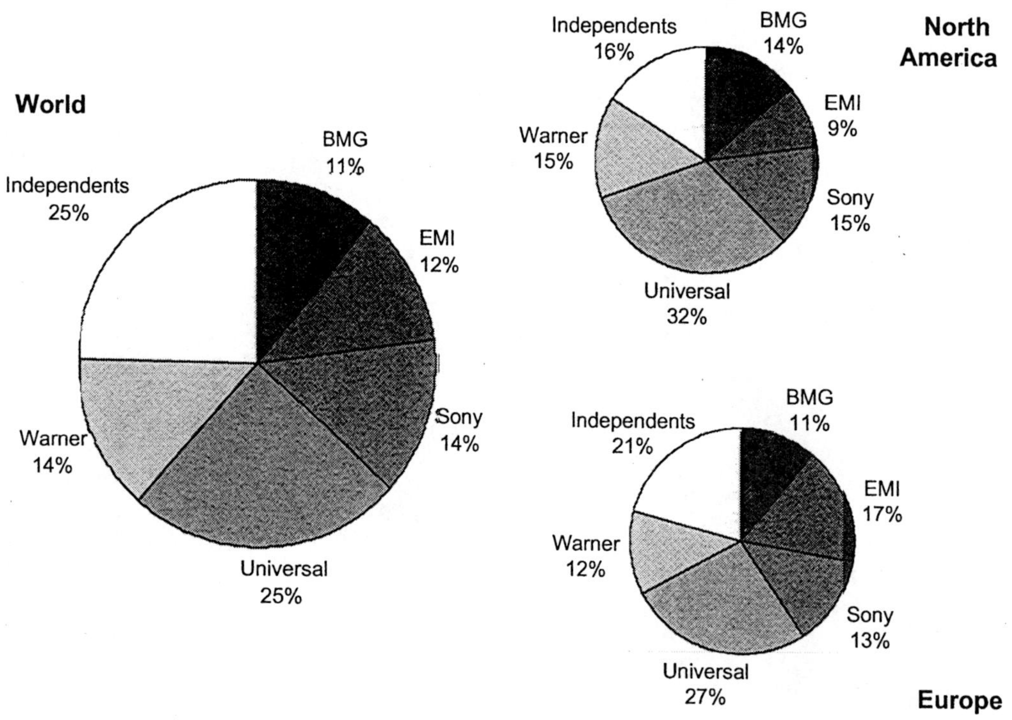

Source: Adapted from International Federation of the Phonographic Industry (IFPI).

Exhibit 7a Top 25 Albums in the U.S. in 2002

#	Album	Artist	Label	Unit Sales
1	The Eminem Show	Eminem	Web/Aftermath/Interscope	7,608,000
2	Nellyville	Nelly	Fo'Reel/Universal	4,916,000
3	Let Go	Avril Lavigne	Arista	4,121,000
4	Home	Dixie Chicks	Monument/Columbia/CRG	3,690,000
5	8 Mile	Soundtrack	Shady/Interscope	3,498,000
6	Missundaztood	Pink	Arista	3,145,000
7	Ashanti	Ashanti	Murder Inc./AJM/IDJMG	3,100,000
8	Drive	Alan Jackson	Arista Nashville/RLG	3,055,000
9	Up!	Shania Twain	Mercury Nashville	2,909,000
10	O Brother, Where Art Thou?	Soundtrack	Lost Highway/Mercury/IDJMG	2,736,000
11	Come Away With Me	Norah Jones	Blue Note/Capitol	2,661,000
12	A New Day Has Come	Celine Dion	Epic	2,645,000
13	Josh Groban	Josh Groban	143/Respire/Warner Bros.	2,569,000
14	Now That's What I Call Music 9	Various Artists	Universal/EMI/Zomba/Sony/UMRG	2,451,000
15	Elvis 30 #1 Hits	Elvis Presley	RCA	2,445,000
16	Weathered	Creed	Wind-Up	2,338,000
17	Hybrid Theory	Linkin Park	Warner Bros.	2,139,000
18	Cry	Faith Hill	Warner Bros. Nashville/WRN	2,089,000
19	Come Clean	Puddle of Mudd	Flawless/Geffen/Interscope	2,071,000
20	Unleashed	Toby Keith	Dreamworks Nashville/Interscope	2,019,000
21	No Shoes No Shirt No Problems	Kenny Chesney	BNA/RLG	2,001,000
22	Word Of Mouf	Ludacris	Disturbing Tha Peace/Def Jam	1,977,000
23	Laundry Service	Shakira	Epic	1,951,000
24	Silver Side Up	Nickelback	Roadrunner/IDJMG	1,921,000
25	Room For Squares	John Mayer	Aware/Columbia/CRG	1,856,000

Source: Adapted from *Billboard Magazine*.

Exhibit 7b Top 25 Singles in the U.S. in 2002

#	Song	Artist	Label
1	How You Remind Me	Nickelback	Roadrunner/IDJMG
2	Foolish	Ashanti	Murder Inc./AJM/IDJMG
3	Hot In Herre	Nelly	Fo' Reel/Universal/UMRG
4	Dilemma	Nelly Featuring Kelly Rowland	Fa' Rell/Universal/UMRG
5	Wherever You Will Go	The Coiling	RCA
6	A Thousand Miles	Vanessa Carlton	A&M/Interscope
7	In The End	Linkin Park	Warner Bros.
8	What's Luv?	Fat Joe Featuring Ashanti	Terror Squad/Atlantic
9	U Got It Bad	Usher	Arista
10	Blurry	Puddle of Mudd	Flawless/Geffen/Interscope
11	Complicated	Avril Lavigne	Arista
12	Always On Time	Ja Rule Featuring Ashanti	Murder Inc./Def Jam/IDJMG
13	Ain't It Funny	Jennifer Lopez Featuring Ja Rule	Epic
14	The Middle	Jimmy Eat World	DreamWorks
15	I Need A Girl (Part One)	P. Diddy Featuring Usher & Loon	Bad Boy/Arista
16	U Don't Have To Call	Usher	Arista
17	Family Affair	Mary J. Blige	MCA
18	I Need A Girl (Part Two)	P. Diddy & Ginuwine	Bad Boy/Arista
19	Gangsta Lovin'	Eve Featuring Alicia Keys	Ruff Ryders/Interscope
20	My Sacrifice	Creed	Wind-up
21	Without Me	Eminem	Web/Aftermath/Interscope
22	Hero	Enrique Iglesias	Interscope
23	All You Wanted	Michelle Branch	Maverick/Warner Bros.
24	Get The Party Started	Pink	Arista
25	Hero	Chad Kroeger Featuring Josey Scott	Columbia/Roadrunner/IDJMG

Source: Adapted from *Billboard Magazine.*

Exhibit 8 Hit Song Science: A Sample Report[a]

HSS Analysis Report
Blue Note Records

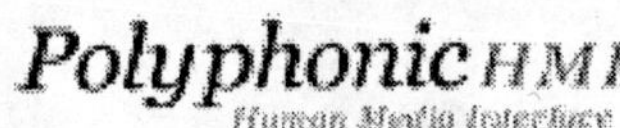

Artist: Norah Jones
Album: Come Away With Me

Album Summary:

Track		HSS Song Rating	HSS Classic Hit Rating	HSS Recentness Rating	HSS Sales Rating
(01) Norah Jones - Don't Know Why		7,21	6,07	6,18	NA
(02) Norah Jones - Seven Years		4,55	5,65	7,97	NA
(03) Norah Jones - Cold Cold Heart	▼	3,31	4,68	7,39	NA
(04) Norah Jones - Feelin' The Same Way		7,29	6,18	6,79	NA
(05) Norah Jones - Come Away With Me		6,97	5,73	6,85	NA
(06) Norah Jones - Shoot The Moon		7,15	6,01	6,37	NA
(07) Norah Jones - Turn Me On		7,32	5,96	7,37	NA
(08) Norah Jones - Lonestar		7,26	5,90	6,07	NA
(09) Norah Jones - I've Got To See You Again	▲	7,59	5,95	5,89	NA
(10) Norah Jones - Painter Song		7,12	5,39	6,97	NA
(11) Norah Jones - One Flight Down		6,13	4,97	6,53	NA
(12) Norah Jones - Nightingale		6,82	4,86	4,53	NA
(13) Norah Jones - The Long Day Is Over		6,29	5,72	7,12	NA
(14) Norah Jones - The Nearness Of You		7,03	5,58	7,04	NA
Global Album Rating:		6,68	5,64	6,70	NA

Key
▲ - Top Rated Song
▼ - Bottom Rated Song

[a]A song that scores an **HSS Song Rating** of 7.0 or above is considered to have mathematical hit potential. A song with a score between 6.75 and 6.99 is considered to have the ability to perform in the market with extra promotion effort and investment. A high HSS Song Rating combined with an **HSS Classic Hit Rating** of 5.5 or greater is considered a song with staying power, which is determined by comparing it to characteristics of classic hits. Finally, a score of 7.0 or higher on the **HSS Recentness Rating** is considered to be a good indicator of its hit potential based on characteristics of recent hits.

Exhibit 8 (continued)

HSS Analysis Report
Blue Note Records

Polyphonic HMI
Human Media Interface

Artist: Norah Jones
Album: Come Away With Me

Song Detail:

Song: Don't Know Why

HSS Song Rating:	7,21
HSS Recentness Rating:	6,18
HSS Sales Rating:	NA
HSS Classic Hit Rating:	6,07

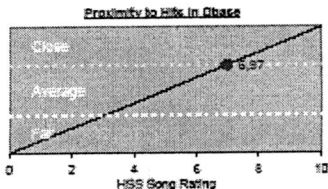

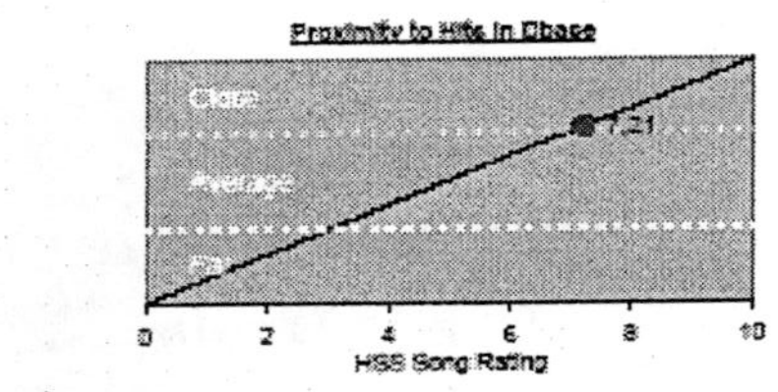

HSS Song Rating: 7,21

Proximity to Hit Songs:

Hit Song	Affinity Value	Single Sales To Date	Album Sales To Date	Release Date
1. Voices Of Theory -- Say It	0,42	0	NA	23/05/1998
2. Lee Ann Womack With Sons Of The Desert -- I Hope You Dance	0,59	0	NA	27/01/2001
3. LeAnn Rimes -- Can't Fight The Moonlight	0,59	0	NA	09/09/2000
4. Boyz II Men -- Thank You In Advance	0,62	0	NA	30/12/2000
5. Shania Twain -- From This Moment On	0,65	0	NA	12/05/1998
6. Nine Inch Nails -- The Day The World Went Away	0,67	0	NA	08/07/1999
7. Mo Thugs Family -- Ghetto Cowboy	0,71	0	NA	21/11/1998

HSS Recentness Rating:	6,18
HSS Sales Rating:	NA

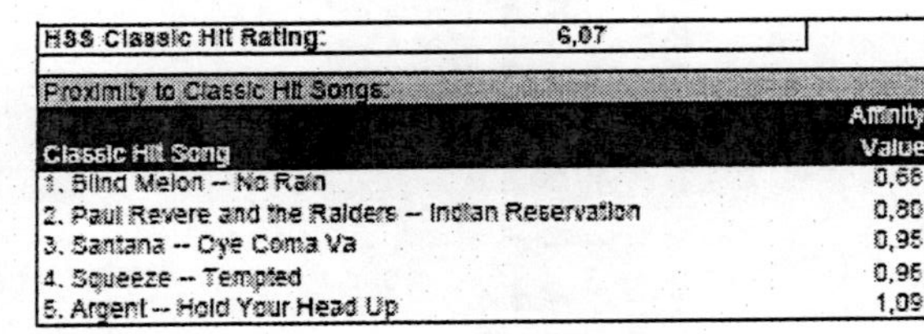

HSS Classic Hit Rating: 6,07

Proximity to Classic Hit Songs:

Classic Hit Song	Affinity Value
1. Blind Melon -- No Rain	0,66
2. Paul Revere and the Raiders -- Indian Reservation	0,80
3. Santana -- Oye Coma Va	0,95
4. Squeeze -- Tempted	0,96
5. Argent -- Hold Your Head Up	1,09

HSS Analysis Report
Blue Note Records

Polyphonic HMI
Human Media Interface

norah jones

Artist: Norah Jones
Album: Come Away With Me

Song Detail:

Song: Come Away With Me

HSS Song Rating:	6,97
HSS Recentness Rating:	6,85
HSS Sales Rating:	NA
HSS Classic Hit Rating:	5,73

Proximity to Hits in Dbase
Close
Average
Far
6,97
0 2 4 6 8 10
HSS Song Rating

HSS Song Rating: 6,97

Proximity to Hit Songs:

Hit Song	Affinity Value	Single Sales To Date	Album Sales To Date	Release Date
1. Brian McKnight -- Win	0,27	0	NA	23/12/2000
2. Brandy Moss-Scott -- Bye-Bye Baby	0,48	0	NA	10/06/2001
3. Sarah McLachlan -- Angel	0,51	0	NA	27/02/1999
4. Jessica Andrews -- Unbreakable Heart	0,66	0	NA	29/04/2000
5. Xscape -- The Arms Of The One Who Loves You	0,77	0	NA	05/02/1998
6. Uncle Sam -- I Don't Ever Want To See You Again	0,80	0	NA	01/03/1998
7. R. Kelly -- If I Could Turn Back The Hands Of Time	0,86	0	NA	09/10/1999

HSS Recentness Rating:	6,85
HSS Sales Rating:	NA

HSS Classic Hit Rating: 5,73

Proximity to Classic Hit Songs:

Classic Hit Song	Affinity Value
1. Dave Mason -- The Lonely One	1,11
2. Culture Club -- Do You Really Want To Hurt Me	1,51
3. Chris DeBurgh -- Lady In Red	1,52
4. Argent -- Hold Your Head Up	1,79
5. Poco -- You Better Think Twice	1,81

Exhibit 8 (continued)

HSS Analysis Report
Blue Note Records

Polyphonic HMI
Human Media Interface

norah jones

Artist: Norah Jones
Album: Come Away With Me

Song Detail:

Song: Cold Cold Heart

HSS Song Rating:	**3,31**
HSS Recentness Rating:	7,39
HSS Sales Rating:	NA
HSS Classic Hit Rating:	4,68

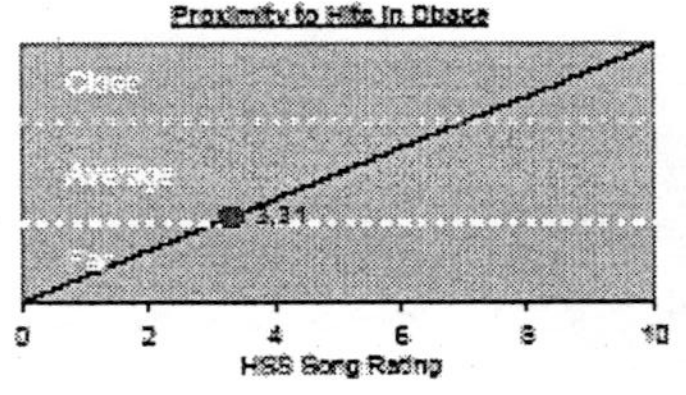

HSS Song Rating: 3,31

Proximity to Hit Songs:

Hit Song	Affinity Value	Single Sales To Date	Album Sales To Date	Release Date
1. JT Money Featuring Sole -- Who Dat	1,14	0	NA	24/04/1999
2. Cuban Link -- Flowers For The Dead	1,33	0	NA	24/06/2000
3. Truth Hurts Featuring Rakim -- Addictive	1,41	0	NA	05/04/2002
4. Pink -- There You Go	1,57	0	NA	03/04/2000
5. Petey Pablo -- Raise Up	1,63	0	NA	08/11/2001
6. Sole Featuring JT Money & Kandi -- 4, 5, 6	1,76	0	NA	18/12/1999
7. R.L., Snoop Dogg & Lil' Kim -- Do U Wanna Roll (Dolittle Theme)	1,80	0	NA	

HSS Recentness Rating:	7,39
HSS Sales Rating:	NA

HSS Classic Hit Rating: 4,68

Proximity to Classic Hit Songs:

Classic Hit Song	Affinity Value
1. Loggins and Messina -- House At Pooh Corner	2,17
2. The Buggles -- Video Killed The Radio Star	3,73
3. Spirit -- Nature's Way	4,07
4. Blood, Sweat & Tears -- You've Made Me So Very Happy	4,24
5. Jim Diamond -- I Should Have Known Better	4,27

HSS Analysis Report
Blue Note Records

Polyphonic HMI
Human Media Interface

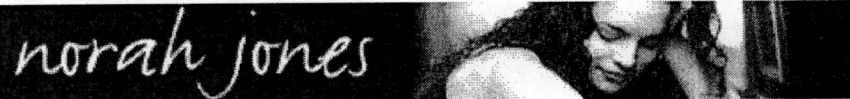

norah jones

Artist: Norah Jones
Album: Come Away With Me

Song Detail:

Song: I've Got To See You Again

HSS Song Rating:	**7,59**
HSS Recentness Rating:	5,89
HSS Sales Rating:	NA
HSS Classic Hit Rating:	5,95

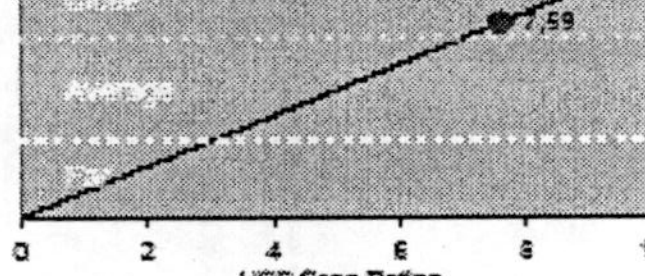

HSS Song Rating: 7,59

Proximity to Hit Songs:

Hit Song	Affinity Value	Single Sales To Date	Album Sales To Date	Release Date
1. Christina Aguilera -- What A Girl Wants	0,22	0	NA	15/01/2000
2. Chico DeBarge -- Give You What You Want (Fa Sure)	0,31	0	NA	23/10/1999
3. Janet Featuring BLACKstreet -- I Get Lonely	0,39	0	NA	23/05/1998
4. Xscape -- The Arms Of The One Who Loves You	0,41	0	NA	05/02/1998
5. Jon B. -- They Don't Know	0,49	0	NA	
6. Travis Tritt -- Best Of Intentions	0,49	0	NA	16/09/2000
7. All Saints -- Never Ever	0,50	0	NA	25/07/1998

HSS Recentness Rating:	5,89
HSS Sales Rating:	NA

HSS Classic Hit Rating: 5,95

Proximity to Classic Hit Songs:

Classic Hit Song	Affinity Value
1. The Hollies -- The Air That I Breathe	1,24
2. Chris DeBurgh -- Lady in Red	1,25
3. Richard Marx -- Hazard	1,26
4. Wang Chung -- Dance Hall Days	1,29
5. Spirit -- Nature's Way	1,30

Source: Polyphonic HMI.

Exhibit 9 The A&R Registry: A Sample Page

UNIVERSAL UNI
8 St. James Square — 44-207-747-4000
London SW1Y 4JU England — 44-207-747-4470
www.universalmusic.co.uk — **ALL**

CONTACT, TITLE — DIRECT

Max Hole *SR VP A&R* — 44-207-747-4298
ASSISTANT RONA LEVENE — 44-207-747-4470
max.hole@umusic.com

UNIVERSAL UNI
1755 Broadway 7th Floor — 212-373-0600
New York, NY 10019-3743 — 212-373-0688
ALL

CONTACT, TITLE — DIRECT

Mel Lewinter *CEO* — 212-373-0775
ASSISTANT JULIE BEARDON — 212-489-8594
mel.lewinter@umusic.com

Monte Lipman *PRESIDENT* — 212-373-0717
ASSISTANT CHRISTINA & AMANDA — 212-373-0678
monte.lipman@umusic.com

Bruce Carbone *EX VP A&R* — 212-841-8677
ASSISTANT ANGELA SPELLMAN — 212-373-0688
bruce.carbone@umusic.com

Kevin Law *SR VP A&R/STAFF PRODUCER* — 212-841-8647
ASSISTANT JENNIFER HAVEY — 212-373-0726
kevin.law@umusic.com

Lee Chesnut *VP A&R* — 212-373-0769
ASSISTANT LEAH LANDON — 212-373-0760
lee.chesnut@umusic.com

Tse Williams *VP A&R - URBAN* — 212-373-0762
ASSISTANT GENEVIEVE ZARAGOZA — 212-373-0768
tse.williams@umusic.com

Dino Delvaille *VP A&R - URBAN* — 212-373-0767
ASSISTANT TORREY TARALLI — 212-373-0699
dino.delvaille@umusic.com

Tabari Sturdivant *DIRECTOR A&R* — 212-373-0748
ASSISTANT GENIEVE ZARA — 212-373-0760
tabari.sturdivant@umusic.com

Sinji Suzuki *ASSOC DIR A&R* — 212-331-2576
ASSISTANT LEAH LANDON — 212-841-8012
sinji.suzuki@umusic.com

Dan Mc Carron *MANAGER A&R* — 212-373-0682
dan.mccarron@umusic.com — 212-373-0726

Sal Guastella *MANAGER A&R* — 212-641-8616
sal.guastella@umusic.com — 212-331-2742

Jennifer Havey *A&R COOR.* — 212-373-0694
jennifer.havey@umusic.com — 212-373-0726

Eloise Bryan *VP A&R ADMINISTRATION* — 212-373-0742
ASSISTANT ASHLEY WHITE — 212-830-0524
eloise.bryan@umusic.com

Meredeth Oliver *A&R ADMINISTRATION* — 212-373-0773
meredath.oliver@umusic.com — 212-331-2740

Nina Freeman *A&R ADMINISTRATION* — 212-830-0802
nina.freeman@umusic.com — 212-331-2740

Jill Rosenthal *A&R ADMINISTRATION* — 212-373-0634
jill.rosenthal@umusic.com — 212-331-2740

UNIVERSAL UNI
9440 Santa Monica Blvd Penthouse — 310-285-2716
Beverly Hills, CA 90210-4610 — 310-285-2616
ALL

CONTACT, TITLE — DIRECT

Jolene Cherry *SR VP A&R* — 310-285-2717
ASSISTANT AMY NADEAU — 310-285-2917
jolene.cherry@umusic.com

Meg Hansen *MANAGER A&R* — 310-285-2716
ASSISTANT AMY NADEAU — 310-285-2616
meg.hansen@umusic.com

UNIVERSAL CANADA UNI
2450 Victoria Park Ave — 416-718-4000
Toronto, ON M2J 4A2 Canada — 416-718-4224
www.umusic.ca — **ALL**

CONTACT, TITLE — DIRECT

Allan Reid *SR VP* — 416-718-4070
allan.reid@umusic.com — 416-718-4224

Dave Porter *DIRECTOR A&R* — 416-718-4045
dave.porter@umusic.com — 416-718-4224

Shawn Marino *INT'L A&R* — 416-718-4066
shawn.marino@umusic.com — 416-718-4224

David Cox *A&R REP* — 416-718-4239
david.cox@umusic.com — 416-718-4224

Ted Selo *A&R DEPT ASST* — 416-718-4048
ted.selo@umusic.com — 416-718-4224

Susan Brearton *MANAGER A&R ADMINISTRATION* — 416-718-4072
susan.brearton@umusic.com — 416-718-4224

UNIVERSAL CLASSICS UNI
825 8th Ave 19th Fl — 212-333-8000
New York, NY 10019-7472 — 212-333-8060
CLASSICAL / JAZZ

CONTACT, TITLE — DIRECT

Evelyn Morgan *ASSOC DIR A&R ADMIN* — 212-830-0586
evelyn.morgan@umusic.com — 212-830-0591

UNIVERSAL CLASSICS GROUP UNI
8 St. James Square — 44-207-747-4004
London SW1Y 4JU England — 44-207-747-4475
CLASSICAL / JAZZ

CONTACT, TITLE — DIRECT

Chris Roberts *PRESIDENT* — 44-207-747-4004
ASSISTANT PEGGY BONNAVENTURE — 44-207-474-4475
christopher.roberts@umusic.com

UNIVERSAL MUSIC GROUP UNI
1425 Collins Ave — 305-604-1300
Miami Beach, FL 33133-4103 — 305-604-1390
LATIN

CONTACT, TITLE — DIRECT

Jesus Lopez *CEO* — 305-604-1300
ASSISTANT ALEJANDRO MAYA — 305-604-1390
jesus.lopez@umusic.com

UNIVERSAL MUSIC LATINO UNI
420 Lincoln Rd #200 — 305-938-1300
Miami Beach, FL 33139-3030 — 305-938-1389
www.universalmusica.com — **LATIN**

CONTACT, TITLE — DIRECT

John Echevarria *PRESIDENT* — 305-938-1300
ASSISTANT NATALIE MEDINA — 305-938-1389
john.echevarria@umusic.com

Walter Kolm *SR VP A&R* — 305-938-1300
ASSISTANT JOANN ACEVEDO — 305-938-1379
walter.kolm@umusic.com

Eddie Fernandez *VP A&R* — 305-938-1300
ASSISTANT LIZ LÓPEZ — 305-938-1379
eddie.fernandez@umusic.com

UNIVERSAL SOUTH
40 Music Square West — 615-259-5300
Nashville, TN 37203-4373 — 615-259-5301
www.universalsouth.com — **COUNTRY/POP**

CONTACT, TITLE — DIRECT

Tony Brown *SENIOR PARTNER* — 615-259-5302
ASSISTANT AMY RUSSELL — 615-259-5301
amy.russell@umusic.com

Tim Dubois *SENIOR PARTNER* — 615-259-5326
ASSISTANT MARTY CRAIGHEAD — 615-259-5373
tim.dubois@umusic.com

Mike Owens *DIRECTOR A&R* — 615-259-5328
mike.owens@umusic.com — 615-259-5301

Ellen Powers *VP RECORDING ADMIN* — 615-880-7326
ellen.powers@umusic.com — 615-880-7410

UNIVERSAL/ISLAND UNI
22 St. Peters Square — 44-208-910-5000
London W6 9NW England — 44-208-741-0369
www.island.co.uk — **ALL**

CONTACT, TITLE — DIRECT

Lucian Grainge *CEO* — 44-208-910-5006
ASSISTANT CAROLINE FOGAZZA — 44-208-910-5423
lucian.grainge@umusic.com

Nick Gatfield *MD-UNIVERSAL/ISLAND* — 44-208-910-3201
ASSISTANT SOFIE RUSSELL — 44-208-741-0206
nick.gatfield@umusic.com

Paul Adam *MD-ISLAND* — 44-208-910-3370
ASSISTANT WENDY AINSLIE — 44-208-910-4799
paul.adam@umusic.com

Chris Rock *DIRECTOR A&R - URBAN* — 44-208-910-3391
ASSISTANT AARON BOAKYE — 44-208-910-3224
chris.rock@umusic.com

Dave Gilmour *SR A&R MANAGER* — 44-208-910-3342
ASSISTANT DOMINIC BASTYRA — 44-208-741-0369
dave.gilmour@umusic.com

Darcus Beese *SR A&R MANAGER* — 44-208-910-3264
ASSISTANT DOMINIC BASTYRA — 44-208-741-0369
darcus.beese@umusic.com

Louis Bloom *A&R REP* — 44-208-910-3302
ASSISTANT DOMINIC BASTYRA — 44-208-741-0369
louis.bloom@umusic.com

74 **THE MUSIC BUSINESS REGISTRY, INC.** 7510 SUNSET BLVD., PMB 1041, LOS ANGELES, CA USA • PHONE: 818-995-7458 • FAX: 818-995-7459 • WWW.MUSICREGISTRY.COM • E-MAIL: INFO@MUSICREGISTRY.COM

Source: The Music Business Registry, Inc.

BRIEF CASES

2073
JUNE 7, 2007

KAREN MARTINSEN FLEMING

Natureview Farm

It was a crisp Vermont morning in February 2000. Christine Walker, vice president of marketing for Natureview Farm, Inc., a small yogurt manufacturer, paused to collect her thoughts from a recently adjourned meeting with the other members of Natureview's senior management team. The team faced a challenging situation—that of finding a path to grow revenues by over 50% before the end of 2001. The central focus of the meeting was whether Natureview should expand into the supermarket channel in order to meet its revenue goal—a move which would represent a major departure from the company's established channel strategy and one which would impact every aspect of Natureview's business.

Despite the growth that Natureview Farm had been able to achieve since it began in 1989, the company had long struggled to maintain a consistent level of profitability. Jim Wagner, hired in 1996 as chief financial officer (CFO), had developed financial controls that brought steady profitability to the company, in line with dairy industry standards. No one at the firm had questioned Wagner's recommendation in 1997 that Natureview arrange for an equity infusion from a venture capital (VC) firm to fund strategic investments. However, the VC firm now needed to cash out of its investment in Natureview. Natureview management had to find another investor or position itself for acquisition, and increasing revenues was critical in order to attain the highest possible valuation[1] for the company. Wagner had advised the management that it would be critical to grow Natureview's revenues to $20 million before the end of 2001—a large jump from the $13 million the company reported in 1999. (See **Exhibit 1** for 1999 income statement.) While Wagner realized the bind Natureview was in, alternative financing would be extremely difficult until the VCs cashed out.

The previous day, Natureview's Chief Executive Officer (CEO) Barry Landers had admonished his management team that he needed a plan:

[1] Organic foods companies similar to Natureview were frequently valued on a multiple of revenues rather than profit or cash flow because these VC firms were investing in order to generate significant revenue growth. Typical sales multiples ranged from 1.5 times to 2.1 times revenue, so maximizing overall revenue was critical to achieving a higher valuation by potential investors.

Karen Martinsen Fleming prepared this case solely as a basis for class discussion and not as an endorsement, a source of primary data, or an illustration of effective or ineffective management. An MBA from Harvard Business School, she has held marketing management positions at major consumer products companies. She currently teaches marketing courses and runs a consulting business in Vermont.

This case, though based on real events, is fictionalized, and any resemblance to actual persons or entities is coincidental. There are occasional references to actual companies in the narration.

> We have to come up with a plan that takes us to $20 million in revenues by the end of 2001. This immediate pressure to grow the top line is going to help us get to the size that we have long aspired to be. As you think through our options, though, you can't lose sight of what has made this company great. I'm proud of the strong brand we've built and what it represents in our marketplace, and I'm even more proud of the unconventional route we've taken to get here. We owe it to our customers, our suppliers, and our distribution partners to make the right strategic choices regarding the revenue growth objective before us.

Those words weighed heavily on the Natureview management team. The first meeting to address the CEO's challenge had not gone well. After much analysis and discussion, the team members were sharply divided.

Natureview Farm's Early Years and the Current Situation

Founded in 1989, Natureview Farm manufactured and marketed refrigerated cup yogurt under the Natureview Farm brand name. The yogurt was manufactured at the Natureview Farm production facility in Cabot, Vermont. The key to the Natureview yogurt flavor and texture was the family yogurt recipe developed by the company's founder. The recipe used natural ingredients and a special process that gave the yogurt its unique smooth, creamy texture without the artificial thickeners used by the major U.S. yogurt brands—Dannon, Yoplait, and Breyers. The company used milk from cows untreated with rGBH, an artificial growth hormone that increased milk production. Because of the special process and ingredients, Natureview Farm's yogurt's average shelf life (the length of time the yogurt stayed fresh) was 50 days. Most of the large competitors' products had a 30-day shelf life, requiring them to build multiple production plants to reduce shipping time to their distributors.

In 10 years, Natureview Farm's revenues had grown from less than $100,000 to $13 million. The company first entered the market with 8-ounce (oz.) and 32-oz. cup sizes of yogurt in two flavors—plain and vanilla. Based on its early success, the company added flavors to both sizes. The 8-oz. flavors were developed by putting fruit puree into the bottom of the cup and adding plain yogurt on top. Producing this "fruit on the bottom" yogurt product required new equipment, but it allowed the brand to expand its product offerings to help increase revenues. Because of the emphasis on natural ingredients and its strong reputation for high quality and great taste, the Natureview brand grew quickly to national distribution and shared leadership in the natural foods channel. This was aided by creative, low-cost "guerilla marketing" tactics that worked well in this channel.

By 2000, Natureview Farm produced twelve refrigerated yogurt flavors in 8-oz. cups (86% revenues) and four flavors in 32-oz. cups (14% revenues). The company had also started exploring multipack yogurt products (children's 4-oz. cups and yogurt packaged in tubes). Natureview shipped its yogurt to retailers in cases, with a typical case containing 12 cups for the 8-oz. and 6 cups for the 32-oz. product lines, respectively. (If the company were to expand into multipack products, their cases would contain four packages.) As a major brand in the natural foods channel, Natureview Farm had developed strong relationships with leading natural foods retailers, including the chains Whole Foods ($1.57 billion revenues in 1999) and Wild Oats ($721 million revenues). The organic foods market, worth $6.5 billion in 1999, was predicted to grow to $13.3 billion in 2003.[2]

[2] "A Step Closer To Defining 'Organic,'" *Natural Foods Merchandiser* 12: 43 (December 1999).

The Refrigerated Yogurt Category and the Yogurt Consumer

Yogurt is a dairy product, the result of milk fermented in a carefully controlled environment. Special bacteria added to the milk change its texture and give yogurt its unique health properties—it is a good source of calcium and improves digestion. Plain yogurt is typically made from whole, low-fat, or nonfat milk without additional flavoring ingredients. Flavored yogurt has sugar and either artificial flavorings or natural fruit (or both) added.

In 1999, total U.S. retail sales of refrigerated yogurt reached $1.8 billion and sales volume was just over 2.3 billion units. The market was fairly concentrated with the top four competitors—Dannon, Yoplait, Breyers, and Columbo—having the dominant share and the top two competitors controlling over 50% of the market. In 1999, when sales through the dominant two distribution channels—supermarkets and natural foods stores—were combined, supermarkets sold 97% of all yogurt consumed, and natural food stores sold the balance. Yogurt revenues were also generated through other channels, including warehouse clubs, convenience stores, drug stores, and mass merchandisers. However, Natureview did not consider entry into these channels because, relative to the supermarket channel, these channels offered limited revenue generation potential; the company's product was not a strong fit for the narrow product offering afforded to consumers through these channels; and volume requirements were prohibitive in certain channels. Warehouse clubs, for example, required multiple unit packages, 24 cups of 8-oz. cups per carton, but Natureview did not view its brand as developed enough to generate the consumer demand necessary to meet this volume requirement. In the previous five years, yogurt sales through supermarkets had grown an average of 3% per year, while sales through natural food stores had grown 20% per year. Because consumers were increasingly interested in natural and organic foods, well-managed natural foods retailers were thriving. Yogurt was an important product in the overall dairy portfolio of natural foods retailers, since stores earned a higher margin on yogurt than on any other dairy product.

Shoppers at natural foods stores tended to be more educated, earn higher incomes, and be older than the typical supermarket shopper. Forty-six percent of organic food consumers bought organic products at a supermarket, 25% at a small health foods store, and 29% at a natural foods supermarket. Generally, shoppers who purchased organic products, regardless of channel, tended to have higher incomes, have more education, and live in the Northeast and West. Organic dairy products were bought by 74% of heavy organic food buyers and 29% of light organic food buyers. Sixty-seven percent of U.S. households indicated that price was a barrier to their purchase of organic products, and 58% expressed that they would buy more organic product if it were less expensive. Forty-four percent of consumers identified the need for a wider selection of organic product in supermarkets.[3]

Yogurt was consumed by approximately 40% of the U.S. population, with women comprising the majority (over 70%) of yogurt purchases. Factors considered when deciding which yogurt to purchase included package type/size, taste, flavor, price, freshness, ingredients, and whether the product was organic, typically in that order of preference. For natural foods shoppers, the product's ingredients and whether or not the product was organic were more important purchase criteria. Among natural foods shoppers, a product's health-promoting qualities were usually more important than price in the purchase decision.

Regarding consumer product preferences, 6- and 8-oz. yogurt cups were the most popular product sizes, representing 74% of total category supermarket sales in U.S. dollars. This segment was

---

[3] "A Step Closer To Defining 'Organic,'" *Natural Foods Merchandiser* 12: 43 (December 1999); "Organic Products Are On One Third of Shopping Lists Enhanced Title," Research Alert 18(7):5 (April 07, 2000); eBrain Market Research, http://www.ebrain.org/ (2002 survey).

growing 3% per year, but also faced stiff competition. Women primarily bought 8-oz. yogurt cups as a healthy snack or lunch substitute and valued a variety of flavors since most consumers did not "add" anything to this size. By comparison, the next largest segment—multipacks—represented 9% of category sales and was growing by more than 12.5% per year. Children (and their mothers, seeking healthier snack alternatives) were the target of the fastest growing multipacks. These included six-packs of 4-oz. cup servings and the "fun and less messy" tube yogurt, which was squeezed from a flexible plastic tube and could be eaten without a spoon; eight 2-oz. tubes were included in the typical multipack. The last segment, the 32-oz. size, represented 8% of sales and was growing at a modest 2%. Buyers of the 32-oz. size were "heavy" yogurt consumers, who either ate the yogurt plain, added other ingredients (granola, fruit, etc.), or used yogurt in recipes (smoothies, cooking). For the 32-oz. size, the most popular flavors were plain and vanilla, and the most important purchase criteria were brand, expiration date, and price. (See **Exhibit 2** for yogurt market share by segment and region in the supermarket channel.)

Stores typically merchandised yogurt product in their own section within the refrigerated dairy case. The size of the yogurt section varied from store to store, although on average, the yogurt section in a natural foods store was smaller (4' wide by 6' high) than that in a supermarket (8' wide by 6' high). In both channels, the small cups (6-oz. and 8-oz.) were displayed on the upper two shelves, most commonly at eye level—where consumers more often purchased items, research showed. Stores usually put multipacks on the next-lowest shelves and 32-oz. containers in the bottom "well" (the least visible spot).

The Sales and Distribution Process: Supermarket Channel vs. Natural Foods Stores

Supermarket Channel

Large consumer products manufacturers, such as Procter & Gamble and Coca Cola, had dedicated sales forces that called directly on category buyers who ultimately controlled dairy product placement in their stores. By contrast, smaller manufacturers like Natureview Farms used sales brokers to sell their yogurt to both natural foods and supermarket chains. These influential brokers, representing several brands of consumer products, used their relationships to arrange discussions between retail chains, wholesalers, and manufacturers, in addition to performing numerous other services for manufacturers. For these services, brokers charged manufacturers such as Natureview a fee or commission that varied from product to product. For yogurt, the broker's fee was 4% of manufacturer's sales.[4]

If Natureview Farm chose to expand into the supermarket channel, it would depend heavily on its broker's knowledge of promotional and merchandising requirements. For each item or SKU (stock-keeping unit) they carried, supermarket chains aimed to maximize sales volume and inventory turns.

Supermarkets carefully monitored sales trends, especially of new items, by region, area, and store, using sophisticated scanner technology. Their relatively streamlined distribution systems also allowed supermarkets to maintain lower prices. Suppliers to supermarkets typically sent products to a large distribution center, which in turn shipped directly to the supermarket chain's warehouse. This facilitated efficient distribution to the individual stores. At each step, the distributor and the retailer charged a markup on products that flowed through their warehouses or stores. The typical

---

[4] Broker's fees were typically accounted for in SG&A (Sales, General & Administrative) expense.

distributor margin in this channel was 15%, and the typical retailer margin was 27%. These margins were consistent across yogurt product type. A supermarket would charge $0.74 for the same cup of yogurt priced at $0.88 in a natural foods store. (See **Exhibit 3** for manufacturing costs and retail prices by channel.)

In order to sell its yogurt into supermarkets, Natureview would be required to pay a one-time "slotting fee" for each SKU only in the first year it was introduced and then to participate in regular trade promotions—both uncommon practices in the natural foods channel. The supermarket retailer charged this slotting fee in order to set up a slot throughout its distribution system for the new SKU and then monitor its sales trends. If the SKU did not prove profitable for the supermarket within the year, the supermarket would discontinue the product and would require a new slotting fee payment in the event the manufacturer sought reauthorization of the SKU. For refrigerated yogurt, the slotting fee averaged $10,000 per SKU per retail chain. For instance, Natureview would need to pay each supermarket chain $80,000 to introduce eight different flavors in the 8-oz. size.

Once an item became part of a supermarket chain's regular inventory, the chain expected or required the manufacturer to participate in regular trade promotions, usually at least every three months. This meant advertising the product in the weekly sales circular that the supermarket distributed to local households. The cost of trade promotion ads varied widely by region and by size of the advertisement. In the Northeast, Midwest, and Southeast of the U.S., advertisements cost $7,500 for the size typically used by Natureview Farm's competitors. In the West, the same advertisements cost $15,000 per ad per retailer. (Nationally, they cost $8,000 on average.) While these were not significant expenses for larger competitors such as Dannon and Yoplait, both of which spent over $60 million per year in marketing their yogurt products, this was an expensive proposition for smaller manufacturers to match.

Natural Foods Channel

Natural foods chains typically charged higher retail prices for the same products than supermarkets did, due to lower price sensitivity among natural foods customers as well as differences in the distribution system. Distribution in the natural foods channel involved four, instead of three, parties. A manufacturer like Natureview first shipped products to a natural foods wholesaler. The wholesaler shipped the yogurt to a natural foods distributor, who in turn delivered the products to a retailer like Whole Foods. (See **Exhibit 4** for a diagram illustrating the length of each channel to market.) In contrast to supermarket distributors, intermediaries in the natural foods channel would "break cases" (i.e., allow natural foods retailers, who tended to be small stores at the time, organized in few chains) to order fewer items than a full case. Furthermore, natural foods distributors would deliver product to individual stores, and in some instances even stock the shelves and track paperwork. The typical natural foods wholesaler margin was 7%, the distributor margin was 9%, and the retailer margin was 35%. These margins tended to be consistent across yogurt product type. Thus, by the time an 8-oz. cup of yogurt had reached the store shelf in the natural foods channel, it had passed through two distribution points plus the retailer, and the retail price of the 8-oz. cup was $0.88.

In contrast to supermarket chains, natural foods retailers did not charge manufacturers monetary slotting fees, but did require a one-time allotment of one free case of product for every new SKU authorized for distribution in its first year. Aside from the large chains—Whole Foods and Wild Oats—most natural foods stores lacked automated scanner checkout systems to track sales from promotions, and price discounts were usually not necessary to achieve sales targets. The competitors that Natureview faced in the natural foods channel versus the supermarket channel reflected the different business models, consumer audiences, and distribution systems inherent in both channels.

Horizon Organic, flush with cash from a recent initial public offering (IPO), was Natureview's greatest competitor to obtaining supermarket distribution. It produced a full range of organic dairy products and was a national brand in natural foods stores. Brown Cow was a smaller company with a strong regional presence on the West Coast. Brown Cow's yogurt was "all natural," but not organic; Horizon's was organic, but it had a shorter shelf life than Natureview's product. (See **Exhibit 5** for market share by brand.)

The Senior Management Team's Three Options

Back in her office, Christine Walker was considering the three options that the senior management team had proposed to grow Natureview's revenues to $20 million by the end of 2001. Two of the options required Natureview to enter the supermarket channel. While supermarket distribution offered Natureview a potential solution to its revenue requirement, it also presented potential problems that required careful evaluation.[5] She wondered what would it really take to thrive in the supermarket channel. The ripple effect of this decision could shake Natureview to its core, changing all aspects of Walker's job, from how she allocated marketing budgets to how she thought about brand strategy.

What concerned Walker even more was the CEO's admonition that kept ringing in her head. "We owe it to our customers, our suppliers, and our distribution partners to make the right strategic choices regarding this revenue growth objective." Natureview accounted for 24% of yogurt sales through the natural foods channel. These retailers had made Natureview what it was today. How would these long-term partners react to seeing Natureview's yogurt at the supermarket down the street at prices at least 15% lower? Would price concessions follow? Worse yet, would the stores in Natureview's traditional channel drop the brand and replace it with competitors' lines? When Natureview's current broker heard about the plan, he would likely let everyone at the company know his displeasure. Clearly Walker would have to minimize the damage to the channel support Natureview had established.

Walker picked up her notebook, which summarized the three options. Fortunately, none of them required building a new facility in the short term, which would have cost $30 million, and capital expenditures for manufacturing were approximately equal across the three options.

Option 1

The first option, to expand six SKUs of the 8-oz. product line into one or two selected supermarket channel regions, was most strongly advocated by Walter Bellini, vice president of sales. (Pursuing six SKUs struck the right balance between having enough cups on the shelf to provide a good shelf presence, while not incurring too large a slotting expense. The six SKUs chosen were the best-selling SKUs of the 8-oz. line.) His argument was based on three key points:

1. Eight-ounce cups represented the largest dollar and unit share of the refrigerated yogurt market, providing significant revenue potential.

2. Other natural foods brands had successfully expanded their distribution into the supermarket channel. Two such brands—Silk Soymilk and Amy's Organic Foods—had increased revenues by over 200% within two years of entering supermarkets. Natureview, the leading

[5] Natureview used a discount rate of 8% to evaluate projects.

natural foods brand of refrigerated yogurt, was uniquely positioned to capitalize on the growing trend in natural and organic foods in supermarkets.

3. Bellini had heard rumors that one of Natureview's major natural foods competitors would soon try to expand into the supermarket channel. Supermarket retailers would likely authorize only one organic yogurt brand. The first brand to enter the channel could therefore have a significant first-mover advantage.

One of Natureview's brokers had told Bellini that supermarket chains—afraid of losing market share to other channels—believed that offering more organic products in their stores would attract higher-income, less price-sensitive customers. Bellini mentioned that some industry experts were predicting unit volume growth of organic yogurt at supermarkets of 20% per year from 2001 to 2006. These predictions were relative to unit growth projections of 2% to 4% for the yogurt category overall in the supermarket channel.

The team acknowledged that this option had great upside potential but also higher risks and costs. The 8-oz. size received the highest level of competitive trade promotion and marketing spending. Natureview Farm's sales broker had indicated that supporting this cup size would require quarterly trade promotions and a meaningful marketing budget. Natureview's advertising agency estimated that a comprehensive advertising plan (comprising television, radio, outdoor, and print advertising) would cost Natureview $1.2 million per region per year. These launch expenditures were in addition to the trade promotion expenditures the company would need to make. Natureview's sales, general, and administrative expenses (SG&A) would increase by $320,000 annually; $200,000 would be incremental SG&A for additions to sales staff required to manage the supermarket brokers in the two regions, and $120,000 would go towards additional marketing staff.

With this level of advertising support, Natureview felt it could achieve a 1.5% share of supermarket yogurt sales after one year, producing an incremental annual sales volume of just over 35 million units. (See **Exhibit 6** for incremental unit sales projections by strategic option.) This projection also assumed Natureview's brokers could take advantage of their relationships with the top 11 supermarket retail chains in the Northeast and the top 9 chains in the West. Research showed that supermarket consumers in the northeastern and western regions were more likely to purchase organic and natural foods than consumers in other regions.

Walker found Bellini's arguments compelling. It was hard to counter his belief that Natureview had to enter the supermarket channel to successfully address the revenue gap. For Bellini, the "go or no-go" decision was clearly a question of "when" and "how," not "if." Walker glanced down at her notebook again.

Option 2

The second option—to expand four SKUs of the 32-oz. size nationally—was advocated by Jack Gottlieb, vice president of operations. His argument was based on three key points:

1. Although 32-oz. cups comprised a smaller unit and dollar share of the yogurt market, they currently generated an above-average gross profit margin for Natureview (43.6% vs. 36.0% for the 8-oz. line).

2. There were fewer competitive offerings in this size, and Natureview Farm had a strong competitive advantage because of the product's longer shelf life. Natureview's brand had achieved a 45% share of this size segment in the natural foods channel. The management team felt that it was realistic to assume that the company could sell approximately 5.5 million

incremental units in the first year. To generate this projection, Natureview's broker advised that the company would need to expand into 64 supermarket retail chains across the United States.

3. Although slotting expenses would be higher because national distribution would require slotting fees across a larger number of retailers, promotional expenses would be lower—the 32-oz. size was promoted only twice a year. For a 32-oz. expansion, marketing expenses would be significantly lower as well—only 10% of what was projected for the 8-oz. size in each region, representing $120,000 per region per year.

Despite the many advantages of this option, the management team doubted that new users would readily "enter the brand" via a multi-use size. Bellini was also concerned about his sales team's ability to achieve full national distribution in just 12 months. Furthermore, as with the first option, Natureview would need to hire sales personnel who had experience selling to the more sophisticated supermarket channel and would need to establish relationships with supermarket brokers. Additions to sales headcount for the 32-oz. expansion option would increase SG&A by $160,000.

Despite these concerns, Walker thought this was an interesting option to consider. Dannon was rumored to be launching a line called Bright Vista, an organic yogurt that would compete directly with Natureview. Supermarkets themselves were also considering launching their own private-label versions of organic yogurt. Would launching a 32-oz. offering be less noticed by the competition? Could it acquaint supermarket customers with the brand before Natureview pursued the 8-oz. size in the supermarket channel? Since the 8-oz. size was the "bread and butter" product for Natureview's competitors, they might view an expansion into the 8-oz. market as a greater threat by Natureview.

Option 3

The third option—to introduce two SKUs of a children's multi-pack into the natural foods channel—was advocated by Walker's colleague Kelly Riley, the assistant marketing director. Riley based her argument on five key points:

1. The company already had strong relationships with the leading natural foods channel retailers, and expansion into the supermarket channel could potentially affect these relationships. Yogurt was an important product to natural foods retailers from both a revenue and a profit standpoint.

2. Riley also was not convinced that Natureview had the necessary resources or skill-set to sell effectively to and through supermarkets. Her recent conversations with Natureview's brokers, who were skeptical of the move, had only added to her concerns, and she feared that her colleagues were not adequately taking into account the impact that a "go" decision would have on the current marketing, sales, brand, and channel-partner arrangements.

3. Natureview Farm's all-natural ingredients would provide the perfect positioning from which to launch its own children's multi-pack product offering into their core sales channel. The sales team was confident that they could achieve distribution for the two SKUs.

4. The financial potential was very attractive. The projected total yearly revenue for the two multipack SKUs would be approximately 10% of the natural foods channel category dollar sales, and Riley estimated potential incremental unit volume at 1.8 million. Gross profitability of the line would be 37.6%. Furthermore, sales and marketing expenses in this channel were lower; the cost of the complimentary cases was estimated at 2.5% of the product line's manufacturer sales, and the marketing expenses were estimated at $250,000. Riley believed

that introducing this product line into the natural foods channel would yield the strongest profit contribution of all the strategies under consideration.

5. The natural foods channel was growing almost seven times faster than the supermarket channel, and Natureview was developing several new products that could further boost sales performance in this highly successful channel. The five-year projected unit growth CAGR of yogurt in the natural foods channel was projected to be 15%, according to industry market research.

For this option, R&D and Operations would need to develop the multipack product. Natureview would incur no additional SG&A costs to introduce the multipack product—this was within the capabilities of the current functional resources.

While the management team sympathized with Riley's concerns, the team argued that potential channel conflict should not be the deciding factor—Natureview could find ways to manage it. But Riley held firm to her belief that supermarkets' emphasis on sales promotion and price was inconsistent with the premium brand positioning that Walker and Riley had worked hard to establish. Walker also recalled Riley describing her fear that Natureview's marketing department was unprepared to handle the demands on resources and staffing that entering the supermarket channel would impose.

Walker thought back to the exploratory conversation she and Riley had not long ago with a dairy buyer at a large Boston-based supermarket chain. He had advised them, "You're going to have to show us a real marketing plan if you want us to distribute your brand. Trade promotion spending and clever public relations stunts alone aren't going to cut it." She also remembered the previous day's conversation with Natureview's fulfillment manager, who had raised concerns about Natureview's ability to handle distribution to supermarket distributors. Such distributors were more demanding from a logistical and technological standpoint compared with distribution partners Natureview was familiar with from the natural foods channel. Instead of incurring the inevitable cost, change, and trauma from entering the supermarket channel, Kelly Riley wanted Natureview to focus on the "shooting star" and create a strategy to gain shelf space at natural foods retailers. Riley could be right, Walker thought, but she also suspected that the natural foods channel would soon be making demands much like those that Riley feared from supermarkets. Walker knew from experience that retailers were likely to demand more and more as they grew.

Just then, the phone rang. It was Natureview's CEO. "Christine, I'm really counting on you to help us figure out what to do here. I trust your instincts about the marketplace—our customers, competitors, and channels. You have the best direct read on all of this, and I need a coherent point of view and an action plan. I know these are not easy decisions, but I have confidence that you'll lead us down the right path."

Exhibit 1 Natureview Farm Income Statement, 1999

Revenues[a]	$13,000,000	100% Revenues
Cost of Goods Sold[b]	$ 8,190,000	63%
Gross Profit	$ 4,810,000	37%
Expenses		
- Administration/Freight	$ 2,210,000	17%
- Sales	$ 1,560,000	12%
- Marketing	$ 390,000	3%
- Research & Development	$ 390,000	3%
Net Income	$ 260,000	2%

[a]Natureview's 1999 revenues were 100% generated from sales of refrigerated yogurt to natural foods stores.

[b]The COGS reflects a product mix of 86% 8-oz. yogurt cups and 14% 32-oz. yogurt cups.

Exhibit 2 Yogurt Market Share by Packaging Segment, 1999 (Supermarket channel, in % U.S. dollars)

	Dollar Share	**Dollar Sales Change vs. Prior Year**
8-oz. cups and smaller	74%	+3%
Children's multipacks	9%	+12.5%
32-oz. cups	8%	+2%
Other	9%	NC
	100%	

Yogurt Market Share by Region, 1999
(Supermarket channel, in % U.S. dollars)

	Dollar Share	**No. of Retailers in the Region**
Northeast	26%	25
Midwest	22%	30
Southeast	25%	33
West	27%	17
	100%	

Note: Market share is given as percentage U.S. dollars for national U.S. market.

Exhibit 3 Yogurt Production Costs and Retail Prices by Channel

Natural Foods Channel	Average Retail Price
8-ounce (oz.) cup	$ 0.88
32-oz. cup	$ 3.19
4- oz. cup multipack	$ 3.35

Supermarket Channel	Average Retail Price
8-oz. cup	$ 0.74
32-oz. cup	$ 2.70
4-oz. cup multipack	$ 2.85

Note: Natureview's manufacturing costs for the three product lines—the 8-oz. cup, the 32-oz. cup, and the children's multipack—were $0.31, $0.99, and $1.15 respectively.

Exhibit 4 Length of Channels to Market

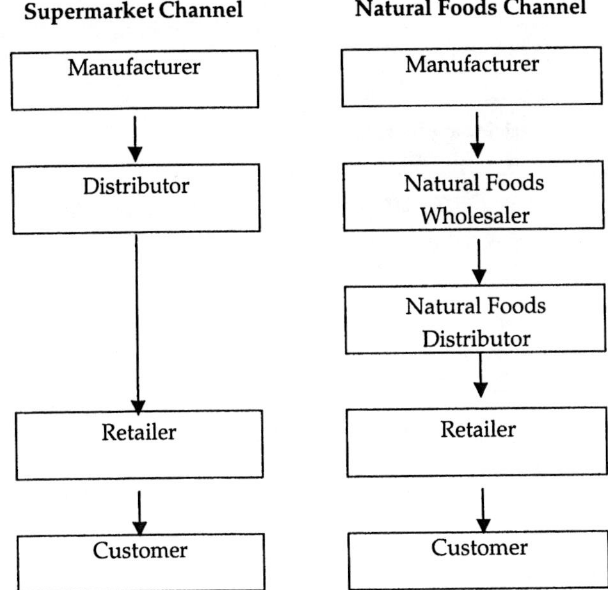

Exhibit 5 Yogurt Market Share by Brand, 1999
(Supermarket and Natural Foods channels, in % U.S. dollars)

Supermarket Channel

Dannon	33%
Yoplait	24%
Others	23%
Private Label	15%
Columbo	5%
	100%

Natural Foods Channel

Natureview Farm	24%
Brown Cow	15%
Horizon Organic	19%
White Wave	7%
Others	35%
	100%

Exhibit 6 Sales Projections for Natureview's Strategic Options

Option	Action	Anticipated Incremental Retail Unit Sales
1	Expand 6 SKUs of the 8-oz. size into eastern and western supermarket regions	35,000,000
2	Expand 4 SKUs of the 32-oz. size nationally into supermarket channel	5,500,000
3	Introduce 2 children's multipacks into natural foods channel	1,800,000

HARVARD | BUSINESS | SCHOOL

9-505-016

REV: APRIL 10, 2007

V. KASTURI RANGAN

MARIE BELL

Comergent Technologies Inc.: Enterprise E-Commerce

At a working lunch with the casewriters and John Mumford, a key venture capital (VC) backer of Comergent, Jean Kovacs, CEO of Comergent, reached into her bag to attend to the chime of her cell phone. She quickly retrieved the phone, glanced at the display, grimaced, and turned it off. She explained that her reaction was not so much to the ringing of the cell phone but her anticipation of a particular call:

> We're supposed to hear back today from a significant prospect. It's a division of a major Fortune 500 company, and it would be a significant breakthrough for us. With a beachhead in the division we could then expand our presence throughout the whole company. The business-people in the organization and the technology group are both supporting us—they love our product and are sold on our people. The stumbling block has been the CIO [chief information officer], who has come from the parent into this newly acquired division. The parent company has dealt with a single vendor, and the CIO is reluctant to introduce another software company even to a subsidiary. That makes it difficult for the CEO to select Comergent. We've met with the CEO and the CIO and his team, done product demos, and I even flew out last week to meet with them personally. We gave them our full customer list and urged them to call anyone on it. They did and got glowing feedback on us. When they asked the installed competitor for referrals, the process was delayed several weeks because the competitor couldn't find comparable implementations. I called the CEO earlier this week, and he promised a decision by the end of the day today.

As Kovacs wrapped up her reflections, she added, "To assure them of our financial viability, I even gave them John's number." Mumford leaned across the table and said, "I spoke with the CEO twice. He wants to go with us."

Returning to the office for further conversations with the casewriters, Kovacs reflected that there had been much to celebrate over the past year. The software company had increased its customer list from 43 customers in 2002 to 57 in 2003. Moreover, it had landed a record number of engagements and successfully increased its footprint in the existing customer base. Customer-satisfaction ratings remained high, and the fledgling company had received increased notice by analysts and industry pundits. Comergent's success was especially remarkable because it had been achieved in the emerging market space of the customer-facing side of the business. The space encompassed all the points and processes that interacted with the customer including product catalog, availability, configuration and selection, order processing, partner (channel) management, service, and so on. Comergent's enterprise e-commerce solution software was targeted at improving the productivity of

---

Professor V. Kasturi Rangan and Research Associate Marie Bell prepared this case. HBS cases are developed solely as the basis for class discussion. Certain details have been disguised. Cases are not intended to serve as endorsements, sources of primary data, or illustrations of effective or ineffective management.

the selling and ordering processes. Yet, despite its progress in a tough economy, Comergent knew it had to accelerate growth even more. In January 2004, Kovacs noted:

> With the economy stalled up until a few months ago, companies had reservations about investing in technology, especially when they were in no-growth or slow-growth environments. Even as the market opened up and began to grow, the combination of the dot-com bombs and poor press on certain major technology investments put a damper on the market's enthusiasm for enterprise software. Our fully configured product involves complex customer-facing solutions that many prospects don't really understand. Because they have been burned in the past with other technology solutions, it has sometimes been difficult to get prospects to come to the table to discuss how Comergent can help them better work with their customers and channel partners. Over the past few months, we've seen a pickup in calls and prospects. If an upswing is coming, we need to accelerate our growth and make sure we have the right product, the right product positioning, and the right sales and customer-acquisition processes in place to bring in prospects and convert them to customers.

Company Background

Comergent was formed in 1998 through a chance meeting of Kovacs and Bill York. Kovacs had recently left Qualix subsequent to its public offering, while York had spent five years at Xerox Company's Palo Alto Research Center and Inxight Software, a Xerox company. They actually met at a company picnic for the law firm at which both their spouses worked. When looking at the most recent trends in the market, they both concluded that by the late 1990s the buy side had been quite thoroughly addressed. E-procurement had developed rapidly and had been widely accepted. Electronic purchasing through business-to-business exchanges and purchasing systems such as Ariba were effectively filling the space.

But the sell side was unexplored.[1] Much of the early work in electronic commerce had focused on going direct to the customer and selling simple products. Corporate customers, on the other hand, often sold complex, configurable products through various sales channels—distributors, resellers, wholesalers, and so on. Until that point, development efforts had focused on the transaction between the customer and the manufacturer. Existing sales channels had been seen as "unnecessary," so little had been developed in connecting customers to channel partners and channel partners to manufacturers. The focus had been on eliminating the channel, not optimizing it. But to Kovacs and York, it was increasingly clear that many channel partners did add value and would continue to add value even in the e-business platform and were, therefore, destined to remain as a part of the sell side of the business. As such, there was an opportunity for the right company to enter and make the sell side more efficient and effective.

Kovacs explained:

> Armed with conviction and not much else, we started some fundamental market research about business needs on the sell side. We did "Market Research 101," that is, driving up and down Highway 101, the major thoroughfare through the Silicon Valley, and talking with anyone who would listen to us. We talked to close to a hundred companies, both in Silicon Valley and scattered across the U.S. What we came away with was a clear understanding that

[1] The terms "buy side" and "sell side" can be confusing. The reader should consider the manufacturer to be in the middle. On the buy side it is purchasing goods and services for the production of products and services. The sell side refers to the activities associated with selling its goods and services to customers and partners.

channel partners were going to remain in the sales process and that customers were telling companies that they needed to make it easier to do business with them.

"By the end of our research, we had a set of market requirements that we could use to build our product and technology," added York, who became the company's chief technology officer.

One of the people with whom Comergent spoke was Mumford, a well-known venture capitalist in Silicon Valley who had been involved in the start-ups of Office Depot, MicroWarehouse, and Ariba, a company that would become the leading solution provider for buy-side commerce.

Mumford, a founding partner of CrossPoint Venture Partners, became a key supporter of Comergent and was instrumental in Comergent's fund-raising efforts and market research. In 1999, Comergent raised $5 million in first-round financing from SoftBank and CrossPoint Venture. The funds from this initial round had been earmarked for research but were quickly converted into product development when Cisco not only became aware of Comergent's activity but also became its first customer, spearheading the development of Comergent 1.0. Using this early version of the Comergent system, Cisco's customers were able to browse the Cisco system for products, select the appropriate product bundle (check compatibility, compare with other products, and choose ancillary products), and send the order to an authorized reseller for fulfillment. Alternatively, customers could contact Cisco's internal sales engineers, who would access the Comergent system and advise the customer on the best product for their needs. Resellers also used the Comergent system to browse Cisco's products and place orders with distributors (such as TechData and Ingram Micro) for fulfillment. In a baptism by fire, Comergent not only brought its product to market but also won the prestigious "Cisco Supplier of the Year" award in 1999.

In February 2000, Comergent planned to raise a further $20 million–$25 million. Ultimately the financing round was capped at $54 million, during a "surreal period when investors with a $4 million–$6 million allocation were sending $8 million and telling us to keep the extra couple of million." In 2002, a $10 million convertible note provided additional funding.

That surreal upswing was followed by a surreal downswing. During the week of April 10, 2001, the NASDAQ fell 25%, signaling the start of the dot-com crash.[2] As one executive noted, "We went from a halcyon period when we literally had to plead with investors to stop giving us money to one when no one wanted to hear the word technology. That presents a challenge when you are a technology company."

Product

As seen from **Figure A,** by 2004, the Comergent enterprise e-commerce system was a "full suite of software applications that increased revenue and profits by streamlining the selling and order-fulfillment processes." Comergent's three-part enterprise e-commerce solution mirrored a typical customer purchase process. In the first stage, customers usually sought information on product functions and features, model numbers, stock-keeping units (SKUs), and so on. In the second stage, once customers had selected a product, they configured it by adding or subtracting features or modules. Finally, once the product was configured and quoted, the order was placed, tracked, and filled.

---

[2] Robert D. Hof and Steve Hamm, "How e-biz rose, and will rise anew," *BusinessWeek*, May 13, 2002.

Figure A Comergent's Enterprise E-Commerce System

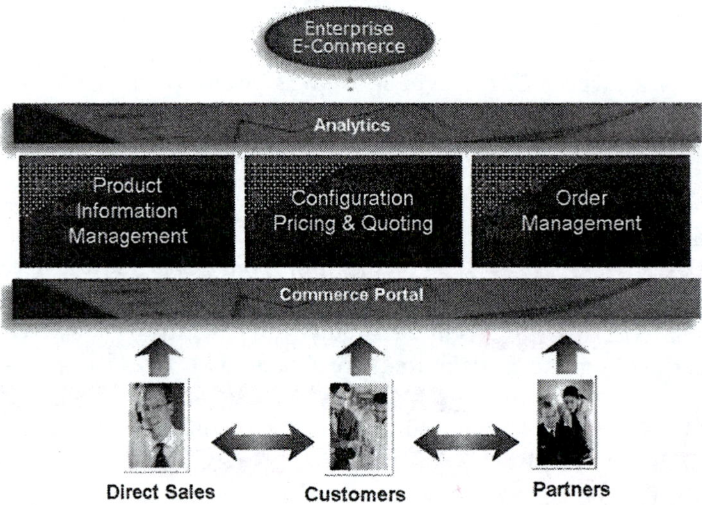

Source: Company records.

As seen in **Figure B** below, Comergent automated the business processes necessary to meet the customer's needs in each of the three stages. As one Comergent executive explained, "Think of each of the product lines as a function in your sales and marketing organization. Product-information management is like your product manager—defining the product, providing a description of its attributes, etc. The configuration, pricing, and quoting module is like your salesperson, taking the list of products and pricing and figuring out the combination that is right for the customer at this time for this purpose. Order management is similar to your customer service reps that take the order, write it up for fulfillment, and ship it out on the promised date." The beauty of Comergent's system was that it could be used within the framework of existing channel partners. A brief description of each of the product lines is listed below.

Figure B Automating the Sales Process

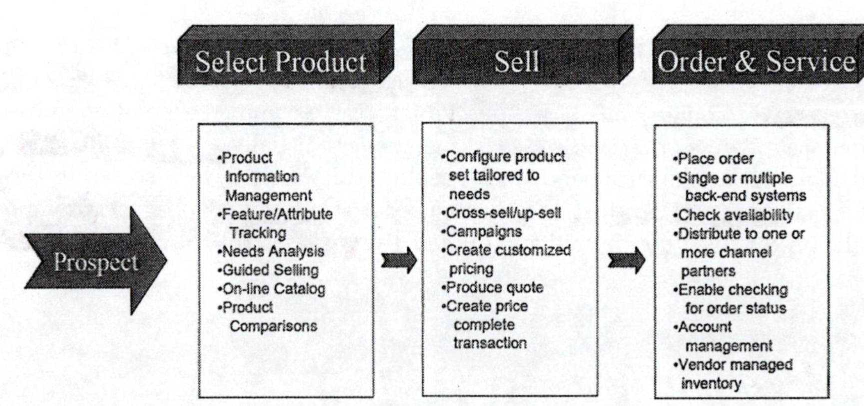

Source: Company records.

Product-information management As their name implied, product-information applications were centered on defining, cataloging, and managing product information. The Comergent system created a single source of product information that could be shared among multiple formats and systems. That product information allowed the end customer to access a full range of products, compare products with side-by-side comparisons, and obtain "catalog" pricing and, where appropriate, associated parts and assemblies. Customers such as Toro, Cisco, and Burger King had purchased components of Comergent's product-information management applications.

Configuration, pricing, and quoting The applications within this module guided customers, partners, and sales reps through the complete process of product selection, allowing users to customize the product solution that worked for them. The system could dynamically recommend the best-suited products and solutions based on the customer's defined needs. During the quoting process, the pricing received by the customer was specific to the customer (based on the negotiated pricing) and also provided real-time inventory availability. In addition, the system could deliver promotional messages to customers as they browsed for their product selections. Symbol, Agfa, and Pearson Publishing were customers that had taken advantage of these applications.

Order management The applications in this product line provided order placement and the brokering and distribution of the order to the appropriate back-end or external systems for fulfillment, shipping, and invoicing. One of the key strengths of the Comergent system was that it provided a single face to the customer for the ordering process even in situations when multiple partners might be involved. Seagate, Dupont, Goodrich, and Brooks were customers using order-management applications.

Customers had the option of purchasing the full system or only acquiring the needed application modules, thereby creating their individual solution. To date, sales had been equally distributed across the three product lines.

Customers licensed the Comergent software and then paid a further 18% of the license fee per year in recurring support and maintenance fees. Licensing costs ranged from $100,000 to over several million dollars, depending on the range of software purchased. Approximately 90% of Comergent's customers renewed their support and maintenance contracts. While upgrades were offered as part of support, customers paid additional fees for new modules added to their systems. Approximately 40% of customers purchased additional Comergent software following their initial purchase. Of those that purchased additional software, 75% purchased an additional module (costing about $100,000–$200,000), with 25% moving to a larger enterprise solution (costing about $600,000–$800,000).

The Comergent product was constructed on a core platform (Release 6.4 in January 2004), but as a result of a major architecture revision in July 2002, Comergent was able to build or upgrade individual modules separately and integrate them into the core system without requiring a major re-write. This was unique in the software industry and gave Comergent and its customers extreme flexibility. The system was scalable and reliable and could be speedily implemented and integrated with a customer's existing systems. Technically, the system was based on Internet messaging capabilities and used a "distributed Internet application architecture that extensively used Web services." This translated into system flexibility, allowing Comergent to seamlessly move data among customers, partners, and suppliers. Sitting on a Java platform, the technologists at Comergent believed that their system was superior to earlier systems from Oracle and SAP. As Dave Burlington, senior vice president of product development, explained:

> Older ERP [enterprise resource planning] systems are very database driven, with the applications [like accounts payable, for example] written directly on top of the database. These systems assume all the information they need to complete a transaction is located in this

database. The systems are monolithic, tightly coupled, and are designed to handle a limited number of internal users. If you change one element in any part of the system, other pieces have to be changed as well. By contrast, the Comergent system is message based. From a development perspective we started out in a different place than ERP; we needed to access information in multiple back-end and partner systems. All of the communications between our applications and the outside world are done through messages. Our applications make no assumptions regarding how or where information is physically stored; our messaging platform resolves that. Our applications are loosely coupled, can accommodate multiple user types and varying information flows, and are designed to exist in a heterogeneous environment. For customers, that means they can implement, make changes to, or upgrade applications easily, which lowers their total cost of ownership. Our implementation costs are usually in the neighborhood of one times the software-license cost. For the traditional ERP vendors it is generally 5–10 times the cost of the software for implementation. The flexibility inherent in our message-based architecture is the primary reason for this cost difference.

In earlier stages, Comergent positioned its system as a demand-chain management set of applications. While this term was useful in describing the functionality of the system, that is, translating and automating customer needs into specific business processes, customers did not have a clear understanding of what demand-chain management entailed. As a result, in June 2004, Comergent began using the more focused term enterprise e-commerce to describe its solution. This way customers could get a better understanding of Comergent's market and how each of the application modules fit into the overall solution.

Comergent Organization and Operations

Comergent's organization reflected the critical functions necessary for the company's long-term success. These core drivers were supported by a lean administrative organization. (**Exhibit 1** outlines Comergent's organization structure.) Several key functions are highlighted below:

Product Development

The product-development team comprised about 35–40 people, about one-third of the company, and was responsible for product management, engineering, quality assurance, documentation, and some sales support.

Sales

As seen in **Figure C** below, Comergent had a well-defined sales process for turning prospects into customers. The process began with an internal and external sales process. After a contract was won, the process moved to the professional services group, which handled implementation, and then ultimately transitioned to the customer services group.

Figure C Sales Process: From Prospect to Customer Service

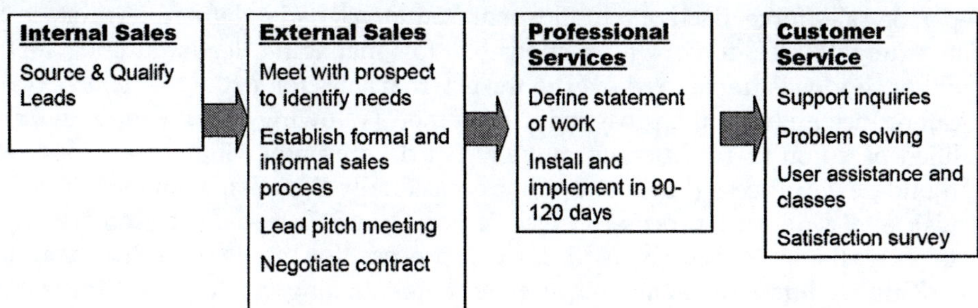

Source: Company records.

Internal sales The process began with the internal sales team. A three-person inside sales team generated leads from cold calls, Webinars (seminars on the Comergent website), and marketing programs. Referrals from other companies were a significant source of leads, as well as mentions in the press and analyst coverage. The internal sales team generated and chased down leads, endeavoring to further qualify the lead as having a real need for Comergent's products and services. While no definitive pattern had been established between leads and real projects, a working estimate was that for every 300 inquiries there were approximately 10 real projects. Although there was a distinct sales staff, as Kovacs noted, "Everyone has sales goals—from the executive team to our service people." The internal sales force was compensated with an annual base salary and a potential team bonus of 25%. As seen from **Table A** below, sales leads were assigned a ranking of A to F. Most of the early leads created through marketing programs began with an E or F ranking. On average, Comergent had 100–120 active leads in an A–E status with about half ranked as an E or F. (See **Exhibit 2** for a representative status report for a single region's A–C leads.)

Table A Comergent Lead Classification System

Classification	Description
S	SOLD
A	Sold, in contract negotiation/signing
B	Won for a defined quote and scope of work
C	Actively competing for business from prospect
D	Prospect has a defined project, budget, timeline, project sponsor
E	Prospect is talking about project/may require more information
F	Just identified from Inside cold call, Webinar, request for information

Source: Company records.

External sales When the customer lead had been qualified by the internal sales force to D status, meaning that there was intent to buy software within the next six months and with a defined customer budget, project, and project owner, the lead was passed from the internal sales force to the external 10-person sales force. Each of the sales representatives had a defined territory in one of three regions. The external sales force was responsible for managing leads in the A–D categories. Generally, when a lead was transferred over to the external sales force, the first course of action was a conference call or meeting with the prospective customer. Following that meeting, the customer was further qualified based on its readiness to move forward. Internally, Comergent classified prospects as having an undefined process (likely D or C or occasionally E leads), a somewhat-defined process (D or C leads), and a defined process (C leads). For D and E leads, the Comergent salesperson attempted to help the prospect create a formal process for navigating the deal through the organization. This included finalizing requirements, conducting product demonstrations, getting executive committee buy-in and approval, and setting budget. In addition, the salesperson played an important role in contract closing and the implementation processes. Because the organization was small, the top management played an active role in the selling process; oftentimes Kovacs herself was involved in the selling process. The sales process generally took four to six months to convert a D-status customer to an A.

Making the sales pitch The "pitch meeting" was the key point in the sales process. The meeting was usually two or three hours long and was attended by the sales executive and the sales engineer, who fielded technical questions and ran the demonstration. Depending on the circumstances, members of the Comergent management team often attended these meetings. Based on a refined understanding of the deliverables from the meeting, Comergent provided a price quote and then after several days and even weeks of providing additional information and clarification a decision followed. Matt Kilguss formerly vice president of sales, summarized the sales challenges:

> It takes much longer to uncover our customer's pain than to relieve the pain. Our biggest challenge is getting the customer to the point where they can define their pain, commit to its alleviation and a willingness to pay for it. Once we have the project definition, the process usually goes smoothly. We have a superb product. The catalog, guided selling, and order management are particularly attractive to customers. Occasionally, we will get interference from the internal organization that might want to build a product in-house, or misinformation from an existing IT vendor that might suggest that our installation could be incompatible with the customers' existing ERP system. But often, when prospective customers try to build it themselves, they soon discover they lack the expertise and come back to us.
>
> As is the standing rule with all enterprise software sales, on a quarterly basis about one-third of prospects close, another one-third move to the next quarter, and the remaining one-third we lose. About half the losses are to established vendors, a much smaller proportion will go to small competitors, and some prospective inquiries simply slip away at the source.

Lead management Every Monday morning, the executive team had a "pipeline call" meeting with sales management and reviewed each salesperson's activities to ascertain new leads and prospects. With the review, the executive team also provided inputs and suggestions to direct efforts and provided support as needed. (**Exhibit 3** provides an abbreviated version of the pipeline report for one of Comergent's three regions.) Every Friday, there was a call of the entire sales team plus management, in which all leads were reviewed.

Over the past 18 months Comergent had begun a trial "land-and-expand" selling strategy, trying to land an account with an entry-level module costing the customer about $300,000 in license fees and then growing the customer over time. This was different from industry practice whereby many software companies tried to sell a new customer a significant software deal in excess of $1 million up front. The idea behind Comergent's strategy was to build customer loyalty early, provide a positive return on investment (ROI) minimizing the investment, and still have several other Comergent applications to sell over time. While the land-and-expand strategy had proven successful, there was some concern that Comergent was selling "point" solutions and not addressing the broader integrated goals of enterprise e-commerce.

Professional services[3] *and customer service*,[4] described in the footnotes, completed the implementation cycle. Ninety-eight percent of Comergent's projects were completed on time and on budget. The 90- to 120-day implementation time was dramatically lower than the one to three years that ERP vendors usually took.

Customer Applications

Comergent had a varied customer list ranging from high-technology companies such as Cisco and Seagate to basic industries such as Windsor Industries, a supplier of cleaning products, and Haworth, a leading office furniture manufacturer. (**Exhibit 4** summarizes Comergent's customer list.) As one Comergent executive noted, "While our customers come from a variety of industries and perspectives, their problems are similar. They need to work through, automate, and optimize their selling and ordering processes. The good news is that our product is robust enough to meet their unique industry or business needs."

A good example was JC Penney, one of the largest retailers in the U.S. with $17.8 billion in sales in 2003. JC Penney was also the country's largest retailer of "hard" window treatments including blinds manufactured by industry leaders such as Hunter Douglas, Springs Window Fashion, and Levolor. Prior to using the Comergent system, when customers came into the store and ordered made-to-measure blinds, the in-store sales associate manually completed the order and faxed the order forms to a specific blind manufacturer. The manual order process was time consuming and error prone. The full order process included completion of the order-entry forms, the point-of-sale transaction, and order transmission to the vendor; follow-up customer service calls with the vendor and customer often took up to one and a half hours of the sales associate's time. Just over a third of the orders received were incorrect or illegible, requiring the blind manufacturer to place the orders into a customer service hold pending notification back to the store sales associate for clarification or correction. This often impacted the customer's shopping experience by either delaying the manufacturing and delivery of their blinds or requiring the company to have to notify the customer their blinds could not be manufactured as ordered. Even so, the customer returned 30% of orders

---

[3] Once the customer was sold and the contract signed, the project transitioned to a professional services team responsible for installation. They customized the modules, populated them with customer data, and configured applications. It was here that the "rubber met the road" and the statement of work was prepared for the contract. Overall, the professional services staff numbered 38 at Comergent. In addition to its own engineers, Comergent had developed a relationship with system integrators such as TechSpan, an independent firm that had engineers trained in the Comergent system who could be called in to work on a Comergent installation. The professional services team was on-site at the customer for the implementation period (90–120 days) working through any issues or idiosyncrasies in the customer system, doing whatever it took to meet customer expectations and get the system up and running. Generally the professional services team members spent little time at Comergent headquarters but moved from customer site to customer site.

[4] The customer service team took over from the professional services group and worked with customers post-installation. The transition was usually initiated with a kickoff meeting to formally recognize the movement from a new product installation to a service phase. The customer service staff had both proactive and reactive functions. From a reactive standpoint, Comergent fielded customer support inquiries. Call levels were generally higher immediately post-installation and then fell off quickly. Proactively, Comergent tried to solve problems before they occurred. Comergent maintained a version of the customer's code in-house for debugging. It conducted training classes for system administrators and developers.

shipped because the product failed to meet the customer's expectations, costing JC Penney half the cost of the order (the blind manufacturer bore the other 50% of the cost). With the Comergent system, order time fell to 30 minutes and the number of wrong or illegible orders fell to 0% within weeks. Moreover, the contract was signed in January, beta-tested in June, and subsequently rolled out to 628 stores in September.

Though every company had its own unique application of the system, there were several common types of business needs that the Comergent system addressed. The first was conducting business through one or more channel partners and/or third-party intermediaries. In these situations, the response to the customer needed to be accomplished through one or more channel partners. For example, Haworth, Inc., an office products manufacturer with $1.75 billion in sales, sold its products through a network of 300 U.S. dealers and a team of 400 sales associates who generated orders for the dealership network. (The top 50 dealers accounted for 80% of the company's sales.) As Haworth's large customers began using e-commerce tools, they wanted to be able to order products online using their Haworth pricing and product agreements. Haworth used the Comergent system to allow customers to place their orders, then have the order forwarded to both the dealer (for ongoing sales and service) and Haworth (for manufacturing). The completed order was forwarded to the dealer for installation and service. Depending on the situation, billing for the order would come from the dealer or Haworth directly into the customer's e-commerce purchasing system, such as Ariba. Haworth was currently considering an expansion of the Comergent application. (See **Exhibit 5** for a more detailed description of the Haworth system.)

Another customer need was for an internal marketplace where Comergent's customers brought together buyers and sellers. A good example of this application was Choice Hotels, a leading hotel chain with an extensive franchisee base. Choice used the Comergent system to allow 3,500 franchisees to purchase from preapproved suppliers with defined purchase agreements. Choice negotiated the agreements; endorsed the supplier; and posted its offering, collateral, and pricing on the site. On the sell side there were about 175 suppliers that represented close to 100,000 SKUs across a broad range of products from televisions to passenger vans. Choice constantly updated its Comergent system with modular upgrades. Systems consultants Deloitte and Touche were primarily responsible for framing and integrating Comergent's solution with Choice's procurement strategy.

From Choice's perspective, the turnover to the Comergent system from its earlier system was without much disruption to franchisees. The overall volume of purchasing rose as did the portion of purchasing volume that was transacted through ChoiceBuys.com versus offline methods of ordering. In total, Choice Hotels managed over $350 million in approved purchasing between its hotel franchisees and approved vendors. The number of service-related calls fell dramatically, allowing the help desk to become more actively involved in the selling process. Importantly for Choice as a franchisor, it provided product enhancements to its franchisees. Even those franchises that did not purchase through ChoiceBuys.com used it to benchmark prices in negotiating with their local, preferred vendors.

Gearing for Growth

At Comergent's June 30, 2003 year-end, revenues had grown to approximately $15 million. By year-end 2004, Comergent expected its annualized revenues to be 40%–50% more. While start-up rates varied from customer to customer, initial customer revenue from software sales and service was about $600,000–$750,000. Comergent's revenues were about evenly split between software and service.

Comergent tried to maintain a fiscally conservative position. Unlike some software companies that recognized revenue when the contract was signed, Comergent did not recognize revenue until the customer was live. Additionally, in 2001, Comergent reduced its headcount from 150 to 100 employees to make it through the crisis in the high-technology sector. Where possible, the company reduced staffing in administration, protecting the core research and development (R&D) team. Like that of many similar software start-ups, most of Comergent's spending was on product development and sales and marketing. Approximately 30% of Comergent's expenditures were on R&D, 30% on sales and marketing efforts, and 30% on professional services, with the remaining 10% on administration. As one Comergent executive noted, "Another way of looking at our costs is that close to 70% of the total is HR related, and another 10% is for outside consultants. Even a chunk of the rest of the 20% is for travel." Overheads were minimal. Most of the expenses were directly related to operations. Based on its increased revenue and cost reductions, Comergent made significant strides in improving its cash position. By year-end 2003, the company projected a net cash loss of $500,000 and anticipated break-even by fiscal 2004, with Comergent actually achieving a first profitable quarter in 2003. Comergent was sufficiently cash resourced to be able to see through the next year's operations.

Comergent's fiscal prudence was based on the company's desire to create long-term value and on its importance for customers. As Christopher Krook, Comergent's CFO, noted, "To sell enterprise software, financial viability is important. Customers want to make sure that you are going to be around to provide the long-term maintenance and support."

Acquisition of Profile Systems

In January 2004, Comergent acquired Profile Systems of Springfield, Massachusetts, in an all-stock transaction. Profile offered two products available through either licensing agreements or hosting applications: a system that standardized product information (including SKUs, pricing, and marketing materials) from disparate systems, and an inventory-replenishment system (called "vendor-managed inventory"). Profile's product line created bookends at either end of the existing Comergent portfolio. On the front end, Profile's product standardization had always been a critical step in a successful Comergent installation as the system aggregated and imported data from varying sources in the customer organization. At the back end, after the order was filled via the Comergent system, the next step was to track and update the inventory in the channel.

Profile Systems also brought new customers to the deal. Profile's customer base included "30 licensed customers and more than a thousand subscribers to its software for managing product-related data and handling vendor-managed inventory." Profile had been particularly successful focusing on industry groups (such as auto replacement parts and medical supplies).

Competition

Although Comergent was the only firm that offered an integrated enterprise commerce solution, Comergent faced competition from a variety of start-ups and established enterprise software companies. Foremost among them were ERP companies such as Oracle and SAP and customer relationship management (CRM) companies like Siebel. Simply put, enterprise software integrated and automated the major business systems within an organization. While many companies had automated systems, it was not until the advent of ERP with its use of relational databases that systems could reach across and coordinate between functions. Generally speaking, ERP systems required more than a year to install; were capital intensive (in excess of $1 million); and often utilized internal IT staff, ERP consultants, and systems integrators. Based on the promise and success of ERP, software vendors like Oracle had seen revenue rise to $10 billion in 2004. Within recent years ERP vendors, facing a downturn in their core business, had begun to add additional applications such as

CRM and partner relationship management (PRM) systems. As recently as June 2004, Oracle had provided enhancements to its PRM software.

During the mid-1990s, companies like Siebel Systems had pioneered CRM systems that automated a company's internal sales force effort and managed customer account information. Traditionally these systems, if they had existed at all, had been built inside the organization and captured the information from one department or business unit. As computing speed and sophistication grew, standardized packages like Siebel's captured customer profile information and in addition lead management data, sales data, and service needs to provide a complete 360-degree view of the customer. By 2002, Gartner estimated that CRM applications were a $23 billion worldwide market. Of that figure, however, custom applications were $20 billion of the market (87%) with $3 billion (13%) in packaged applications. Siebel Systems, the market leader, had a $700 million share of the $3 billion packaged applications. The next largest player, PeopleSoft, had CRM license revenues of $94 million,[5] which represented only a small segment of PeopleSoft's $2.3 billion in revenue.

As CRM systems rolled out it became apparent that understanding the customer and the company's relationship with the customer was only part of the solution. There was a need to better coordinate and manage channel intermediaries, and with this recognition PRM systems began to emerge. (**Exhibit 6** summarizes PRM vendors and the more broadly defined sell-side e-commerce vendors.) These emerging systems were a corollary to CRM systems and were designed to link with channel partners. Key components of PRM systems were presales information management (lead management, marketing campaign management, training, and certification) and measurement and analysis tools that helped assess partner performance, training, and certification status.

But for Comergent, neither the CRM nor the PRM systems provided the needed integrated solution from the customer through the partner to the company and to its internal ERP systems. As one sales executive explained:

> CRM systems are primarily used by sales management to assist in sales forecast reporting and contract management. Additionally they are used by customer service representatives for call tracking and dispute resolution handling with customers. PRM systems are used by channel managers to manage channel-partner profiles, marketing campaigns, lead generation, and ongoing training materials for your partners. Enterprise e-commerce does more than basic CRM. It focuses on the order-to-cash business process and provides self-service capabilities for customers and partners. These include product and catalog management, configuration, quoting, pricing and order management, and e-commerce capabilities.

Forging the Future

It had been over a month, and in spite of much back and forth, there still seemed to be little movement on the Fortune 500 customer. Kovacs sportingly declared:

> This customer is really a metaphor for our customer-acquisition challenges. We have a technologically superior product, a product that better meets customers' needs, and better pricing, and we still face the possibility of losing to an entrenched competitor. We need to decide what prospects to target and how to convert them to customers. Yet at the same time, we need to remember that it is a marathon, not a sprint. Customer acquisition and satisfaction

[5] As quoted in the Siebel Annual Report, cited by M. Maoz, "Large Enterprise CRM Suites: Melodic or mediocre?" Gartner, Inc., March 2003.

will ultimately help us win the race. We may be small now, but make no mistake; we want to be a significant enterprise software company.

There was no internal consensus in the company as to what the future strategy ought to be in order to achieve the status of growing into a significant player in the enterprise software space. Some felt the company was too focused on solving "today's particular pain." Instead, they argued that the company "should invest more time in helping the decision makers, CEOs, and marketing directors understand the value we bring to their organization." In sharp contrast, several of the company's field executives argued, "We have to face today's reality. Customers don't want to hear about big concepts. They have particular problems that they want resolved. Once we get them in the door, we can sell them additional modules."

Another set of debates within the company had to do with partnering and who the appropriate partners might be. Here again, the field-level people had urged, "We should think broadly and creatively about partnerships. We could partner with an ERP firm or even the consulting division of an IT company. There are many large firms that have prospects approach them every day for services they don't provide but that we do. We need a partner to point those prospects to us."

A senior executive at Comergent countered this view: "Partnering is great when business is good. The story is different today. These companies are far more likely to believe that they can build it themselves instead of forwarding a lead to another vendor even if it is ostensibly a partner."

"These larger debates aside, the real guts of this company are the entrepreneurial spirit of our developers and sales force; to tell you the truth, it is lead prospecting and customer acquisition that turns us on. I spend more time on these issues than strategizing the future," a visibly energized Kovacs offered as she prepared for the October 1, Friday conference call with her sales force and sales management.

She glanced at the three sales leads. All were in different stages of development, Ds and Cs, but each had created considerable interest in the company. As she prepared for the week's pipeline call, she debated the merits of each and wondered how to approach them.

Customer A: Alpha Cooperative was a $750 million agricultural cooperative located in the Midwest region of the United States. Alpha had two major operations—the distribution and sale of agricultural products (fertilizer, machinery, tools) to its members, and the sale of its members' refined products (vegetable oil, seed cake, grain) to the retail market. Alpha used a combination of its own sales reps and several national distributors to sell into the retail market. Alpha had approached Comergent about using the Comergent system for order management and perhaps inventory management with its member co-ops. After initial contact with the prospect, Comergent's sales rep thought that there was potential. Alpha had recently promoted its long-standing logistics chief to also oversee the IT function. The company's sales vice president felt there was a defined need for the order management module with potential growth both within the member business management as well as the retail distribution. However, given that the business was a cooperative, major capital spending on all items had to be approved by the membership. Comergent's sales representative had come upon this lead from an existing customer in the same geographic region.

Customer B: Beta Corp. was a $2 billion auto-parts manufacturer that distributed aftermarket parts to national retail chains, regional distributors, and individual body shops and garages. Product identification was a significant challenge in the auto-parts business. Often the original equipment manufacturer, the auto-parts maker, the distributor, and the retailer would all have unique product numbers to identify the same part. Also, as "under the hood" sophistication had increased, the mechanics, increasingly known as technicians, needed more information about parts and the configuration of groups of parts. Given the tough channel environment in which Beta Corp. operated, its relationship with key distributors was at times rocky, but in the end the company and its distributors realized they were in it together. While the sales process was still in its early stages, Beta Corp. had made it clear that the Comergent system would need to be compatible with its installed ERP system. Moreover, because Beta Corp. was also a certified tier-one supplier to a large auto manufacturer, the ERP systems compatibility was a must. Given this priority, the CIO was also investigating the channel management capabilities of its ERP vendor. On the up side, Beta Corp. was a Fortune 500 company with sister divisions engaged in supplying to the U.S. Defense Department. A Comergent sales rep had caught wind of this lead through a contact in the automotive industry, and Comergent's internal sales force had validated the opportunity.

Customer C: Gamma Company was a fast-growing, $100 million high-end telecommunications instrument assembler that sold 85% of its products through value-added resellers and 15% direct to customers. The direct-to-customer initiative with a Web interface was recent, started on the advice of a systems consulting company. Initially, however, the "direct sale" products were limited to refurbished products and larger direct telecommunications service providers. Gamma Company's competitive advantage was its customized systems. Customers and value-added resellers had the option of either ordering standard components or creating a customized package. With the rise of networked communications, the packages were in high demand. For some time, the company had used a fax-based ordering system, but with the rise in demand and increased complexity of the packaging, Gamma Company lost many orders due to poor communication, improper configurations, and out-of-stock positions. The owner and CEO had heard about Comergent from a colleague in Silicon Valley and had participated in a Comergent-sponsored Webinar.

Exhibit 1 Comergent Organization Structure

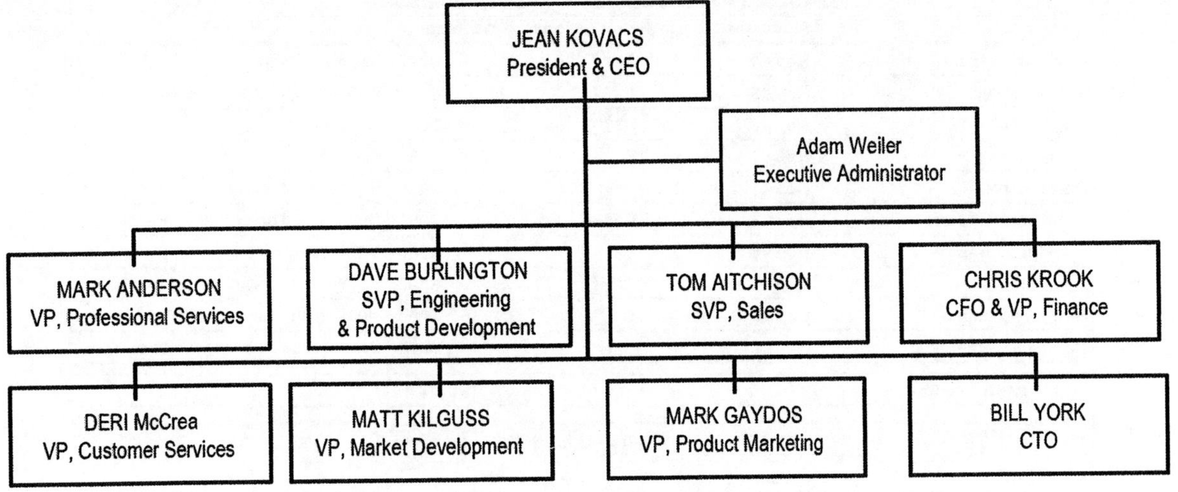

Source: Company records.

Exhibit 2 Representative Lead Status Report

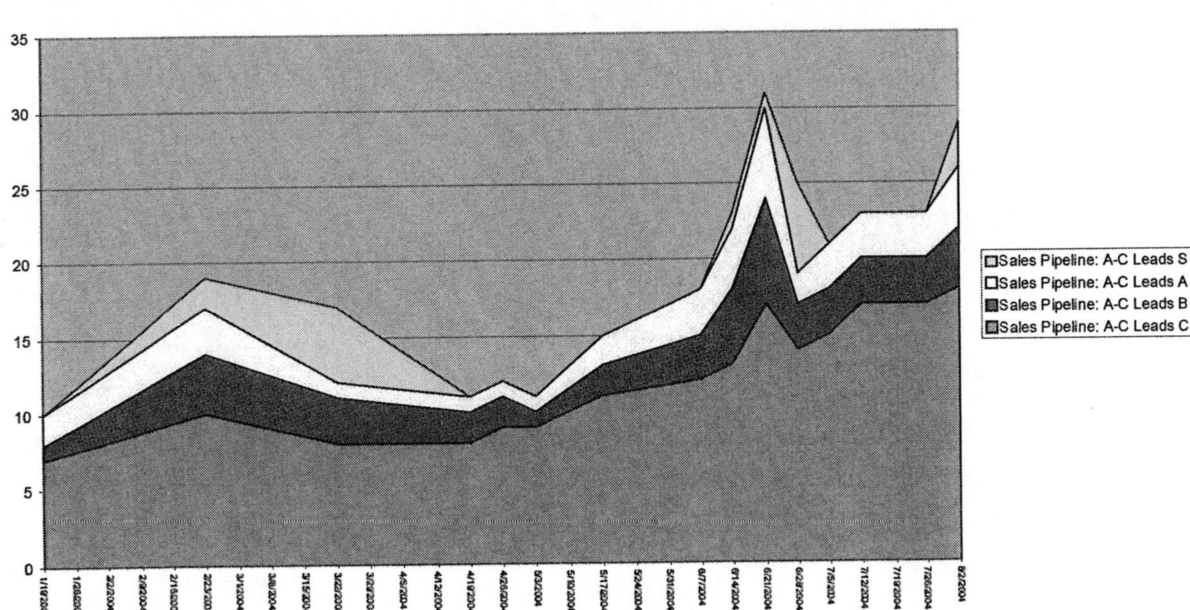

Source: Company records.

Exhibit 3 Comergent Pipeline—Fourth Quarter 2004—Single Region (disguised) ($000s)

Q4 FY2004 "High Probability" Deals				
Account	**Account Rep**		**License Amount**	**Notes**
Communications Company	Rep #1	A	$395	Signed, contingent
Retail Market	Rep #3	A	$350	Catalog and order management
Large Retailer	Rep #6	A	$3,500	Configurator
Distributor	Rep #1	B	$250	Extension
Retail Market	Rep #2	B	$250	B2C and Extension
Retail - on-line store	Rep #3	B	$300	Catalog and order management
Industrial Company	Rep #4	C	$300	Configurator
Retail Market	Reo #5	C	$300	Catalog and order management
Software company	Rep #5	C	$200	Quoting and pricing
Consumer Appliances	Rep #6	C	$400	Catalog and order management
Total High Probability			**$6,245**	
Q4 FY2004 "Upside" Deals				
Account	**Account Rep**		**License Amount**	**Notes**
Software Company	Rep #1	D	$200	Catalog and order management
Franchisee	Rep #1	D	$300	Order management
Industrial Manufacturer	Rep #2	D	$100	Proposals
Automotive	Rep #7	E	$125	Product Depot
Automotive	Rep #7	E	$125	Product Depot
Total High and Mid Probability			**$7,095**	

Source: Company records.

Exhibit 4 Comergent Customer Base

Source: Company records.

Exhibit 5 Haworth, Inc.—Single-Channel Implementation

Haworth was the number three office furniture manufacturer in the U.S., with about 12% share. All orders were built to order in the company's facility in Holland, Michigan. The company's product line was broad—33 million SKUs before accounting for color options. Haworth had three major product segments: stand-alone furniture (a desk, a chair, etc.); commercial, configurable furniture (the ubiquitous office cubicle); and architectural products. The configurable market represented about 80% of Haworth's volume.

During the mid-1990s, Haworth's large customers became involved in electronic commerce, and their involvement soon began to force Haworth to engage with the new technology. Subsequently, the company decided to purchase a sell-side solution and considered several potential vendors, including enterprise solution providers such as SAP and PeopleSoft, but finally selected Comergent.

From the outset Haworth brought its dealer network into the design of the Comergent system (shown below). Haworth had made it clear that they were not considered a "transactional element" and were considered an important part of the selling process in the major market segments. The Comergent system was hosted by a third party and required no investment from the dealer, merely access to an Internet browser. Since installation of the Comergent system, Haworth's dealers spent more time actively selling to customers rather than managing the account. Haworth realized a 30% reduction in the cost of order fulfillment and a 50% reduction in the sales cycle time.

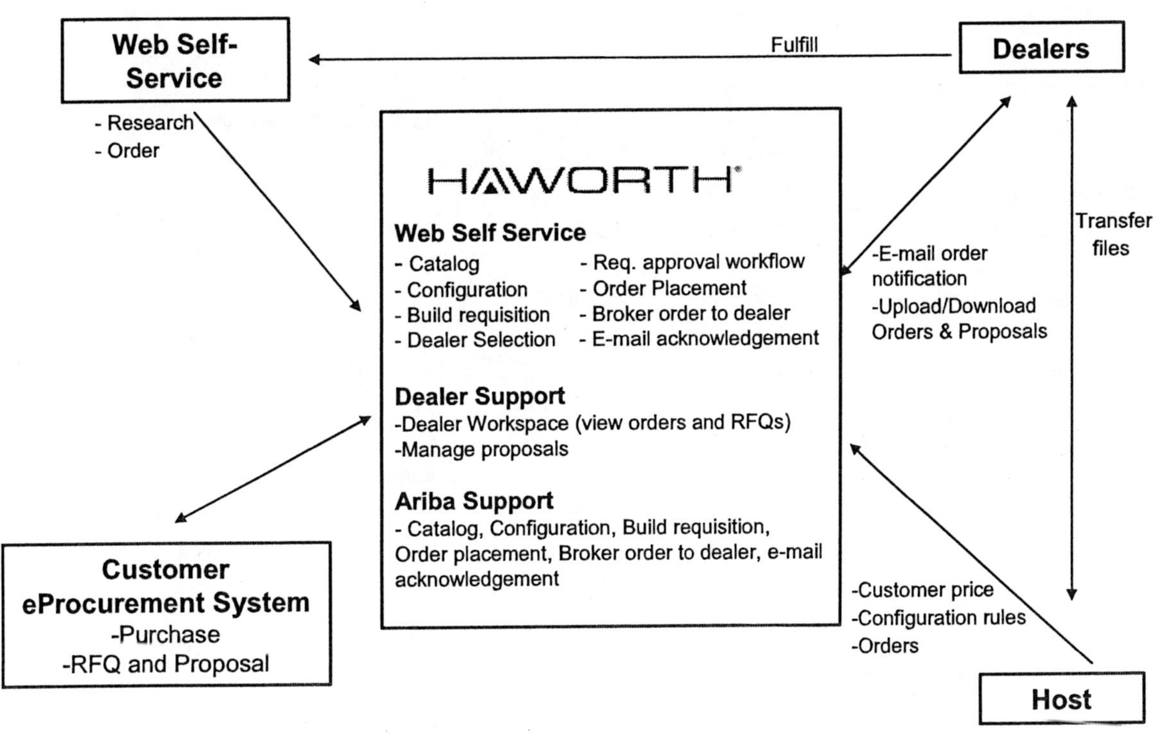

Source: Company interview and records.

Exhibit 6 Competition in Sell-Side E-Commerce and PRM Applications

	Gartner Rating[a]	Ownership	Remarks
Sell-Side E-Commerce:			
ATG	Promising		
Blue Martini	Promising	Public	Loss of $61.3 mm in 2002 but continued visibility
BroadVision	Caution	Public	B2C focus, loss of $170.5 mm in 2002 ($110 mm from restructuring)
Click Commerce	Promising	Public	Loss of $11.4 mm in 2002; loyal customer base in industrial products purchased Allegis, a PRM vendor
Comergent Technologies	Positive	Private	
HAHT Commerce	Caution		Commerce front end to SAP, but threatened by SAP in-house offering
IBM	Positive	Public	
Oracle	Promising	Public	
PeopleSoft	Caution	Public	Tied primarily to CRM products
SAP	Promising	Public	
Siebel Systems	Promising	Public	
PRM:			
Azerity	Caution	Private	Electronics industry focus
Blue Martini	Promising	Public	
ChannelWave	Promising		
Click Commerce	Promising	Public	Recent acquisition to expand and strength PRM functionality
Comergent Technologies	Promising	Private	
Info Now	Caution		
Onyx Software	Caution		
Oracle	Caution	Public	Revamped product with Oracle Partners
PeopleSoft	Caution	Public	Limited use of CRM package to manage partner relationships
Pivotal	Caution	Public	
SAP	Caution	Public	Lagging, but large installed base in core products
			Strong CRM and PRM functionality, but deployments are complex even with basic packages

Source: "Marketscope: Partner Relationship Management, 1H04," January 22, 2004; "Sell Side Electronic Commerce, 1H04," both Gartner, Inc.

[a] Scale for ratings was strong negative, caution, promising, positive, strong positive. Ratings based on financial viability and commitment, targeted delivery, functionality and vision, and application agility.